3rd
PAM

THE NIGHT OF THE HUNTER

THE NIGHT OF THE HUNTER

A BIOGRAPHY OF A FILM

JEFFREY COUCHMAN

NORTHWESTERN UNIVERSITY PRESS

EVANSTON, ILLINOIS

Northwestern University Press
www.nupress.northwestern.edu

Printed in the United States of America

10   9   8   7   6   5   4   3   2   1

Library of Congress Cataloging-in-Publication Data
Couchman, Jeffrey.
    The night of the hunter : a biography of a film / Jeffrey Couchman.
        p. cm.
    Based on the author's thesis (doctoral): City University of New York, 2006.
    Includes bibliographical references and index.
    ISBN 978-0-8101-2542-1 (pbk. : alk. paper)
    1. Night of the hunter (Motion picture) 2. Grubb, Davis, 1919–1980. Night of
the hunter. I. Title.
PN1997.N5213C68 2009
791.4372—dc22
                                                                    2008039038

∞ The paper used in this publication meets the minimum requirements of the
American National Standard for Information Sciences—Permanence of Paper for
Printed Library Materials, ANSI Z39.48-1992.

To my mother and father, who got me started

and

To Barbara and Ella, who keep me going

CONTENTS

ILLUSTRATIONS

Art

Music

ACKNOWLEDGMENTS

I am indebted to three superb teachers at the Graduate Center of the City University of New York, where *The Night of the Hunter: A Biography of a Film* began life as a Ph.D. dissertation. Morris Dickstein gave incisive notes that were of help to me as a writer and a model of analytic commentary for me as a teacher. Royal Brown and William Boddy were steadfast in their support and made shrewd suggestions that helped me to clarify many ideas.

At Northwestern University Press, the entire staff has been a pleasure to work with. Mike Levine was the first to insist that the manuscript should be turned into a book. He has remained an ardent champion and a levelheaded editor. Henry Carrigan has been nothing but gracious and enthusiastic. I am deeply grateful for their confidence and encouragement. Many thanks to Marianne Jankowski, responsive and reassuring during our several conversations about artwork in the book; Jess Biscamp for efficiently guiding the volume through production and giving swift answers to all my editorial questions; Jenny Gavacs for her cheerful e-mails about permissions and other administrative matters; Katherine Faydash for her attentive copyediting and thoughtful suggestions; and Jon Resh for his superb cover design.

I am also thankful to librarians and archivists around the country. Rosemary Hanes and Madeline Matz at the Library of Congress made life easy for me during many hours of research. Barbara Hall at the Academy of Motion Picture Arts and Sciences Library went out of her way to help me before, during, and after my visits to Los Angeles. She and Anne Coco patiently worked with me over the phone as I selected drawings by Davis Grubb for use in the book. Brad Roberts performed xeroxing magic on the drawings and provided first-rate reductions. Jenny Romero carefully answered my several bibliographic queries and expedited a couple of last-minute requests. Thanks also to the staff at New

York Public Library's Billy Rose Theatre Division, particularly Susan Chute, who took time to help me identify some obscure sources. Charles Silver and Ron Magliozzi, longtime friends at the Museum of Modern Art's Film Study Center, were, as always, genial and accommodating. I thank Nick Wyman for making me feel so welcome and at home in the Special Collections Library of the University of Tennessee. Also friendly and helpful were David Houchin of the Clarksburg-Harrison Public Library, Harold M. Forbes and Michael Ridderbusch at West Virginia University's Regional History Collection, John R. Waggener at the University of Wyoming's American Heritage Center, Geoffrey D. Smith, head of Rare Books and Manuscripts at Ohio State University, Deborah Winkler of Fordham University's Quinn Library at Lincoln Center, and the outgoing staff of the Paley Center for Media in New York.

At appropriate places in my preface, I mention colleagues who have helped me. But I will add here additional words of thanks to Preston Jones, expert on *The Night of the Hunter,* for his conviviality and generous spirit, to Bob Gitt for being such a considerate host at the UCLA Film and Television Archive, to Nancy Mysel of the UCLA archive for spending time during a hectic week to verify several quotations from *Night of the Hunter* outtakes, to Nigel Algar of the British Film Institute for his help and inspiration from across the waters, and to David Schumann for all his friendly correspondence and support. Paul Sprecher of the James Agee Trust also deserves additional thanks for his kind support throughout this project. I am grateful to Paul for introducing me to Michael Lofaro, whose good humor and scholarly advice have enriched my life. Professor Lofaro in turn introduced me to John Wranovics. With great enthusiasm, John put into my hands correspondence from Agee's agent, Ilse Lahn, and a letter from Laughton to Agee. I value his professionalism and his friendship. I am grateful to Thomas E. Douglass for providing me with an unpublished essay by Davis Grubb. Thanks to Jack Garcia for his many acts of kindness and for sharing his encyclopedic knowledge of film. Jack, with able aid from Teresa Machin, helped me locate many hard-to-find films. Greg Pliska put thought and care into notating the musical examples in chapter 6. Listening to him play and talk about *The Night of the Hunter*'s score gave me renewed appreciation for the work of Walter Schumann. Margo Scott moved with remarkable speed to help in securing music permissions. Nicole Verity, ever eager to offer assistance, gave me tireless help with computer problems and online research.

A great benefit of this project was meeting some of the people who made *The Night of the Hunter*. Having spent time with this group, I understand why the film shoot in 1954 was so harmonious. Paul Gregory treated me like an old friend from the minute I met him, and our continued conversations over the phone have been a delight. Stanley Cortez concluded our interview by taking me on a tour of the American Society of Cinematographers' clubhouse and giving me advice on driving in L.A. Hilyard Brown, bubbling with life, let me spend hours with him and his wife, Audrey, and their son John. Robert Golden was a splendid storyteller and host, who treated my wife and me to a first-rate lunch at his country club. Sy Hoffberg, a true gentleman, was also a fine raconteur, and he continued to call every now and then with news from Hollywood. Terry Sanders affably took time away from a busy filmmaking schedule to meet with me. Besides offering vivid recollections, he worked overtime one night to make excellent copies of several preproduction drawings. Peter Graves, though on vacation in Lake Tahoe, gave me a cordial and highly articulate telephone interview. Robert Mitchum, just back from a shoot in Vancouver, also gave me time on the telephone and let me ask all the questions I wanted to ask. Special thanks to Dick Berg for putting me in touch with Mitchum. I spent a pleasant evening with Davis Grubb's agent, Don Congdon, who talked to me at length about the author and made certain that I went home with several pages he had written about Grubb. I am also grateful to Sally Jane Bruce, who, though she did not remember Laughton well (she was five when she made the film), took the time to respond to my query.

The two people who would most enjoy this book are no longer here to read it. My mother, Barbara Couchman, thought always of others before herself and was as wise and loving as Rachel Cooper. This was her strength: she could banish the fears of childhood. My father, Gordon Couchman, combined the fervor of Laughton with the compassion of Agee and added a strong measure of civility that was his own. Together, they gave me all.

My wife, Barbara Hogenson, has sustained me in every way imaginable through the research and the writing of these pages. She started it. Years ago, she went to the Library of Congress to do her own research and came back full of excitement because she had discovered piles of material on *The Night of the Hunter.* She had even copied the sheet music for "Willa's Waltz." Eventually, she returned with me to the library and volunteered to do more xeroxing than any spouse should have to do. I could not have maintained my equilibrium without her quiet efficiency, her love, and, beyond all reasonable expectations, her laughter.

Then there is our daughter, Ella. I am grateful to her for climbing onto my lap to see what I was writing and for asking to hear the story. But I am especially grateful to her for pulling on my arm and saying to me, "Come on, let's go play," and for reminding me that these are, in any endeavor, the most important words of all.

NOTE ON THE TEXT

Unless a screenplay is cited as a source, quotations from *The Night of the Hunter* and other films are my transcriptions of spoken dialogue.

Quotations from *Night of the Hunter* outtakes are also my transcriptions, taken from footage at the UCLA Film and Television Archive.

Interviews that I conducted and transcripts of interviews by Nigel Algar have been edited for ease of reading: repetitions and verbal fillers have been silently eliminated. Substantive omissions from the interviews are indicated by ellipses.

ABBREVIATIONS

AF   James Agee, *The Night of the Hunter,* in *Agee on Film,* vol. 2, *Five Film Scripts by James Agee* (New York: McDowell, 1960), 261–354.

FM   Walter Schumann, *"The Night of the Hunter," Film Music* 15, no. 1 (1955), 13–17.

"GF"   Davis Grubb, "Gentleman Friend," typescript of unpublished story (August 10, 1950), A&M 2797, West Virginia and Regional History Collection, Charles C. Wise Library, Morgantown.

HH   Preston Neal Jones, *Heaven and Hell to Play With: The Filming of "The Night of the Hunter"* (New York: Limelight, 2002).

NH   Davis Grubb, *The Night of the Hunter* (New York: Harper, 1953).

"NH"   James Agee, "The Night of the Hunter," typescript of first-draft screenplay (1954), box 4, folder 29, James Agee and James Agee Trust Collection, Special Collections, University of Tennessee.

A Case Study

In the autumn of 1953, Harper and Brothers published *The Night of the Hunter,* a first novel by a West Virginian named Davis Grubb. Set in the Depression, the book was about a man claiming to be a preacher who murders a widow and pursues her two children down the Ohio River to rob them of $10,000. Atmospheric, lyrical, and suspenseful, the novel was a hit with critics and readers; it remained four months on the *New York Times* best-seller list.[1] Hollywood, of course, noticed. In conventional hands, a film based on the novel would no doubt have been a straight-forward thriller. But it was the independent producer Paul Gregory who bought the book, convinced United Artists to produce the film (because Robert Mitchum agreed to star), and gave Charles Laughton the chance to direct his first motion picture. The result was nothing like the usual Hollywood product. Laughton's *Night of the Hunter* is at once a fairy tale, a horror film, an allegory, a thriller—a mixture of realism and stylization that even now is hard to define. Released in the autumn of 1955, the film was a flop with critics and audiences.

Today, the novel is known mainly as the source for Laughton's film, which has achieved the status of a classic. As one of Laughton's biographers puts it, "Despite its flaws, *The Night of the Hunter* remains one of the few uncompromised masterpieces of the American cinema."[2] Because this is the only film that Laughton directed in its entirety (he directed a few scenes in *The Man on the Eiffel Tower* [1949]), the work gains even greater significance. *The Night of the Hunter* is among the motion pictures selected by the Library of Congress for the National Film Registry, and it often turns up on lists of the world's best films, including a recent list in the *Guardian* for "the best family films of all time." The *Guardian*'s blurb for Laughton's feature reads, "No film on the list sparked as much debate as *Night of the Hunter*. While all were in agreement over the film's merits, some felt that it was just too terrifying to inflict on the family. That said, one could argue that *Night of the Hunter* is the perfect children's fable (albeit of a dark and twisted variety)."[3] The film has indeed captured the imagination of more than one child. Preston Neal Jones, author of *Heaven and Hell to Play With*, a production history of *The Night of the Hunter* told through superbly edited interviews, "was one of those fans . . . who first encountered the film when he was young and impressionable."[4] Before a screening of the movie at the New York Film Festival in 2001, Martin Scorsese said, "I saw [*The Night of the Hunter*] at the age of 12. It's never left my consciousness."[5] My own childhood viewings of the film left a lasting impression on me. They are, in fact, the source of this book.

In looking closely here at the film's screenplay, its cinematography, the novel on which it is based, and other aspects of the work, I am in a sense replaying moments of discovery from the past. I was about ten years old when, with my father's assurance that the film was one I would never forget, I sat down to watch *The Night of the Hunter*. Two scenes in particular made me believe my father's prediction: the evil preacher on a horse in the distance singing "Leaning on the Everlasting Arms" and the corpse of the murdered mother bound to an old car at the bottom of the river. No film I watched on the late show (and I watched a lot of them) had anything that looked as strange and frightening and beautiful as those scenes. Several years later my father, once again my mentor, gave me a gift of *Agee on Film:* two volumes containing James Agee's film reviews and screenplays. I was just beginning to realize that someone actually *wrote* the movies I watched. The fact that one of my favorite films was written by the author of one of my favorite novels, *A Death in the Family*, gave me a startling awareness of the interconnection between books and films. In college, I found another surprising connection. I took film courses that naturally stressed the importance of Orson Welles, and one day I realized that the cinematographer on Welles's *Magnificent Ambersons* (1942), a man named Stanley Cortez, had also created the images in *The Night of the Hunter*. Not until I was a few years out of college did I pay attention to the fact that *The Night of the Hunter* was based on a novel called . . . *The Night of the Hunter*. When I read the book by Davis Grubb, I almost felt that I was reading the screenplay again. The film re-created the book nearly scene by scene. Dialogue in the movie came straight from the page. And yet it fascinated me that the movie, with its impenetrable shadows and its otherworldly music (by Walter Schumann), created an emotional experience very different from the one generated by the novel.

My interest in Laughton's adaptation of Grubb's work led me to read about *The Night of the Hunter* in books and scholarly journals. What I read, or rather what I did not find in what I read, ultimately prompted me to write the present study. Before I explain what the book is, however, it will be helpful to say a few words about what it is not. My book does not look at the adaptation process as a means to a theoretical end. This is not a work in the vein of George Bluestone's seminal *Novels into Film*, which analyzes several adaptations to help the reader understand "how a linguistic medium is changed to a visual medium,"[6] or Seymour Chatman's *Coming to Terms*, which "is concerned . . . with the different solutions that novels and films prefer for common narrative problems."[7] Many other studies of adaptations focus on the issue of fidelity. Writers such as Geoffrey Wagner, Morris Beja, Michael Klein and Gillian Parker, and J. Dudley Andrew establish categories that characterize a film's fidelity to the original work. Wagner's terms for a sliding scale of fidelity (*transposition, commentary,* and *analogy*) typify the taxonomic approach.[8] Robert Stam, among others, finds fault with criticism that "has often been profoundly moralistic, awash in terms such as *infidelity, betrayal, deformation, violation, vulgarization,* and *desecration.*"[9] The question of fidelity comes up in *The Night of the Hunter: A Biography of a Film* because Laughton and Gregory themselves raise the issue: they were intent on creating what they considered a faithful adaptation of Grubb's novel. I do not, however, attempt to define Laughton's *Night of the Hunter* according to a system of classification. Nor do I make an ideological case for or against the idea of fidelity. I consider Laughton's "faithfulness," or lack of it, to understand what the director hoped to achieve on screen and to analyze the effect of his choices on the film as a whole.

Thus *The Night of the Hunter: A Biography of a Film*, which from another angle could be subtitled *A Biography of a Book*, examines the genesis and the eclectic form of each work and the process of transformation by which the novel became a motion picture. The film that came out of the novel is an especially good illustration of the tension between the idea of a director as auteur and the collaborative nature of filmmaking.

Although Andrew Sarris, in his classic discussion "Notes on the *Auteur* Theory in 1962," points out that "the *auteur* theory emphasizes the body of a director's work rather than isolated masterpieces," he also speaks of the theory's being grounded in a concern with an "interior meaning" that he calls "an *élan* of the soul."[10] *The Night of the Hunter*, different from any other film in American cinema, is an expression of that élan in Laughton's soul. With this single film, Laughton joins the ranks of such acknowledged auteurs as Orson Welles and Alfred Hitchcock. Like Hitchcock in particular, he controlled every phase of production so closely that the film bears his unmistakable signature. "There wasn't an inch of that footage that wasn't Laughton, not an inch," said Gregory.[11] Robert Golden, editor on *The Night of the Hunter*, agreed that the film was "as close to being a one-man show as anyone could imagine." Yet he also said that the production was a "cooperative effort of the highest degree."[12] As a first-time director of genuine humility, and as an artist who respected talent in any field, Laughton worked with his crew in a surprisingly democratic fashion, often allowing a creative freedom that was unique in the experience of his collaborators. The film, then, both illustrates the auteur theory and reminds us of its limits. The contradictory nature of Laughton's directorial method perfectly fits a film of stylistic contradictions. The complexity of the movie allows this particular adaptation to withstand detailed scrutiny. *The Night of the Hunter* is a prismatic work that can be looked at from many angles and still reveal new aspects of itself. In an essay from *Sight and Sound*, Paul Hammond says, "Two or three times the number of words contracted for would not be enough to do justice to the film."[13]

Outline of The Night of the Hunter: A Biography of a Film

The story of *The Night of the Hunter* is a tale of pairings between Laughton and various colleagues. The first in a remarkable series is the partnership with Paul Gregory, a talent agent who became Laughton's promoter and producer. He inaugurated a series of cross-country tours, in which Laughton, alone onstage, read selections of prose and poetry. The success of those tours was matched by other well-received stage shows that Gregory and Laughton put on in the early fifties. Although the productions are discussed in biographies of Laughton and in a dissertation on Gregory by James Lester Johnson, books and articles about *The Night of the Hunter* rarely go into any detail about the four works: Laughton's one-man show, *An Evening with Charles Laughton;* the concert staging of George Bernard Shaw's *Don Juan in Hell;* the more elaborate concert staging of Stephen Vincent Benét's epic poem *John Brown's Body;* and a production of Herman Wouk's play *The Caine Mutiny Court-Martial.* These stage presentations provide an important context for understanding Laughton's film. There is a notable continuity between *The Night of the Hunter* and the theatrical ventures that precede it. Chapter 1 details what Gregory and Laughton achieved onstage and relates their work in the theater to their screen version of Grubb's novel.

What exactly that novel is and why it seemed the perfect choice for Laughton's debut as a director are the subjects of chapter 2. Little has been written about Grubb and *The Night of the Hunter.* In an article for *Western Humanities Review,* James R. Fultz discusses the book in relation to Agee's adaptation. David Thomson, writing about Laughton's film in *Sight and Sound,* gives careful consideration to passages in Grubb's book. Jack Welch has written a dissertation about Grubb's life and work, and he devotes an interesting chapter to the author's first novel. In a foreword to a reprint of another novel, *Fools' Parade,* Thomas E. Douglass, who is at work on a biography of Grubb, sheds light on the author's background and literary influences. At times, however, the novel is mentioned simply to dismiss it. In an early article on Laughton's film, Robin Wood believes that style and tone in the work are "highly suspect, characterized by that gooey, pseudo-poetic self-indulgence that too often passes for 'lyricism.'"[14] Charles Higham, in a biography of Laughton, concurs: "Davis Grubb's novel has not worn well; it can now be seen to belong to that odd, hybrid 'lyrical' genre that included works like *Dark of the Moon* and *Finian's Rainbow* on the stage. The author aimed at a kind of folksy poetic approach that never quite comes off: a cross between Thomas Wolfe and Sherwood Anderson."[15] The novel deserves better. It may not be as adventurous as Laughton's film, but it is a well-plotted, well-told story. It is also, in its own way, as eclectic as the film. Chapter 2 traces the literary streams feeding into Grubb's work and looks at its reception by critics and audiences—and by Gregory and Laughton.

Laughton wanted to film the book that Grubb wrote. To that end, he established a close working relationship with the author. He asked Grubb, who had studied art at the Carnegie Institute of Technology, to supply drawings that would help him to visualize scenes and characters from the novel. Ultimately, Grubb drew more than one hundred pictures for Laughton. In 1973, 119 *Night of the Hunter* drawings, along with an explanatory letter from Grubb, were assembled and put up for sale to collectors. By 1986, a Philadelphia dealer in rare books and prints had the collection on the market for $3,000.[16] Martin Scorsese eventually purchased the drawings, then donated them to the Margaret Herrick Library of the Academy of Motion Picture Arts and Sciences (*HH*, 63). Grubb's illustrations, alongside the novel itself, are an important source for Laughton's film. Several sketches, provided by Barbara Hall, Anne Coco, and Brad Roberts at the academy's library, are on display in chapter 3, which explores the way Laughton and Grubb worked together and analyzes the influence of various drawings on the movie. In particular, the chapter makes a point that has never been raised before: certain nonrealistic drawings by Grubb appear to have inspired Laughton to create his own expressionistic visuals.

The most controversial of Laughton's collaborations is that with his screenwriter, James Agee. The long-standing account of their relationship is found in a recent *Newsday* review of a book on screenwriting: "As almost anyone knows who has made an even cursory study of 'Hunter,' director Charles Laughton threw out Agee's script, the writer being in the final stages of alcoholism, and rewrote the film himself."[17] By tracing the history of Agee's work with Laughton on *The Night of the Hunter*, chapter 4 strives to dispel myths about Agee's contribution and to resolve the question of the screenplay's authorship. That task has been made easier by an important find: Paul Sprecher of the James Agee Trust discovered a copy of Agee's "lost" first draft for *The Night of the Hunter*. I was told about the draft by Preston Neal Jones, who put me in touch with Sprecher. He in turn graciously sent me a copy and, in conjunction with the Wylie Agency, has allowed me to quote at length from the script. Thus, chapter 4 provides a critical examination of Agee's draft— its form, its adaptation of Grubb's novel, and its relationship to the shooting script, which was published initially in 1960 and republished in 2005 by the Library of America.

Chapter 5 moves into the production phase of Laughton's film. Although my book is not a production history in the vein of such works as *The Making of "The Wizard of Oz,"* by Aljean Harmetz, or *The Making of "Citizen Kane,"* by Robert L. Carringer, I use many production details to illustrate points within my analyses of Laughton's adaptation. To better understand the way Laughton worked, I interviewed several people involved with *The Night of the Hunter:* Paul Gregory, cinematographer Stanley Cortez, art director Hilyard Brown, editor Robert Golden, assistant cameraman Sy Hoffberg, second-unit director Terry Sanders, Robert Mitchum (who played Preacher), and Peter Graves (who played Ben Harper). Another collection of unpublished interviews has proved immensely helpful. In 1995, Nigel Algar produced a fine segment about *The Night of the Hunter* for the BBC2 program *Moving Pictures.* (A videocassette of the show arrived at Hilyard Brown's house on the day I met him, and although he could no longer see, his wife put Algar's tape in, and he happily sat with me while I watched the documentary.) Algar generously supplied me with transcripts of the interviews he conducted for his program. In addition, I have drawn on the interviews published in what is now an essential volume for studies of Laughton's film: Jones's *Heaven and Hell to Play With: The Filming of "The Night of the Hunter."* The *Night of the Hunter* production was unusual in that Laughton, while maintaining control over how he wanted Grubb's novel to be presented on film, gave his crew extraordinary latitude. Chapter 5 studies Laughton's close working relationships with key members of the crew: Cortez, Brown, Golden, and Sanders. Laughton's clear vision of what he wanted on screen is evident in line drawings that he made for his second unit, as well as in subsequent images that Sanders sketched in his production notebook. I am grateful to Sanders for allowing these drawings to be presented here for the first time. Nearly everyone who writes about the film mentions stylized scenes reminiscent of German expressionism. Nearly everyone also mentions that Laughton studied D. W. Griffith movies in preparation for *The Night of the Hunter.* But no discussions—and I include passages from articles that I have written about the film—look deeply enough into *The Night of the Hunter's* connections to these and other film traditions. Chapter 5 attempts to fill this gap by looking closely at the way Laughton mingles film styles.

Disparate styles do not cause *The Night of the Hunter* to fragment into chaos. Rather, they become part of a visual scheme that gives the work unity. Chapter 6 analyzes that scheme and looks at two other unifying elements: stories that are told in the course of the film and the score by Walter Schumann. The beauty of the film's music has often been commented upon. Wood even offers a keen analysis of the way "Leaning on the Everlasting Arms" is used structurally to "mark [the film's] essential progress."[18] Schumann himself wrote a piece for *Film Music* about his discussions with Laughton and the way he composed the score. Yet here again, no full-scale study of the music exists. Chapter 6 concludes with a close reading of the score, which demonstrates how the music mirrors the film's visual contrasts and repetitions. This chapter, too, benefits from a fortunate find. At the University of Tennessee's James Agee Celebration in April 2005, I learned from psychology professor Doris Ivie that Walter Schumann's son is on the faculty of the university's business school. I contacted David Schumann, who took the time to look through boxes of his father's musical scores. He found the original, handwritten score for *The Night of the Hunter*, which he cheerfully lent to me. His discovery was especially helpful, because some of the *Hunter* cues that had been deposited with the Library of Congress for copyright purposes in the fifties had been misplaced. Thus, thanks to Schumann, I was able to study the missing pieces, and the library received a new copy of the complete score.

In writing chapter 7, I received invaluable help from another direction. Robert Gitt, preservation officer at the UCLA Film and Television Archive, had for many years overseen the restoration of outtakes from *The Night of the Hunter*. Elsa Lanchester, Laughton's widow, had donated some eight hours of *Hunter* outtakes to the American Film Institute, which in 1981 turned the material over to the UCLA archive.[19] With the help of Nancy Mysel and others, the outtakes were assembled and restored "as a labor of love off and on over a period of years." They were ready to be seen by 2001.[20] I am grateful to Gitt for allowing me to spend several pleasant days in a dark editing room at the UCLA facility screening all the outtakes. They make up, as F. X. Feeney aptly puts it, "a ghostly second film by Laughton."[21] Chapter 7 uses that "second film" to show how Laughton shapes performances to create a contrast in acting styles that matches other oppositions in *The Night of the Hunter*. Studies in adaptation too often neglect acting as an important component in the transfer of material from page to screen. Chapter 7 analyzes the way the principal actors and their techniques relate to the characters found in Grubb's novel. It also looks at the actors in other roles to put their *Hunter* performances in context and to illustrate how Laughton uses, or plays against, established screen personas.

Chapter 8 is a melancholy chapter: it tells the story of the film's poor reception in 1955, the failed attempt by Gregory, Laughton, and others from *The Night of the Hunter* crew to adapt Norman Mailer's *Naked and the Dead,* and the breakup of the Gregory-Laughton partnership. The bulk of the chapter is devoted to examining why the film failed with critics and audiences. Newspaper ads are analyzed to suggest that the film's marketers were not sure how to promote a film as hard to categorize as *The Night of the Hunter.* The chapter does reveal, however, that the film was promoted on various fronts and still never reached a wide audience. A sampling of reviews shows that while the notices were not universally bad, they did little to help advance the film. Writers in later years have sometimes claimed that *The Night of the Hunter,* as a small, black-and-white film, was simply out of place at a time when the industry was turning to such processes as Cinerama or CinemaScope in its battle with television. A chief point of chapter 8, however, is that the very essence of *The Night of the Hunter* was at odds even with smaller-scale, black-and-white films of the fifties. Where the many literary strands within Grubb's novel made his book familiar to a reading audience, the confluence of cinematic styles made Laughton's film confusing to a viewing audience. Chapter 8 illustrates how *The Night of the Hunter* fails to fit comfortably into any genre from the fifties.

The story, fortunately, does not end in 1955. Chapter 9 tracks *The Night of the Hunter*'s critical reassessment and its subsequent growth from a cult movie to a classic in the pantheon of American film. Laughton's work, especially the image of Preacher and his tattooed fingers, is now ingrained in popular culture, and chapter 9 analyzes references to the movie in songs and films. The chapter concludes with a look at two later adaptations of Grubb's novel: a 1991 television production and a 1996 stage musical. Neither adaptation is able to escape comparison to Laughton's version, which, as a film that can truly be called "unique," casts a long shadow.

THE NIGHT OF THE HUNTER

INTRODUCTION

Three Men and a Book

Not a moment of screen time is wasted in *The Night of the Hunter*. Every scene, every frame, propels the narrative. The source of that economy is the novel on which the film is based. Davis Grubb has a story to tell, and he tells it swiftly, without digression. He breaks the tale into five sections (four books and an epilogue) and thereby gives his narrative a formal sense of order—the feel of a drama with five acts or, more accurately, given the pulse of his prose, a musical composition in five movements. His sentences teem with adjectives and rhetorical figures, yet every word contributes to the mood and the atmosphere of his lyrical nightmare.

Both the taut structure and the extravagant language of the novel appealed to the two men who stepped forward to make a film version of Grubb's story. Charles Laughton was an actor of extravagant effects that were carefully controlled. Paul Gregory was a producer who combined a flair for showmanship with the spirit of a minimalist. Together, in such stage shows as *Don Juan in Hell* and *John Brown's Body*, Gregory and Laughton offered high drama in the restrictive form of reader's theater.

The Gregory-Laughton theatrical presentations also turned literature into mass-market entertainment. *Don Juan in Hell,* for instance, achieved such widespread fame that on the night Laughton made a television appearance with Abbott and Costello, semiliterate Lou Costello casually mentioned that he had seen Laughton's show (he said he had not understood a word) and found it unnecessary to mention its name

(*The Colgate Comedy Hour*, NBC, April 6, 1952). To Laughton and Gregory, no barrier existed between so-called highbrow and lowbrow endeavors. Grubb shared their belief that art and commerce could coincide. His faith was vindicated by the commercial success of his artistic thriller *The Night of the Hunter*. It is a sad irony that when these proponents of literate entertainment joined forces to put the novel on screen, Laughton's own artistic vision could not find an audience.

The careers of these three professionals, each a careful craftsman in his own sphere, form an essential background to the story of the book's progress from page to screen. That story will be more fully appreciated if I provide, along with a detailed synopsis of Grubb's novel, biographical sketches of Grubb, Laughton, and Gregory. This introduction, then, truly introduces the reader to a novel much less familiar today than it was in 1953 and to the three men who united briefly to create a lasting film.

Synopsis of Davis Grubb's Novel

"Book One: The Hanging Man."   In Cresap's Landing, West Virginia, the Depression has hit hard. Ben Harper, a clerk in a hardware store, is worried about supporting his family. He steals $10,000 from a bank and kills two men during the robbery. His children know where the money is hidden, but Ben has sworn them to secrecy. In Moundsville Penitentiary, where he awaits execution, Ben shares a cell with Harry Powell, imprisoned for stealing a car. The man calls himself a preacher, but the God he follows is one who tells him to murder widows for their meager savings. Powell has lost count of the women he has killed in the Ohio Valley. Although Preacher tries to wheedle the whereabouts of the stolen money from Ben, Harper goes to his death without revealing the secret. Released from prison, Preacher goes straight to Cresap's Landing and finds Ben's widow, Willa, working at an ice cream parlor run by Walt and Icey Spoon. Preacher says he quit his job as chaplain at the penitentiary and is stopping by to give comfort to Willa. He delivers a sermon about hate vanquished by love. To illustrate the point, he uses his hands, which are tattooed with the words *love* and *hate*. John alone is unimpressed and remains suspicious of Powell. Between the boy and the preacher, a silent, deadly game begins.

"Book Two: The Hunter."   Preacher stays on in Cresap's Landing. He charms the townspeople and courts Willa. When he tells her that Ben sank the stolen cash in the river, any suspicion that he might be wooing her for the money is cleared away. Willa marries Powell. On their honeymoon night, Preacher expresses his revulsion toward sex and refuses to consummate the marriage. Willa prays to become clean, "so I can be what Harry wants me to be." Soon she is preaching with Powell at tent meetings along the Ohio River. From time to time, Preacher attempts to pry the secret of the money from John, who cannot make his mother believe the truth about Powell. Preacher nearly discovers the money just before bedtime one evening, when Pearl opens her doll, Miss Jenny, and takes out bills to play with them (thus revealing to the reader where the money is hidden). That night, John dreams of the day his father returned from the robbery and gave his son the fateful charge to protect Pearl and the money. Meanwhile, Willa dreams of her past life with Ben and wakes feeling sinful. Across town, Walt Spoon tells his wife that he senses something about Preacher is not right, but Icey persuades him that his fears are groundless. "It's true," he thinks, just before he falls asleep. "He's a Man of God."

"Book Three: The River."   John's only friend is Uncle Birdie, an old riverman who lives in a wharf boat. He knows something is wrong at the house and he vows to help John if the boy is ever in trouble. On a night of river mists, Willa returns home and overhears Preacher threatening Pearl if she refuses to tell him where the money is hidden. Knowing the truth about Preacher now, Willa nevertheless lies in bed that night, serene in the belief that the Lord sent Powell to her for the salvation of her soul. Preacher himself hears the voice of God, opens his switchblade, and murders Willa. He tells the Spoons that Willa ran off and, alone with the children, tries to worm the secret of the money from them. John tricks Preacher into looking for the money in the basement. To save John's life, Pearl blurts out that the money is in the doll. John douses a candle, and in the darkness he locks Preacher in the basement and flees with Pearl. The children run to Uncle Birdie for help. The old man, however, has seen Willa's body, with its throat slit, bound in a Model T at the bottom of the river. The terrified man is now in a drunken stupor. "There is still the river," thinks John. He loads Pearl into a skiff just as Preacher appears at the river's edge. With the killer bearing down on them, John pushes off and glides to safety on the river.

While the children drift down the Ohio, Preacher pursues them on land. After days on the river, John and Pearl are discovered by a widow named Rachel Cooper in the shallows near her farm. She is already mother to three homeless girls, and now she has "two more peeps" in her brood.

"Book Four: A Strong Tree with Many Birds." Living with Miz Cooper, John feels that he has found home. Preacher, however, catches up to the children. In town, he uses his charms on Ruby, Miz Cooper's adolescent charge, to discover where John and Pearl are. He comes to the farm to collect his children, but Miz Cooper believes John when he tells her, "He ain't my dad." She chases Preacher off at gunpoint. That night, Preacher stalks the house and sneaks in. Miz Cooper blasts him with a shotgun, and he takes refuge in the barn. By morning, state troopers arrive and arrest Powell in a scene that for John is a traumatic replay of his father's arrest. At the trial, where Preacher's murderous past becomes public, John recedes into himself and is unable to identify Powell. The townsfolk, however, are vocal in their hatred of the hypocritical Bluebeard. Led by Icey and Walt Spoon, a mob storms the county jail to lynch Harry Powell.

"Epilogue: They Abide." Christmas Eve at Miz Cooper's. She reflects on Christmas and on the endurance of children. Then it is time for presents. John wraps a McIntosh apple that he selected from the cellar and gives it to Miz Cooper. She gives John the dollar watch that he has coveted since just after his father was taken away. He lies in bed under calico quilts, listening to his watch tick and staring at shadows on the wall. He is no longer afraid, and he drifts into peaceful sleep.

The Author

Like William Faulkner, who founded his fictional realm of Yoknapatawpha County in the Mississippi he knew so well, Davis Grubb created his own fictional landscapes—the towns of Cresap's Landing, Adena, and Glory—from his native West Virginia. He was born in Moundsville on July 23, 1919. "I remember it as a place of daily astonishment, entertainments, mysteries, myths, brags, facts and holy awe," Grubb says in an article he wrote forty years later.[1] The place helped to give his imagination the gothic cast that would shade his fiction. In the center of town was a burial mound some seventy feet high built in approximately the third century B.C.E. by a tribe known as the Adena. Close by was the West Virginia State Penitentiary.[2] Grubb recalls the effect of these two monuments:

> The great dirt mound stood imponderable in the midst
> of my river town, kept secrets among the roots of gigantic
> trees that were saplings when the Wars of the Roses raged.
> It . . . stood higher than the bleak, black bastions of the
> State Penitentiary two blocks away.
>
> In the innocence and confusion of my child's mind the
> great mound and the penitentiary were bound together in
> ambiguous and dreadful brotherhood. One was the burial
> place of the unknown dead; the other of the unknown
> living. These two were the great, dark, earth-colored pre-
> eminences in my town, each full of its secrets, riddles and
> whispers of ritual killing.[3]

In *The Night of the Hunter*, Grubb does not describe the penitentiary beyond mentioning the "cold, wet bricks of the prison courtyard,"[4] yet in Laughton's film, after Ben Harper's execution, a wall of the penitentiary is given a presence as foreboding as that in Grubb's recollection.

Another feature of the town would become even more central to Grubb's imagination. "I am river-born," he wrote at the time his first novel was published, "and, although I have not been to the bottom-lands in more years than I can remember, the music and grandeur of the Ohio River has never left me and I think it never will."[5] The river of his childhood—it was only a few blocks from Grubb's house—runs through Grubb's writing as forcefully as the Mississippi runs through Mark Twain's.[6] In *The Night of the Hunter*, Preacher's revival meeting in the river town of Welcome (*NH*, 110–12) has its roots in scenes that Grubb recalls in his nostalgic article from 1960: "many a roaring, evangelic tent meeting of the little torchlit Chautauquas which sang and flickered along the river shores in the nights of my childhood."[7]

He was raised in a nine-room, Victorian house supposedly haunted by a ghost with a clubfoot, though for Grubb it was a place of enchantment. The home, filled with books, was literate and creative. He once described his mother, Eleanor, as "a woman of great intellectual curiosity, great intellectual mischief. She liked to throw in an outrageous question and get everybody thinking in new lines." His father, Louis, was an architect, "who taught Grubb to draw before he could write."[8] An idyllic childhood, however, was shaken by the Depression. A few years after the birth of another son, Louis, the father's architecture business began to totter, and just before Christmas in 1934, the family was evicted from their beloved house. "We moved to a shabby suburb of Moundsville: to a grey salt box of a house with awful fumed oak floors and stairways," Grubb wrote to his agent in October 1953, on the very day he received his first copies of *The Night of the Hunter*.[9] Within two years of moving to "the shabby suburb" called Glen Dale, Grubb's father died of a heart attack. Eleanor once again moved her two sons, this time to the coal-mining region of Clarksburg, where she became a social worker for a community ravaged by the Depression.[10] Given this history, it is understandable that Grubb's work, exemplified by *The Night of the Hunter,* is suffused with a sense of transient joy, of chaos lurking below the deceptively placid surface of life.

In 1938, Grubb entered the Carnegie Institute of Technology in Pittsburgh. He stayed only a year, but his training would serve him well when Charles Laughton came to ask him for drawings to help with his visualization of *The Night of the Hunter*. In any event, Grubb's true creative outlet was writing. Between 1946 and 1953, Grubb published thirteen stories, completed two novels that he preferred to forget,[11] and wrote some forty thousand words of another book that was, as his agent, Don Congdon, recalls, "a somewhat typical first novel, dealing with his efforts as an art student at Carnegie Tech, . . . more of an exercise than anything of interest to the public." Grubb's next book was *The Night of the Hunter*. In Congdon's view, it was "the best first novel of any consequence I've ever represented as an agent."[12]

The Night of the Hunter contains themes and characters that Grubb would continue to use in his fiction until his death on July 24, 1980, just a few weeks after he delivered the manuscript for his long, surrealistic novel *Ancient Lights*.[13] Religious fanaticism turns up frequently, linked to violence, sex, or a combination of the two. In *Fools' Parade* (1969), the story of an ex-con who fights a coterie of dishonest businessmen to cash a $25,000 check from the state of West Virginia, a hired assassin named Kilfong exults over shooting atheists:

"I jist love it when they repent," he said. "Jist before I do it to them."

Gravely he threw the safety catch.

"We both loves it," he went on. . . . "Me and Jesus."[14]

In *The Barefoot Man* (1971), a Depression-era novel about a showdown between strikers and the owners of a coal mine, Tom Turley gives his son "a real Christian education" by forcing him to watch the crucifixion of an illiterate Polish scab.[15] After the gruesome murder, Tom has "the expression on his face of a man who had just been to a whorehouse— or a church."[16] As a counter to such horror in his fiction, Grubb creates variations on the compassionate Rachel Cooper. She herself is based on a woman from West Virginia named Rachel Kutscher, who took in homeless children and was a lifelong friend of Grubb's.[17] The two Rachels fuse with characters like Marcy Cresap, the public-health nurse in *The Voices of Glory* (1962), who fights daily battles with greedy, small-minded citizens of her town, and Preacher Twining in *A Tree Full of Stars* (1965), the only minister in Elizabethtown with true Christian charity; he alone does not turn on a family that continue to celebrate Christmas after their Christmas tree roots itself in their house. Grubb's faith in the resilience of children, central to *The Night of the Hunter*, also reappears in later works, notably in *A Dream of Kings* (1955), about a young couple's loss of innocence during the Civil War era, which ends with a Wordsworthian vision of children in a meadow "washed with morning light" who represent "that holy and precious wonder that is the time of man on earth."[18]

With one exception, however, none of Grubb's subsequent books holds together as well as *The Night of the Hunter*. Only *The Golden Sickle* (1968), an adventure tale in the vein of *Treasure Island*, in which a twelve-year-old orphan boy outwits a vicious gang of thieves in a search for hidden treasure, has the narrative vigor of Grubb's first novel. Grubb is at his best writing about boys threatened by evildoers. Otherwise, his novels become diffuse, as in the many plot strands of a novel about racial hatred, *Shadow of My Brother* (1966), or repetitious, like *The Voices of Glory*, which also suffers from a feeling that it is reworking material that Edgar Lee Masters, Sherwood Anderson, and Sinclair Lewis made their own decades before. Although in his later work Grubb is still capable of plain, strong language ("Dark was settling now, it stood in pools among the laurel, and a curl of moon lay high among the pines"[19]), too often his writing is bloated, as in the following picture of a man who has been shot and is now lying on the ground, his head propped on a large lump of coal: "In a sleep that was deep as the mile-down seam from which his dark pillow had been man-lifted, Sizemore's stunned mind strove and twisted among the meshed and motionless fibers of his wound-shocked body."[20]

In a way, Grubb's experience with *The Night of the Hunter* is similar to Laughton's. The film is Laughton's single venture as a director. Although Grubb published nine novels and two collections of short stories in his lifetime, no other book enjoyed the virtually unanimous critical praise heaped on *The Night of the Hunter*. No other book became a best seller. Reprints of his books often announce him as "author of *The Night of the Hunter*." His first novel was a singular phenomenon even for Grubb.

Although several of Grubb's short stories were adapted for *Alfred Hitchcock Presents* and other television shows,[21] *Fools' Parade* is the only other book of his to reach the big screen, in a lackluster 1971 film starring James Stewart. Grubb says that he wrote the first draft of *The Night of the Hunter* in six weeks, working at night after a nine-to-five job, and revised the book within another six.[22] Perhaps that period of concentrated writing helps to explain the book's forceful story and taut structure, qualities that in turn explain why the book transfers well to the screen. The book also combines more successfully than his other novels a "popular" form (a suspense tale about a serial killer) with "artistic" content (a spiritual fable of good and evil). It was partly that combination that appealed to Laughton and Gregory.

The Actor

In reminiscing about creative influences from his childhood, Grubb once said, "If I'm going to talk about the actors I learned from when I was growing up, I can't leave out the name of Charles Laughton. . . . We kind of worked together till the time when he started to direct movies" (*HH*, 50). By the time Grubb and Laughton began truly working together, the fifty-five-year-old actor had long been an international star. He was presented with a flourish to American film audiences in *Devil and the Deep* (1932). His credit reads:

And introducing
Charles Laughton
The eminent English
character actor

Throughout the 1930s, Laughton divided his time between film and theater. On the London stage, he appeared in works by Shakespeare, Congreve, Chekhov, and Wilde. On screen, he quickly became more than an eminent character actor, even if his method, as Simon Callow points out, remained that of the character actor intent on transforming himself for each role.[23] Laughton became a true star through transformations in films as diverse as *The Private Life of Henry VIII* (1933), *The Barretts of Wimpole Street* (1934), *Ruggles of Red Gap* (1935), *Les misérables* (1935), and *Mutiny on the Bounty* (1935). He reached the pinnacle of cinematic fame when Disney artists put Laughton's Captain Bligh in the cartoon *Mother Goose Goes Hollywood* (1938). In creating his various personalities, Laughton seems never to have made a distinction between the supposedly "artistic" realm of classical theater and the "popular" world of film. In a 1938 interview with *Film Weekly,* he said, "Fundamentally, both cinema and theatre are places for emotional relaxation and most of the theories aired by highbrows are nothing more than snobbery." He believed that "by stimulating the emotions of the great film public one might achieve tremendous artistic heights."[24] To Laughton, art was entertaining, and even light entertainment could be an art. If one looks at *The Night of the Hunter* in the context of American cinema, its visual style and fabulist quality stand out as something unusual. Seen from the perspective of Laughton's history, the film looks perfectly familiar. It takes its place alongside his many performances that display, within a popular form, artistic effects created in a style different from that of his Hollywood peers. The Laughton technique, aptly defined by Callow as a "combination of intense physical projection and deep emotional realism," was "a completely new kind of acting" in American films.[25]

Whatever role he played, Laughton was obsessive in his quest for perfection. As director on *The Night of the Hunter* he would also seek perfection, but he would do it in a steady, efficient manner that might have surprised a few of his own directors. To Elsa Lanchester, William Dieterle recalled that on the first day of production for the big-budget, cast-of-thousands *Hunchback of Notre Dame* (1939), Laughton announced that shooting would have to be postponed. "I am sorry, so sorry," Dieterle reported him saying, "but I thought I was ready, but it just did not come, but it will come and will be good." Dieterle's dry response: "Please, Charles, the next time you are not yet ready, let me know it previously, so I can plan accordingly."[26] The BBC documentary *The Epic That Never Was* (1965), about the aborted Josef von Sternberg production of *I, Claudius,* offers rare glimpses of Laughton on the set, tortured with self-doubt and struggling with his characterization.[27] Years before his association with Gregory, Laughton teamed up with two other producers and was able to immerse himself even more deeply in his films. Alexander Korda's *Private Life of Henry VIII,* for instance, marked "the first time he was in on a project from the beginning. He was all but co-producer of the film."[28] In the late thirties, Laughton formed Mayflower Productions to produce films with Erich Pommer, the German exile who had headed up Universum Film A. G. (UFA) and overseen many of the expressionist films that would influence Laughton's *Night of the Hunter.*[29] The films that Laughton made in the forties, however, did not generally offer the challenging, substantial roles that allowed the actor's creativity to flourish. "Acting in the movies was only using a tenth of my energy," Laughton says in the preface to his anthology of literary selections, *Tell Me a Story* (1957). "The unused energy, as it always does, was churning inside me and turning me bad."[30] That energy was applied to other activities, all of which helped to prepare him for directing *The Night of the Hunter.*

Naturally enough, Laughton turned first from film to theater—specifically the theater of Bertolt Brecht. He met the exiled playwright among other artists who banded together at the Santa Monica home of Salka Viertel. (Another frequent visitor to Viertel's salon was James Agee.)[31] Laughton and Brecht formed a personal bond that led to professional partnership: they collaborated on a new American version, titled simply *Galileo,* of Brecht's 1938 play *The Life of Galileo.*[32] As Brecht explained, because Laughton did not know German, "we had to decide the gest of each piece of dialogue by my acting it all in bad English or even in German and his then acting it back in proper English in a variety of ways until I could say: that's it."[33] By this process, *Galileo* was tightened and restructured, and Galileo himself became more human, full of contradictions and passions that had not existed in the original text. (The two versions can be compared in a well-annotated edition of the play by John Willett and Ralph Manheim.)[34] In 1947, Joseph Losey directed a production of the new version, though Laughton himself took a director's interest in casting and costumes and the overall look of the presentation. *Galileo* played Los Angeles and New York, but "in neither city did it have any great critical or commercial success."[35] Nevertheless, the play was a milestone for Laughton: he had taken his first steps toward directing. (Despite a directing credit for the 1932 play *The Fatal Alibi*, it was Jed Harris who was in charge.)[36] And he had gained editing skills that would serve him well in his stage productions with Paul Gregory and on the script that James Agee would deliver for *The Night of the Hunter*.

Laughton found another outlet for his creative energy when friends invited him to teach classes in acting. Among some twenty students who gathered in the evenings at Laughton's house were well-known names: Arthur O'Connell, Robert Ryan, Jane Wyatt, and Shelley Winters, who was only a few years away from being cast in a leading role for *The Night of the Hunter*. In the summer of 1950, Laughton directed his group in *The Cherry Orchard* at Eugénie Leontovich's tiny Stage Theatre. He himself played Gaev.[37] As director, Laughton gave "minute attention to every aspect of the production" and achieved critical and popular success. Laughton's joy in his students and in directing led to preparations for a production of *Twelfth Night*, in which Laughton would play Sir Toby Belch.[38] But by then Laughton and Gregory had joined forces, and Laughton's first reading tours had proved a surprising success. Gregory believed that Laughton's teaching was mainly for the instructor's ego. "Get rid of these people, and let's do something," he told Laughton.[39] Teaching gave way to a new life on the road. That vaudeville existence would further Laughton's directing and storytelling skills even as it finally exhausted him and prompted Gregory to seek out a film project that would allow Laughton a chance to stay home in Hollywood.

The Producer

"My whole thing in my lifetime has been to take the good stuff to the public. . . . Money follows achievement. . . . I believe this. I've lived it all my life." There, in plain language, is the credo of Paul Gregory. His career is marked by a willingness to take risks, to pursue improbable ventures in the belief that, because they interest him, they will interest an audience. "I've never known what [the public] wanted," he said. "But I know what I can sell."[40]

From an early age, Gregory combined that confidence—the chutzpah of the showman—with a love of literature and language. It was a combination that allowed his partnership with Laughton to flourish. Growing up as Jason Burton Lenhart in Waukee, Iowa, he was entranced with stories told him by his aunt Edda, a full-blooded Cherokee who lived to the age of 107. In 1934, at age fourteen, he opened a suitcase that she had left him and discovered a cache of books that included the Bible, Emerson, and the Rubáiyát, along with a note from his aunt that told him the books were "the best things you can read." In that same year, he took a job on a morning radio show at station KSO in Des Moines.[41] A United Artists press release from 1955 claims that Gregory read "the classics" on the air.[42] What he read were the funny papers.[43] The funnies also served for his first theatrical enterprise, in which he and his friends staged their favorite comics in a henhouse, and Gregory took the part of Li'l Abner.[44] A more literary endeavor, as part of a class presentation, soon followed: scenes from *John Brown's Body*. Gregory wrote to Stephen Vincent Benét for permission to perform his forty-five minute cutting. The author was impressed with the excerpt and granted permission to the young man, who would one day produce a two-hour adaptation of the epic poem, edited and directed by Charles Laughton. Gregory's precocious business sense is revealed even more clearly in a piece he wrote at age sixteen for a national essay contest. His essay, on the topic of lowering prime interest rates, won him a scholarship to Drake University. On the Des Moines campus, Gregory began his career as a promoter when he persuaded local sponsors to fund concerts by performers like Burl Ives and the dancer Ruth St. Denis. He would use skills honed in college to finance Laughton's first reading tours fifteen years later.[45]

Show business was ultimately too strong a lure for Gregory. At age nineteen, he left Drake and moved to Hollywood.[46] It was 1939, the same year that Charles Laughton suffered through a summer of record heat in torturous makeup to play Quasimodo in *The Hunchback of Notre Dame* and achieve what Callow calls "a cornerstone of this century's dramatic achievement."[47] The handsome newcomer Jason Lenhart, on the other hand, signed with Metro-Goldwyn-Mayer (MGM), which envisioned him as a second Gregory Peck and gave him a name better suited to a marquee before putting him into a few quickly forgotten films. The newly christened Paul Gregory eventually decided that film acting was not for him.[48] He did subsequently tour for several months with a Gilbert and Sullivan troupe as a member of the chorus—not, as later reports have it, in the role of manager—but when he returned to L.A. he took a job as a soda jerk.[49] While serving up phosphates and banana splits, Gregory met the man who would set him on his life's true course. Dr. Charles Hurt, who conducted the choir of the Hollywood Presbyterian Church, introduced Gregory to a member of his group, the actor and singer Dennis Morgan. With Hurt's encouragement, Gregory organized successful concert dates for Morgan in San Diego, Fresno, San Francisco, and Sacramento. Morgan was represented by the Music Corporation of America (MCA), which was looking for someone to head up its concert bureau. Gregory, already in business with MCA's client, was an obvious choice. In 1947, he moved to New York and joined the ranks of the city's theatrical agents. As vice president in charge of MCA's concert division, Gregory booked tours for such performers as Ralph Edwards, Spike Jones, and Tommy Dorsey.[50] "I didn't like it," he recalled. "It was against my basic nature to be out all night with Gene Krupa."[51] The artist who better suited Gregory's nature was about to enter his life.

It is at this point, two years before Davis Grubb even imagined writing a novel about a mad preacher, that the story of *The Night of the Hunter* begins.

One

PARTNERS

An Evening with Charles Laughton

One night in March 1949, Paul Gregory sat at the bar of an East Side restaurant called the Chambord, waiting for Dennis Morgan and his wife, who were coming in from Chicago. "I got the call from Dennis that they were snowbound in Buffalo and wouldn't make it," recalled Gregory. "And just at that time, I looked up on the television screen over the bar, and there was Laughton on the Ed Sullivan show."[1]

Charles Laughton was reading chapter 3 from the book of Daniel, the tale of the burning fiery furnace and Nebuchadnezzar's sudden conversion.[2] As *Time* magazine described the scene a few years later, Gregory "stared entranced at the bar's TV set as Laughton dramatized his readings by balletlike turnings of his heavy body, ducking his dewlapped chin into his collar, shooting sly glances from his spaniel-sad eyes."[3] The spectacle remained vivid in Gregory's mind some thirty years later: "I noted that nobody spoke while Laughton was speaking—even the bartender looked respectful."[4]

For Gregory, the moment was an epiphany. "I thought, 'My goodness, I can take him and send him all over the country, doing his readings.'" He raced across town to West Thirty-ninth Street and waited for Laughton to emerge from the stage door of the Maxine Elliott Theater, from which *Toast of the Town* was broadcasting.[5] (The name of the program would change to *The Ed Sullivan Show* on September 25, 1955, and on that landmark telecast, Robert Mitchum, Lillian Gish,

Shelley Winters, and Peter Graves would play scenes from *The Night of the Hunter.*)[6] "I approached him," Gregory recalled, "and he said, 'Talk to my agent.' And I said, you've just thrown away a million dollars, Mr. Laughton," a statement that brought the actor up short. "There isn't an agent in the world who would understand what the hell I'm talking about. And he said, 'Well, let's have a drink, old boy.' So we went to the Algonquin Hotel bar, . . . and we talked, and about four in the morning I left with a contract on Algonquin stationery to represent him to do [the readings]."[7] Laughton's widow, Elsa Lanchester, tells a story similar to Gregory's, though she ends it more sedately: "Paul and Charles met, and they went to a quiet bar to talk." In her account, Laughton was "enchanted with the idea" for the readings and called her up "at once," full of excitement.[8] (For the record, other versions of the encounter say that Gregory contacted Laughton the day after the *Sullivan* performance.[9] One hopes that these more prosaic reports are untrue.)

The result of Gregory's impetuous trip across Manhattan was a compelling show that starred Laughton, a lectern, and a pile of books. Simon Callow offers a vivid description:

> It started with him shambling onto the platform in an
> overcoat from which, balefully eyeing the audience, he
> would remove books, one by one, making a pile out of
> them. Then the overcoat would come off to reveal him
> attired much as he would be in the street, i.e., shabbily.
> He'd chuckle: "Here we are again—an actor and an audi-
> ence . . . ", and he'd be off, with the first reading, after
> which, "I'll tell you a story," he'd suddenly say, and it might
> be a four-line gag about a little boy he spoke to in Athens,
> Ohio, or it might be an anecdote about Henry Moore.[10]

The books were merely for show—some were hollowed-out props—because Laughton had his texts memorized. Indeed, Gregory called Laughton's performance one of "rehearsed spontaneity," a phrase that nicely describes Laughton's method of directing *The Night of the Hunter.* From night to night, depending on the mood of the audience, Laughton would change the order of his program, though he always maintained a balance between lighter works—short poems or a piece by James

Thurber, for instance—and weightier passages from, say, the Bible or Shakespeare.[11]

Without knowing it, Laughton for years had been preparing himself for the show eventually called *An Evening with Charles Laughton*. He had offered readings in his films (the Gettysburg Address in *Ruggles of Red Gap* [1935], the Bible in *Rembrandt* [1936]) and to hospitalized soldiers during World War II, and in 1944 he released a record on which he read from the Christmas chapter in *The Pickwick Papers*.[12] Despite that groundwork, it took someone of Paul Gregory's imagination to conceive a one-man show. Indeed, during his five-year association with Laughton, Gregory exhibited remarkable acumen in recognizing projects that allowed for the creative expression his partner craved.

Paul Gregory Presents

"Beyond acting," Elsa Lanchester observes, "Charles' chief talent, I think, was construction. You might call it editing. He was never a creative playwright, but he was a master cutter. He would have liked to have been a writer, because in fact he really knew how to build a dramatic house."[13] Laughton had already gained experience in dramatic construction from his adaptation of *Galileo*, but the productions with Gregory—*Don Juan in Hell*, *John Brown's Body*, and *The Caine Mutiny Court-Martial*—prepared him more thoroughly for his most challenging editorial job: working on James Agee's long first draft for *The Night of the Hunter*.

The text of *Don Juan*, from the third act of George Bernard Shaw's *Man and Superman*, is a discourse on reason and sensuality, marriage and womanhood, and as many other topics as Shaw could cram into a single, extended scene. Although Shaw had asked that his entire text be used without any cuts,[14] Laughton found it necessary to eliminate lines here and there, chiefly in the interest of pacing and time, though a few bits dismissive of religion seem to have been cut to avoid offense (an ironic self-censorship in light of the way Laughton and Gregory offended church organizations with *The Night of the Hunter*). Laughton edited the scene lightly and maintained the progression of Shaw's philosophical argument.[15]

To adapt *John Brown's Body* for three performers and an onstage chorus, Laughton had to edit more extensively, and he did the job with a sure poetic touch. In a foreword to a 1941 edition of the poem, Stephen Vincent Benét says that "three meters do most of the work: blank verse . . . ; the light, swift meter . . . ; and the longer, rougher line."[16] In the 1953 recording of the Gregory-Laughton show, one discovers that Laughton maintains the balance of those meters in the way he distributes lines among individual performers and the chorus. Even in compressed form, Laughton captures both the sweep of history and the details of human life within Benét's epic scheme.[17] (Laughton had performed in a version of the poem on radio for Norman Corwin's CBS program *The Pursuit of Happiness* [1939–40]. Lanchester, who costarred with her husband, describes the program as "using music, chorus, and sound effects"—a precursor, then, to the 1953 production.[18] Although that program seems to be lost, it sounds similar to a Corwin production on *The Columbia Workshop* [1939]. Corwin's own skillful condensation of the poem is a model for Laughton's later version.[19])

For his first two shows, Laughton was able to adapt the scripts at his own pace in his own way. The script for *The Caine Mutiny Court-Martial* had to be shaped in collaboration with its author, Herman Wouk, while the show was in its pre-Broadway tryout. Laughton had not initially been involved in the play. He came in when the original director, Dick Powell, was fired.[20] The first order of business for Laughton was to create a workable script. Wouk's first draft ran to four hours. Over one weekend, Laughton cut out more than an hour. In a *New York Times* piece published the week before the play's successful Broadway opening, Wouk recalls his reaction: "When Laughton gave me back my script, . . . I felt like saying, 'Look you fat sonofabitch, you can't do that to me.' But actually I know his editing was the thing. He took the script and made it into a play."[21] The published script bears the following testament to Laughton's work:

> This play is dedicated to
> Charles Laughton
> in admiration and gratitude.

Laughton recalls that in Boston he was having trouble articulating to Wouk what was needed to make the script hold together. He took the playwright to the Boston Art Museum, and together they studied a Japanese screen composed of gray monkeys and black birds descending in an arc that, to Laughton, sealed "the pattern of the picture." In reference to *Caine Mutiny*, Laughton said to Wouk:

> "The birds are missing." I looked at Herman. He was
> blushing.
> "Damn you, Charles, damn you," he said and he burst
> out laughing. The screen had said what I had been unable
> to say.
> The following day we had a script with the necessary
> emphases beautifully written.[22]

Laughton's indirect method of conveying ideas would become familiar to the crew on *The Night of the Hunter*. At production meetings, he would read from Davis Grubb or Dickens or the Bible to help convey what he was after on screen.[23] The preceding story is significant, too, for the way it illustrates Laughton's visual acuity. He naturally thought in terms of images, even when constructing the script for a play. Laughton's imagination seems ready to be set loose in the world of film, where a story can be told in pictures. In his description and analysis of the Japanese screen, one sees the director who, with Stanley Cortez at his side, would compose the beautifully balanced shots that are a hallmark of *The Night of the Hunter*.

One also sees an anticipation of the film in the minimalism of the Gregory-Laughton stage productions. "When I was in school and interested in play producing," Gregory explains in a profile for the *Los Angeles Times*, "I had the habit of undressing a production, that is, trying to estimate what a play was like in its essentials, without extraneous decor."[24] *Don Juan in Hell* and *John Brown's Body* are extensions of Laughton's readings. In *Don Juan*, instead of one man at a podium "reading" from texts he had memorized, there were four actors (Charles Boyer, Cedric Hardwicke, Agnes Moorehead, and Laughton) in evening dress on stools—"those damnable stools," as Hardwicke remembered them[25]—"reading" from scripts they knew by heart. If Gregory turned to *John Brown's Body* because he "wanted to follow *Don Juan in Hell* with something panoramic,"[26] the show nevertheless used a bare setting—part of a balustrade, a red bench—and only a trio of actors in evening dress (Raymond Massey, Judith Anderson, and Tyrone Power) to play dozens of parts alongside a chorus of twenty men and women.[27] *The Caine Mutiny Court-Martial*, which featured Henry Fonda, Lloyd

Nolan, and John Hodiak, was also presented in a spare style. The courtroom was suggested by a judge's bench, a round witness stand, and a long table for the prosecution so that viewers could concentrate on the words and ideas of the drama.[28] In the *Times* profile, Gregory says, "One cannot be this restrained in the treatment of decor for films. Reality is demanded."[29] Yet on *The Night of the Hunter*, Laughton crafted scenes that drew on the design principle of the stage shows he had done with Gregory. For the revival meeting, the shooting script reads, "No set necessary for this scene. Flare or flares, in every SHOT. Faces lighted by flares."[30] On film, the scene is indeed stripped to essentials—flares and faces against a backdrop that suggests a tent. Later, at Preacher's trial, we never see the full courtroom. John sits in a witness chair, while we hear the prosecutor's offscreen voice and see his arm reach into frame. Even in some shots that contain more realistic decor, the image has a spare, presentational quality, such as Preacher's dark form beside the gas lamp in Willa's yard or Preacher crossing the horizon in the moonlight on a horse.

The musical aspects of *Don Juan in Hell* and, especially, *John Brown's Body* form another connection to *The Night of the Hunter*, where music plays a vital role in the film's overall effect. While the stage adaptation of *John Brown* was still being prepared, Gregory brought in the composer Walter Schumann, well known at the time for records of popular songs with his choral group, the Voices of Walter Schumann, to develop a score for the show. In the LP recording of *John Brown's Body*, one can hear lyrical melodies, sung a cappella, that look ahead to the lullabies in *The Night of the Hunter*.[31] In both works, the overused word *haunting* is an apt term for Schumann's ethereal themes. For *John Brown*, Schumann created musical bridges between dialogue—a waltz, for example, or a Yankee melody—that allowed Laughton to condense Benét's poem and make swift transitions from scene to scene.[32] When Schumann signed on to write the score for *The Night of the Hunter*, he once again composed music even before production began.[33] Laughton and Schumann's close working relationship on the film was a happy extension of their stage work.

Alongside Schumann's melodies, music in a figurative sense adds dimension to Laughton's theatrical presentations and film. The director chose not to use the Mozart theme that Shaw wrote into *Don Juan*, but the musical nature of the show is conveyed by the name that Gregory gave the ensemble of actors, who sat onstage with music stands in front of them: the First Drama Quartette.[34] In liner notes for the 1952 recording, Jacques Barzun calls *Don Juan in Hell* a "fugue for four voices."[35] Kurt Singer grasps the show's inherent musicality when he describes Laughton's direction: "He was like a Toscanini conducting his orchestra."[36] Writing about Laughton's direction of *John Brown's Body*, in which the actors pass dialogue and narration back and forth, Raymond Massey also turns to musical imagery: "He conducted us like a maestro, bringing the performance to dramatic climaxes and modulating us to the moments of horror, pity and doom."[37] The sound of each actor for the stage played a significant role in the casting. "I always first cast with my eyes closed," Gregory once said. "I think that if you can't hear the sounds of a given piece, you shouldn't try to produce it."[38] Laughton evidently felt the same way, because the resonance of the actors in *Don Juan in Hell* and *John Brown's Body* looks ahead to *The Night of the Hunter*, where the voices are carefully balanced against one another: Mitchum's booming baritone as he delivers his "Right-Hand-Left-Hand" sermon; Evelyn Varden's sickly sweet drawl, "And you don't get a smidgen of my fudge unless you *stay* for the pick-nick"; and Lillian Gish's mellifluous lilt as she recalls "them olden days, them hard, hard times."

The importance of a musical quality in the actors' delivery is made clear in the typescript of *The Night of the Hunter*'s final screenplay. After Willa's murder, we see the faces of John and Pearl at a basement window while Preacher playfully calls for them. On page 74 of the typescript, his line is written out in musical notation not found in the first draft and not suggested by any description in the novel:[39]

PREACHER'S VOICE (O.S.)

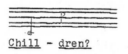

Chill - dren?

Example 1.1
Preacher's call to John and Pearl, typescript of final screenplay
for *The Night of the Hunter*, 1954.

In the film, Mitchum approximates the specified octave jump. A later scene on page 89 of the typescript—a scene photographed but cut from the film—uses the same notation for the same offscreen words when Preacher is locked behind the basement door and speaks with false sweetness to the children. It is unfortunate that the musical notes are not reproduced in the version of the shooting script published in *Agee on Film: Five Film Scripts* (1960) and republished in 2005 as part of the Library of America's *James Agee: Film Writing and Selected Journalism.* They are essential to Laughton's conception of the film.

John Brown's Body demonstrates that even before making *The Night of the Hunter,* in which nonrealistic sounds heighten the drama, Laughton was fascinated with stylized sound and used it in imaginative ways. The onstage chorus chants as though in a Greek drama ("Horses of anger trampling, horses of anger/Trampling behind the sky in ominous cadence") or creates crowd noises and sound effects (drums, marching feet, a faraway bugle). The voices of *John Brown's* lead performers frequently blend with the chorus. Judith Anderson, for instance, draws out the word *wind* to mingle with a wind sound being created by the group.[40]

In all of his work with Gregory, Laughton's chief aim is to serve the author, to respect the creator's original words. The productions demonstrate how closely Laughton identifies with his material. Although he himself chose *Don Juan in Hell,* it was Gregory who selected the other projects. Gregory's ability to match the director with the ideal text, combined with his skill at casting for stage and screen, made him a creative force in his partnership with Laughton. Yet for all that, Gregory's chief strength, as he himself admitted, was as a businessman and marketer.

"Merchandise Man"

Lillian Gish noted the balance that Gregory and Laughton achieved in their relationship. "An artist is like a six month old kitten in business matters usually," she said, "and he needs someone he can trust, someone to manage the business for him."[41] During production on *The Night of the Hunter,* for example, Gregory shielded Laughton from interference by United Artists, which he liked to call "united against the artists."[42] As Gregory explained it, "I encouraged Charlie to not be bound by the number of pages that he was supposed to shoot every day. I said, 'You be satisfied with your scenes, you be satisfied that when you say "cut," you've got what you want. And I'll fight the battles for you.' "[43]

Gregory, however, did not win a battle over the film's marketing strategy. That loss was particularly bitter for a producer who once defined himself in these words: "I am a merchandise man."[44] United Artists chose to release *The Night of the Hunter* into theaters nationwide. "I tried to get [United Artists] not to, but I just ran into a stone wall," said Gregory (*HH,* 351). He recognized that Laughton's unusual film required an unusual marketing plan. "I wanted to road-show it. I had been all over the country, . . . and I knew these towns. . . . It was a matter of . . . taking the film under your arm and going out and selling it. And it could have been done."[45]

It had certainly been done for *An Evening with Charles Laughton.* The first ten-week reading tour did not attract large audiences.[46] Things changed when Gregory left MCA and took charge of the tours himself.[47] He drove from town to town in Southern California, renting halls and selling tickets in bulk to church and civic groups. "We did those towns for almost five years," said Gregory. He and Laughton were eventually making $5,000 to $7,000 a night.[48] A list of the dates Laughton played in just one year looks like a schedule from the days of vaudeville—or rather, as Gregory pointed out, "more like the old Chautauqua than vaudeville."[49] During one tour in 1953–54, the performance halls ranged from the Shubert Theater in New Haven, Connecticut, to the Knife and Fork Club in Sioux City, Iowa, with stops at dozens of other clubs, churches, and colleges around the country.[50] "Charles' reputation as a reader grew and grew," says Lanchester, who goes on to offer a description of Laughton's new career: "He read on the Dinah Shore and Jack Paar television programs, in the same way as other performers went on to sing or dance. He became Charles the Reader . . . and Teacher. Audiences wanted and waited for him to read and tell them stories about America."[51] As a result of his fame onstage, in 1953 Laughton appeared in twenty-nine episodes of his own syndicated television series, *This Is Charles Laughton* (edited by Robert Golden, who would soon become editor on *The Night of the Hunter*). At a podium in front of a gray curtain, he read for fifteen minutes from, say, Shakespeare, *The Arabian Nights,* or fables by Aesop and James Thurber. A few years later he released records on which he read from the Bible and, in a two-disc set titled *The Story-Teller,* offered a version of his road-show program.[52]

Gregory's success at creating audiences for Laughton's readings was repeated with *Don Juan in Hell* and *John Brown's Body*. Both productions toured extensively before coming into New York for successful limited runs.[53] *Don Juan in Hell*, in particular, received a good deal of attention in the press, including an article by John Houseman and a cover story in *Time* magazine.[54] Given Gregory's achievements with the Laughton tours and his ability to make a popular success out of "highbrow" material, it is understandable why the producer wanted his chance "to road-show" *The Night of the Hunter*. It is tantalizing to think about what Gregory, with his "great toughness and flair" and his "smooth, persuasive manner," might have accomplished if he had been active in the selling of Laughton's film.[55]

The Storyteller

Although Gregory was unable to employ marketing strategies he had used for Laughton's stage shows, Laughton himself did find ways to use his theatrical success in connection with *The Night of the Hunter*. For instance, the "original soundtrack recording" of the film, released by RCA in 1955, is not the usual collection of musical cues. It presents, as the cover explains, "Charles Laughton in a reading of *The Night of the Hunter*." The recording is its own adaptation of Grubb's work. A credit even reads, "Based on the United Artists Film and Davis Grubb Book." Grubb wrote a script that condenses his novel into some thirty minutes of narration. Here the children's flight to the skiff that will carry them away from Preacher is compressed into a new form with new words: "One last chance, John. Take Pearl's small hand and the doll with its cursèd treasure and run to the boat, John. To the boat, quickly! Already the swift, razor-edged blade of the madman's knife glints in the moonshine. Hear it whisper as it slashes its way through the brush, filth, and vines upon your very heels, John. Push, boy! Free the boat from the clasp of the shore. Quick, boy! He's nearly to the water's edge." Laughton's dramatic reading of the script is accompanied by music from Walter Schumann's score. The production is essentially a radio program. Grubb creates his scenes with sharp, visual details and varies the rhythms of his spoken sentences to maintain a suspenseful pace. The unique recording, however, did not help to bring customers into the theaters. (The LP eventually became a high-priced collector's item. Several years ago, a copy at Footlight Records in New York City was selling for $125. In 1999, the recording was rereleased as a more reasonably priced CD.)[56]

Laughton also considered using his storytelling persona in the film itself. Among nearly eight hours of *Night of the Hunter* outtakes at the UCLA Film and Television Archive is footage of Laughton speaking directly to the audience and reading from the Bible. He was experimenting with ways to begin his film. The shooting script starts with children playing hide-and-seek while a narrator's voice reads Bible verses. Toward the end of production, on October 2, 1954, Laughton filmed a prologue in which Lillian Gish speaks to offscreen children and reads passages from the Bible. Some three weeks later, Laughton decided to try his own hand at opening the movie.

In the outtakes one can see that Laughton, keeping with his directorial technique all through production, does not cut between takes. The camera rolls while he tries out different approaches to his lines. If he stumbles, he simply begins again. "No, don't cut it, don't cut it," he tells his offscreen crew at one point. "This is all voice." If he intended for part of his recitation of the Bible to become voice-over, like Gish's readings in the finished film, he planned to be on camera at the start of the scene. The prologue opens with Laughton in suit and tie seated at a table, peering through glasses at an open book before him. In one take he removes the glasses, looks up, and says, "Hello." In another he looks up as though surprised to discover an audience: "Oh, hello." (The effect is laughable, and he does not repeat it.) He goes on to say, "Before we start this, uh, epic"—he gives a wry chuckle—"I wanted to remind you of some words in the Sermon on the Mount." Throughout the takes, he ad-libs various comments about the Bible verses: "Here's a good one. . . . There's a lovely one here that you remember. . . . 'Judge not, that ye be not judged': it's a wonderful thing that we all try to live by and find it very hard to." The outtakes allow us to see Laughton developing the "rehearsed spontaneity" that Gregory mentioned in describing his reading programs. From take to take, Laughton works through various possibilities to achieve a casual voice and attitude. He acts as though he is just discovering a verse on the page, or he pretends to be searching his memory for the words. He tries a take with glasses off completely, another in which he holds the glasses, then puts them on to read. In episodes of *This Is Charles Laughton,* he uses his glasses as a prop in the same calculated way.

For this abandoned opening, Laughton uses the image of himself familiar to viewers in the fifties to invite the audience in, to welcome them to the reading of yet another story. Gregory felt that the image was out of place within the film. Hinting at another marketing strategy that was never used, he said to Laughton, "If we took [the film] on tour, . . . and you walked out on the stage, you could sit on the stool, and you could talk to the audience, and we could get twenty dollars a night from all over the country instead of two-fifty."[57] Gregory's instincts were right. The effect of a self-referential filmed prologue is to subvert the story, which becomes, in Laughton's ironic phrase, "this epic." The viewer is kept at a distance from the tale by the incongruity of Charles Laughton, reader from the realm of theater and television, preparing his audience for a motion picture. The Gish prologue, on the other hand, establishes a dreamlike aura that is essential to *The Night of the Hunter* and introduces the audience, however obliquely, to an important character in the story. Laughton the director wisely rejected Laughton the storyteller to frame his movie.

Yet Laughton's peripatetic career as a reader did inform his direction of the film. In his anthology *Tell Me a Story,* Laughton writes, "I have traveled all over the United States on reading tours. Once I traveled 23,000 miles in thirteen weeks and played eighty-seven engagements. I suppose I have been at more places in the United States than any other actor before me."[58] His experiences on the road gave the transplanted Britisher an understanding of the country that would help him in transferring Grubb's American landscape to the screen. As Lanchester puts it, "Charles' love and respect for America grew as he toured the little towns and cities across the country."[59] In *The Night of the Hunter,* expressionistic sequences, as well as the film's overall sense of experimentation, have what one might call a European sensibility. But the movie's feel for the countryside and the small towns of West Virginia comes from someone with a profound affection for the regions of "the fabulous country," as Laughton calls it in the title of his second anthology of readings.

Laughton continued his lucrative reading tours to the end of his life, even though he "had come to hate them."[60] Gregory recognized that the tours were becoming burdensome and looked to yet another career for

Laughton. "I wanted to bring Charlie into focus as a top [film] director and have him eventually quit performing," he said.[61] At the time, late 1953, Davis Grubb's first novel was still in galleys. Gregory received a call from Harold Matson, who headed up his own literary agency in New York. "He knew me, and he knew me well," Gregory recalled. "He said to me one day, 'You know, I've got a writer that's absolutely crazy, Paul, but you would understand him, and he would understand you.'"[62] Gregory and Laughton were both in New York, staying on the same floor at the St. Moritz. Matson sent *The Night of the Hunter* galleys to Gregory, who, certain the book would make a first-rate movie, passed the galleys on to Laughton. As Gregory later told Grubb, "Here came Laughton wallowing down the hallway in his nightshirt, waving this book, saying, 'We've found it, we've found it!'" Although it was the middle of the night, Laughton and Gregory talked for some two hours about turning the novel into a film.[63] Gregory offered the Matson Agency $75,000 for the book. "I owned it before it was published," he said.[64]

For Laughton, directing a movie offered yet another way to tell a story. He could apply principles of construction and direction learned over four years of theatrical collaboration, but he could move his tale forward on images even as he reveled in language, voices, and music. Although his circle of collaborators would grow to meet the demands of a technological medium, the only person whose help he sought at first was the man who wrote the words for *The Night of the Hunter*. More than once Grubb recalled that Irving Thalberg had told Laughton, "You can't make a good motion picture unless you have the writer sitting in a chair beside you."[65] It was advice that both Laughton and Gregory took to heart. "I encouraged Laughton to be in touch with Davis," Gregory said. "I felt it was essential."[66] When Laughton discovered that Grubb was living in Philadelphia, he picked up the phone and gave the astonished author a call. Years later, Grubb could still remember Laughton's first words: "My God, man, who are your Masters?"[67]

Two

DAVIS GRUBB
AND HIS "RIVER BOOK"

Many Masters

William Blake and Charles Dickens, William Faulkner and Thomas Wolfe, Hans Christian Andersen and Sax Rohmer (author of the Fu-Manchu mysteries): these are but a few of Grubb's "Masters."[1] The list reads like a program from one of Laughton's reading tours. Laughton, who writes that Hans Christian Andersen "is one of the best of all story-tellers" and who calls Thomas Wolfe "one of the great masters," found in Grubb a soul mate.[2] In *The Night of the Hunter* he found a multifaceted novel that appealed to his eclectic taste. According to Grubb, on that first night when Laughton and Gregory stayed up to talk about the novel as a film, Laughton told his partner, "It's a really nightmarish sort of Mother Goose tale. A beautiful ballad, folk-tale, and real Americana."[3]

Laughton's description points out how hard it is to classify Grubb's novel. To reviewers from the fifties the work is by turns a "fairy story," a "little masterpiece of horror," a book of "suspense and terror," and a "poetic thriller."[4] *Time* saw a connection with tales about criminal life, noting that Grubb's book "has some of the tension of Marie Belloc Lowndes' famed story of a psychopathic killer, *The Lodger*," and Anthony West in the *New Yorker* calls Preacher "a sort of Jack the Ripper," implicitly linking the book to a history of tales and dramas about the Victorian slasher.[5] Scholarly attempts to define these genres only confirm that *The*

Night of the Hunter slides in and out of various categories. The book has attributes of the thriller, in which "crime is always heinous,"[6] and "the audience knows who the culprit is from the start—even if the characters in the fiction do not."[7] In defining two other genres, David Punter suggests that horror "has to do with what frightens, or disgusts, us to death" (which Preacher is capable of doing), while terror offers "the thought of an escape into a realm where . . . we can re-emerge from our hiding-place" (an escape that Miz Cooper effects for the children and the reader).[8] *Thriller, horror, terror*—the terms all eventually lead back to the "public 'ancestor' form" of works that dabble in fear and dread: the gothic.[9] A stream of gothic literature is at the center of Grubb's novel.

Gothic Echoes

Critical consensus identifies the source of English gothic fiction as Horace Walpole's *Castle of Otranto,* published in 1764. Although gothic elements may be found in earlier works, notably Tobias Smollett's *Adventures of Ferdinand Count Fathom* (1753),[10] Walpole's short novel "introduced all the paraphernalia of classic Gothic: the unscrupulous tyrant; the youthful, virtuous hero; the persecuted virgin heroine; the medieval castle with its attendant caves, forests and crags; the brooding, doomladen atmosphere; supernatural interventions."[11]

Tracing the evolution of the gothic form through the centuries, Elizabeth MacAndrew notes that "its weird tales [were fed] into the mainstream of realistic fiction." She points out that "settings were changed from medieval to contemporary," and "a man's house turned out to be still his Gothic castle."[12] In many ways, the realistic narrative of *The Night of the Hunter* is far removed from the supernatural events of Walpole's tale, in which a gigantic helmet crushes a young aristocrat to death and a ghost rises from the ruins of a castle. Yet one can, following MacAndrew's lead, find analogues to the gothic "paraphernalia" listed here. Grubb offers Preacher as an "unscrupulous tyrant," John as a "youthful, virtuous hero," and Willa as a "persecuted heroine," who, though not virginal, has the naïveté often associated with a virgin. When John tells Pearl a story about a king who lived with his son and daughter "in a castle over in Africa," he seems to be speaking of his own father and implicitly transforms his house into a castle (*NH,* 47). It soon becomes a place of nightmares ("I am having a bad dream," John thinks during one conversation with Preacher [*NH*, 94]), haunted by a kind of demon:

> The house loomed silent in the faint shine of the young spring moon. . . .
>
> Is somebody there? he said to the house, as he tiptoed up the steps. . . .
>
> But there was no reply, no sound, and he opened the screen door and closed it softly and stepped into the shadowed hallway. He knew almost at once that Preacher was there or had been there not an instant before because there was a Preacher smell in the silent air and it was the smell of dread in his nose, and doglike his flesh gathered and bunched at the scent of it. (*NH*, 92)

This passage is one of many that match the "doomladen atmosphere" of *Otranto,* in which, for example, "an awful silence reigned throughout [the castle's] subterraneous regions" while the Princess Isabella, attempting to escape the tyrant Manfred, "frequently stopped and listened to hear if she was followed."[13] As for otherworldly effects, when Rachel Cooper enters the story to become the children's protector, her appearance has the force of a "supernatural intervention." For the film version of the story, Laughton seizes on that unspoken supernatural quality and opens with an image of an angelic Miz Cooper superimposed over a night sky.

Gothic novels subsequent to *The Castle of Otranto* develop other elements that form a link to *The Night of the Hunter.* In Matthew Lewis's *Monk* (1796), Ambrosio, the eponymous character renowned for his virtue, rapes the young and beautiful Antonia, "and in the violence of his lustful delirium, wounded and bruised her tender limbs."[14] In response to Lewis's novel, Ann Radcliffe wrote *The Italian* (1796) and vividly created the murderous Schedoni, "a demon in the garb of a monk." There is, Radcliffe tells us, "something terrible" in the figure of Schedoni, "something almost superhuman."[15]

Grubb's Preacher is a twentieth-century version of these villainous holy men. Preacher may not burn with Ambrosio's lust and sense of sinfulness—or if he does, he sublimates his feelings into homicidal rage—but he shares a revulsion for the female that Lewis's monk ultimately feels. Preacher is a woman hater drawn to watching strippers and patronizing whores; Ambrosio finds himself "at once repulsed from and attracted towards" Antonia, whom he finally murders with a dagger.[16]

Grubb also writes of Preacher in such a way that he, like Radcliffe's Schedoni, takes on superhuman characteristics—specifically, characteristics associated with the devil. Just as the devil in medieval theology smells of sulphur,[17] the Preacher gives off a foul odor. It fills the house in the previously quoted scene, and "the hot breath" and "bad smell" oppress John when he is trapped beside Preacher on a boat in a thunderstorm (a storm that is, with its "high keening shrills of the river wind and the bombardment of the thunder" [NH, 83–84], a classic gothic effect in the vein of, say, the howling winds and roaring thunder of a tempest in The Monk[18]). Rachel, the only other character to see through Preacher, can smell his odor "like I can smell burning brush filth in October even when there ain't no smoke on the sky to mark it" (NH, 244). Preacher becomes the very image of the devil, who proverbially never sleeps, when John, on the run from the killer, wakes in a hayloft in the middle of the night and sees Preacher in the distance "moving still in that infinitely sinister slowness." The boy asks himself, "Don't he never sleep? Don't he never find a barn and climb up in the hay and shut his eyes like other mortals do at night or does he just keep on hunting me and Pearl to the end of the world?" (NH, 201).

As a type of the demonic, Preacher is related to the title character in another significant work of gothic literature, Melmoth the Wanderer (1820), by the Irish curate Charles Robert Maturin. Paul Hammond's 1979 article on the film version of The Night of the Hunter, "Melmoth in Norman Rockwell Land," implicitly points to a kinship between Maturin's and Grubb's characters. Melmoth has sold his soul to the devil and wanders the globe seeking release from his Faustian bargain. Preacher submits to the will of a wrathful God as he wanders American small towns seeking widows to rob and murder, yet he, too, craves release: "Lord, won't I never settle down? Lord, won't you never say the word that my work is done?" (NH, 25).

Melmoth, like The Night of the Hunter, is suffused with an atmosphere of fevered, misguided religion; Maturin even includes a passage in which a Father Superior, as outraged by sex as Grubb's Preacher is, entombs an adulterous couple in a room deep in his monastery.[19] The author wryly lets a fiend express an essential idea of the book: people of different faiths agree on one thing, "making their religion a torment;—the religion of some prompting them to torture themselves, and the religion of some prompting them to torture others."[20] In short, Maturin's "real subject is the absurd distortion of the psyche created by systems of belief."[21]

The Night of the Hunter is not so all-encompassing in its religious skepticism. To Grubb, the subject of his book was simply "religious fakery."[22] In opposition to that fakery, he presents Rachel Cooper—a true believer, an ideal of goodness. Nevertheless, Grubb paints his own gothic pictures of religion's "absurd distortions." Preacher, who waits for commands from the Lord to commit murder, sees himself as "the dark angel with the sword of a Vengeful God" (*NH*, 26). Willa, denied sex in her marriage to Preacher, funnels her passion into a hysterical evangelism. As Grubb writes, "Willa had discovered Sin. It seemed somehow that this discovery was something that she had sought and hungered after all her life" (*NH*, 109). Even Walt and Icey Spoon, an everyday couple of everyday piety, become hatemongers in the name of God when they form a mob to lynch Preacher because "he taken the Lord's name in vain and he trampled on His Holy Book!" and "he dragged the name of Jesus through the mud!" (*NH*, 252).

A violent mix of religion, sex, and demonic predators is also found in a significant outgrowth of the gothic novel—the tale of horror. As Noël Carroll explains, "the horror genre proper" stems from "the supernatural gothic, in which the existence and cruel operation of unnatural forces are asserted graphically."[23] Throughout his career, Grubb dabbled in supernatural horror stories, such as "The Horsehair Trunk" (1946), in which a man's spirit leaves his body to commit a murder, or "The Siege of 318" (1976), in which toy soldiers come to life and wage war against a boy's harsh father. *The Night of the Hunter,* like most of Grubb's other novels, remains grounded in realism. Yet the novel's villain shares characteristics with creatures of the horror tale's landscape.

Carroll makes a distinction between monsters in fairy tales, which are "part of the everyday furniture of the universe," and those in horror tales, where "the humans regard the monsters they meet as abnormal, as disturbances of the natural order."[24] John instinctively views Preacher as a disturbance of his "natural order," and Rachel's prayer on the night Preacher lays siege to her house turns the man into a less-than-human force of evil: "Dear God, there is something awful out there in my garden and I've got to keep it from my lambs" (*NH*, 239). Even Willa is troubled by a vague figure who "wandered in and out among the trees of her consciousness," the figure of "something frightful beyond telling—something with the body of a child in its arms" (*NH*, 90). Once the townsfolk know the truth about Preacher, they see him as an abomination, an affront to God, and are bent on destroying him, just as Dr. Frankenstein in Mary Shelley's *Frankenstein* (1818) becomes obsessed with destroying his unnatural creation. In the way Preacher relentlessly stalks his victims, he is indeed kin to Frankenstein's monster—and to the vampire of various tales, especially the smooth-talking, fiendish count in Bram Stoker's *Dracula* (1897). Like the vampire, Harry Powell drains the life from female victims and is a creature—a hunter—of the night. Rachel assures the children that "it'll be sun-up directly and he won't dare to come pokin' around by daylight" (*NH*, 242). The horror story, of course, forms the basis for many classic Hollywood films that are related to the look of Laughton's *Night of the Hunter*. (I will discuss that cinematic connection in chapter 5.) In a complicated circle of influence, the visual echoes of horror films in Laughton's adaptation strengthen the literary connection between tales of horror and Grubb's novel.

American Gothic

For all of its ties to various European forms, *The Night of the Hunter* is finally, as Christopher Morley puts it in *Book-of-the-Month Club News*, "a truly American Gothic."[25] During the age of Lewis and Radcliffe, on a great wave of popularity, the gothic crossed the Atlantic. It was Charles Brockden Brown "who most thoroughly founded the Gothic tradition in American fiction with his novels *Wieland* (1798), *Arthur Mervyn* (1798), *Edgar Huntly* (1799) and *Ormond*, completed in 1799."[26] As Donald A. Ringe points out, Brown prefigures the work of Edgar Allan Poe and Nathaniel Hawthorne, "and his strong affirmation of the use of American materials links him to practically all the American writers who came after him in the early nineteenth century."[27] One could extend that link to writers in the twentieth century, including Davis Grubb.

Brown's first novel, *Wieland*, looks back to European forebears even as it looks ahead nearly two centuries to *The Night of the Hunter*. Where gothic works of Lewis and Radcliffe brought religion and violence, often tinged with a sexual edge, together in the terrors of the Inquisition, Brown combines these elements in an American, evangelical fanaticism. It is God, Wieland believes, who commands him to murder his wife and children. "My sacred duty is fulfilled!" he exclaims after the first killing.[28] Grubb's preacher, with the "knife beneath the wool, the Sword of Jehovah beneath his wrathful fingers," also follows the will of the Lord: "God sent people to him. God told him what to do. And it was always a widow that God brought to him" (*NH*, 21).

In other ways, too, a new literature in a new world altered the face of the gothic genre. Gone are what Brown, in a preface to *Edgar Huntly*, calls "puerile superstition and exploded manners; Gothic castles and chimeras." In their place are such elements as "Indian hostility, and the perils of the western wilderness," features indigenous to the American landscape, full of their own terrors.[29] As Ringe, discussing *Edgar Huntly*, puts it, "The world that the characters face is by and large the natural one, and the sense of mystery and terror derive . . . from the inner workings of their individual minds."[30] Grubb's novel, a tale of psychological terror set in a distinctly American region of back roads and river towns, is a true descendant of Brown's fiction.

Grubb's roads and towns are in a West Virginia haunted by a knife-wielding preacher—one of literature's "grotesques," who help us "to confront the demonic and fix its nightmares in art."[31] *The Night of the Hunter*'s locale and grotesquerie place the novel in a tradition of so-called Southern gothic, a strain of American literature that reaches back at least to Poe and encompasses such latter-day authors as Robert Penn Warren, Flannery O'Connor, and William Faulkner.[32]

In *World Enough and Time* (1950), set in nineteenth-century Kentucky, Warren creates a vivid portrait of his own preacher—a wandering evangelist with the resonant name Corinthian McClardy. He describes McClardy in rolling rhythms that would not be out of place in *The Night of the Hunter*: "He belonged to that old race of Devil-breakers who were a terror and a blessing across the land, men who had been born to be the stomp-and-gouge bully of a tavern, . . . or a raper of women by the cow pen, but who got their hot prides and cold lusts short-circuited into obsessed hosannas and a ferocious striving for God's sake."[33]

Still another tormented relationship with God is depicted in Flannery O'Connor's *Wise Blood* (1952). Hazel Motes, furiously trying to deny Christ, creates a religion from his own psychological needs. He climbs onto the hood of his car to preach the doctrine of "the Church Without Christ." In the course of his violent career, Hazel murders a fraudulent preacher by running him over with his Essex (coincidentally, the same make of car stolen by Grubb's Preacher) and, "to pay" for sins he leaves unnamed, puts out his own eyes and lacerates himself with broken glass and barbed wire.[34]

Wise Blood and The Night of the Hunter each create a world of perverse religion and ever-present threat. O'Connor, however, was a devout Catholic, writing, as she puts it in a prefatory note on Wise Blood's tenth anniversary, "a comic novel about a Christian malgré lui." She allows Hazel Motes a mysterious sanctification; he becomes, in the vision of his bewildered landlady, a "pin point of light."[35] Grubb was skeptical of organized religion because he saw in it so much "outward show and hypocrisy."[36] He creates an earnest novel in which Harry Powell, a type of Antichrist, remains unredeemed at the end, and a mob of sanctimonious Christians storms the county jail to lynch him. Wise Blood and The Night of the Hunter may be, to use O'Connor's phrase about the American South, "Christ-haunted,"[37] but O'Connor resolutely affirms humanity's need for Christ while Grubb remains ambiguous about the means to salvation. Grubb's novel, it is true, concludes on Christmas Eve in the house of the saintly Miz Cooper, thus suggesting that the way out of darkness is through Christian faith. In the final pages of the book, Rachel offers a long benediction for children, the essence of which is in her words "Lord save little children! They abide. The wind blows and the rain is cold. Yet, they abide" (NH, 268). John is proof of that endurance. Released from fear and the shadow of the hunter, he nestles into bed under a quilt stitched with the "gentle shepherds" of the Bible (NH, 273). The soothing lyricism of Grubb's finale nearly persuades one that characters in this story live happily ever after in the grace of a Christian world. Yet religious doubts expressed earlier by John cannot be laid to rest even under a Gospel quilt. When Miz Cooper reads to her children about the way Christ "and His folks put up for the night in a barn," John tells us, "I went and looked out the window at the barn while she was reading but I never seen no one so I reckon it is just a story. Or maybe they ain't got here yet and they'll be getting set up in the barn after we're all in bed asleep. You never know what they tell you. You never find out if it's real or a story" (NH, 271–72). If the story of Christ is not true, then perhaps salvation is a secular matter and rests on the actions of a Miz Cooper—on human efforts to bring one another comfort and peace.

Grubb also offers a darker cosmic possibility. While John reflects on the "blue men," enemies who came and took his father away, and on the tattooed fingers of his other enemy, Preacher, the boy wonders, "Is God one of them? Is God on the side of the fingers with names that are letters? . . . She says he is a man of God. And so God is one of them; God is a blue man" (*NH*, 74, 75). Like William Blake, who ponders the figure of a tiger to ask, "What immortal hand or eye / Could frame thy fearful symmetry?" ("The Tyger," lines 3–4), or Herman Melville, who suggests that there is a "vulturism of earth" divinely ordained,[38] Grubb raises a question about the nature of God: is there a demonic dimension to the Almighty?

Along with their theological differences, *Wise Blood* and *The Night of the Hunter* offer a revealing contrast in styles. O'Connor writes understated prose that maintains a distance from the outlandish or horrific events being described: "Haze drove about twenty feet and stopped the car and then began to back it. He backed it over the body and then stopped and got out."[39] Grubb has no use for laconic irony. He sees a world bursting with beauty and horror, with wonder and madness, and he is intent on describing it in full, sensory detail.

American Lyricism

The Night of the Hunter reverberates with the voices of other writers. Consciously or unconsciously, Grubb has adapted them to create his own lyrical medley, which serves as a counterpoint to the novel's gothic effects. Here, for instance, is a sample of a monologue from Faulkner's *As I Lay Dying* (1930). Dewey Dell recalls the time she had sex with Lafe in the woods: "And so it was because I could not help it. It was then, and then I saw Darl and he knew. He said he knew without the words like he told me that ma is going to die without words, and I knew he knew because if he had said he knew with the words I would not have believed that he had been there and saw us."[40] Faulkner's tone and rhythms echo through *The Night of the Hunter* in John's interior monologues. In the following passage, the boy reflects on why he must go to a picnic:

John thought: I will go with them because not going would make them think: What does he know? Why is he afraid for us to see him? Is he afraid we'll make him tell?

He thought: Because Mr. Powell knows. He knows I know where the money's hid. He has always known and that's why he told Mom that fib about Dad saying the money was in the river. (*NH*, 72)

At times, Grubb falls under the spell of Thomas Wolfe. Words from *Look Homeward, Angel* (1929)—"O lost, and by the wind grieved, ghost, come back again"[41]—lurk behind Grubb's sentence, "It had begun to snow and the wind grieved in the stark river trees—a wind like a moaning song—a wind like a hunter's horn" (*NH*, 37). Among other reminiscences, the following exaltation of the Ohio River is perhaps the most Wolfelike: "the dark stream of the river flowed like the blood of the earth itself: old, dark Time coursing to the oceans and never stopping whatever the calendar or clock might say" (*NH*, 267). Wolfe himself tells us: "the river, the dark, immortal river, full of strange tragic time is flowing by us—by us—by us—to the sea."[42]

In the course of his novel, Grubb sings more than one hymn to the Ohio. It is the river on which the children elude Preacher, the river that brings them to Miz Cooper. Grubb deemed the Ohio of such importance in his tale that he could write his agent Don Congdon, "about ten minutes ago I finished the second draft of my river book. I have decided to call it 'The Night of the Hunter.'"[43] Inevitably, Grubb's novel evokes the spirit of Mark Twain, who wrote more than one river book. In *Life on the Mississippi* (1883), Twain exalts his river, "the great Mississippi, the majestic, the magnificent Mississippi, rolling its mile-wide tide along, shining in the sun."[44] In *Adventures of Huckleberry Finn* (1885), he sends Huck and Jim downriver in a raft: "Sometimes we'd have that whole river all to ourselves for the longest time. Yonder was the banks and the islands, across the water; and maybe a spark—which was a candle in a cabin window. . . . It's lovely to live on a raft. We had the sky, up there, all speckled with stars, and we used to lay on our backs and look up at them, and discuss about whether they was made, or only just happened."[45] Glimmerings of that description can be seen in Grubb's picture of John and Pearl in their skiff: "All the long hot day after their escape they had drifted upon the swift river channel and then the river night dropped abruptly upon them and there were no lights but the stars and the shantyboat lamps along the shore and the drifting dust of fireflies against the black, looming hills above the narrows" (*NH,* 195). Thanks to Twain, Grubb's depiction of "two floating innocents," as Margaret Atwood describes John and Pearl, becomes "a quintessential American image."[46] Then, too, John and Huck are boys who, thrust headlong into adulthood, learn truths about both the depravity and the goodness of human nature.

Although I have suggested that *The Night of the Hunter*'s conclusion does not completely dispel religious doubts within the book, Grubb himself, writing from John's point of view, insists on untainted hope: "the night of the hunter was gone forever and the blue men would not come again" (*NH,* 273). Jack Welch tells us, "This kind of belief in the triumph of good persisted in Grubb even to his old age. He has the kind of Emersonian confidence that actually shocked a group of academics in 1978 when he expressed it to them."[47] Reviewers of *The Night of the Hunter* may not have been shocked by Grubb's optimism, but they found the happy resolution of the novel worth commenting on. L. A. G. Strong, writing in the *Spectator,* finds that the novel "in scene and theme . . . suggests Mr. William Faulkner," and he believes Preacher to be "own brother to Faulkner's Popeye," the sexual predator of *Sanctuary* (1931). Yet he makes a distinction between the two authors by noting that if Faulkner had written the novel, "the story would not be so painfully clear or have a happy ending."[48] In the *Saturday Review,* Harriette Arnow writes, " 'The Night of the Hunter' is most impressive for its refreshingly unorthodox treatment. First, the author has dared give a serious work a happy ending."[49]

The sense of hope that rises up steadily through *The Night of the Hunter* aligns the book with work by Appalachian writers like Jesse Stuart and Arnow herself, who shy away from the gothic to present realistic portraits of a region and its inhabitants. Rachel Cooper, mother to five orphaned children, capable of fending off Harry Powell with a shotgun, would not be out of place in *Hunter's Horn* (1949), Arnow's carefully observed novel set in the hills of Kentucky. In that book, Milly Ballew presides with love and fortitude over a family of four children and a husband struggling to maintain a poor farm. Arnow's forthright style is different from Grubb's lush lyricism, but each book portrays human sympathy and familial love as saving graces in a hard world.

Similar graces can be found in works by Jesse Stuart. In his story "Split Cherry Tree" (1939), for instance, a farmer goes to school with a gun to confront the teacher who has kept his son working after school to pay off a debt for a damaged cherry tree. The conflict is resolved without violence on a note of affection between father and son. Like *The Night of the Hunter,* "Split Cherry Tree" concludes with a quiet contentment and the feeling that a new phase of life has begun.

Given *The Night of the Hunter*'s faith in the resilience of the human spirit and the redeeming power of love, it is surprising that Walter Allen, in his review for the *New Statesman,* finds that Grubb's characters are "reminiscent of Mr. Erskine Caldwell's cretinous Georgians."[50] Caldwell maintains a mordantly comic distance from characters like Dude Lester, who in *Tobacco Road* runs over his grandmother's body with a car, and Jeeter, who callously lets the old woman, "with her face all mashed," lie dying in the yard.[51] Grubb enters into the minds and emotions of his characters to understand them. They are not, as Robert D. Jacobs describes Caldwell's creations, "so dehumanized that one can scarcely feel compassion for their plight."[52] The author even allows a twinge of pity for Harry Powell. A victim of his own obsessions, Preacher "sometimes . . . cried in his sleep he was so tired" (*NH,* 25).

If, as Leslie A. Fiedler puts it, "the primary meaning of the gothic romance . . . lies in its substitution of terror for love as a central theme of fiction,"[53] then Grubb's novel has both main themes; it is a synthesis of terror and love. For his film adaptation, Laughton seizes on this literary split and gives it visual form. He draws on cinematic traditions to tell his version of the story in two distinct styles—expressionistic and realistic. Grubb, however, makes no stylistic distinction between the opposing strains in his novel. Here he describes a time soon after Rachel has taken in John and Pearl: "The river brought the time of gold into the valley. Up in the woods the hickory nuts rained their dry patter throughout the still afternoons and there was smoke in the air. . . . John had come home. . . . And yet despite this capitulation John kept his eyes on the river road, . . . harking ever for the clop of that strange horse on the windy, midnight highway, for the creak upon the threshold, the whisper of the hunter's steel" (*NH,* 216–17). Idyll and menace are both wrapped in a sensual, rhythmic prose. They are, Grubb seems to say, inextricably bound together in the fabric of life.

Myth and Fairy Tale

The novel's tale of terror is driven by Preacher. The tale of love is nurtured by Miz Cooper. The opposition of these characters adds another dimension to *The Night of the Hunter*. For all their psychological realism, they function in the novel as archetypes—devil and angel—and they help give the story the quality of a myth. One influence on this religious, mythical aspect of the novel is the poetry of Blake. "He has so many wonderful things to tell us, so many truths," Grubb once said. "He has something for everyone, everywhere."[54] In his foreword to Grubb's novel *Fools' Parade,* Thomas E. Douglass points out that Grubb was drawn to "the collision of opposites" in Blake's work. "The influence of Blake gave Grubb the go-ahead to draw strong, larger-than-life characters who were embodiments of good and evil, love and hate."[55] Margaret Atwood, writing about Laughton's film but speaking implicitly about the novel from which it came, notes the Blake influence in the fact that "for every Song of Experience, there's a Song of Innocence."[56] Thus, Rachel's "Songs of Innocence"—heartfelt stories about Moses and Jesus—are countered by Preacher's hypocritical sermon "Right-Hand-Left-Hand—the tale of Good and Evil" (*NH,* 57). In his film, Laughton creates Blakean contrasts in tune with the novel. When we first see the children, John is helping Pearl button the clothes on her doll. Later we see John, in terror, stuff the stolen money back into the doll while Preacher looms over the children in the background. David Ashley King points out that the film's opening lullaby—a children's chorus over the credits—is matched by the chant "hing, hang, hung," with which a group of children taunt John and Pearl.[57]

Laughton more than once expressed his interest in another aspect of the book: the story's resemblance to a fairy tale. In an interview with Hollis Alpert at the time of the film's release, he repeated an idea he had once expressed to Gregory in private: "It's really a nightmarish sort of Mother Goose tale we were telling."[58] During preproduction, he told his second-unit director, Terry Sanders, that for the scene with John and Pearl in the hayloft he wanted, in words that Sanders copied down in his production notebook, a "fairy tale quality."[59]

Bruno Bettelheim's *Uses of Enchantment* helps us understand *The Night of the Hunter*'s relation to fairy tales. "The fairy-tale hero proceeds for a time in isolation," explains Bettelheim. "The hero is helped by being in touch with primitive things—a tree, an animal, nature."[60] When John and Pearl embark on their river journey, they do beg food from the wives of farmers along the way, but always they are returned alone to the natural world of the river, and one night they take comfort by sleeping among cows in a barn. In the film, the force of nature is precisely what Laughton and his crew emphasize through shots of animals along the river, images of stars, and a vision of cattails blowing into a misty light. The river sequence becomes a visual poem that brings out the fairy-tale quality Laughton saw in the book. Both the novel and fairy stories "abound in religious motifs," and evil in both "is as omnipresent as virtue." At the plot level, "many fairy stories begin with the death of a mother or father. . . . Only by going out into the world can the fairy-tale hero (child) find himself there; and as he does, he will also find the other with whom he will be able to live happily ever after; that is, without ever again having to experience separation anxiety."[61] John's father is executed soon after the novel begins, and eventually his mother is killed. Adults whom John has trusted—his father, his mother, Uncle Birdie—fail him one after the other. Ultimately, they leave him stranded and force him out into the world. There he does indeed discover his courageous, resilient self. When at the end of the story he snuggles under his quilt in Miz Cooper's house, the suggestion is that he will live happily with someone who will never abandon him.

Grubb emphasizes the nature of his story in the script he wrote for the RCA soundtrack. That emphasis is even clearer in the rough script—two single-spaced pages—housed at the Library of Congress. Its language and sentence rhythms are those of a fairy tale (even as they also echo the Bible): "Once upon an evil time of hunger and depression in our land [two children] lived with their mother and father in a house by a river, cradled in the green arms of the great Ohio Valley. . . . And the boy was called John and the girl was Pearl. And their mother was Willa and their father Ben. And Ben was a good man in an evil time—a hungry time—and one day he took a gun to the bank where he drew his pay each week and he slew two men."[62]

Although Grubb identified Hans Christian Andersen as one of his masters, *The Night of the Hunter* seems more strongly connected to the darker stories of the brothers Grimm—"Snow White," for instance, in which a girl is forced to wander alone in a wood to escape the wicked stepmother who eventually tracks the girl down, or "Hansel and Gretel," in which a brother and sister are abandoned by a cruel stepmother in a wood and then must outwit an old witch who keeps them prisoner in her house.

Popular Author

Despite *The Night of the Hunter*'s many literary strands, its story is simple, its plot straightforward, and its characters readily understandable. Although Grubb "always wanted to be known as a serious, artistic writer who was telling the world something important, something religious, something philosophical," he also "intended to earn his living by his writing, thus making commercial appeal a necessity in his life."[63]

It is clear, then, why Grubb would count among his influences mystery stories, which he read "avidly" as a child. Sax Rohmer was a particular favorite. "I loved him," Grubb once said. "I still do" (*HH*, 51). In thirteen books published between 1913 and 1959, Rohmer revels in diabolical deaths generated by the master criminal Dr. Fu-Manchu. For all the overt racism of Rohmer's novels—the government agent on Fu-Manchu's trail says he is working "in the interests of the entire white race"[64]—they demonstrate how to create a suspenseful story and how to move a narrative forward on dialogue. Grubb learned his lessons well, because *The Night of the Hunter,* with its own diabolical villain, is a compelling narrative, rich in dialogue that improves on the functional, melodramatic speech in Rohmer's work.

Another popular writer who exerted significant influence on Grubb was Howard Pyle. Grubb read Pyle as a boy and remained devoted to him all his life.[65] Because Pyle illustrated his own medieval adventure tales, he was a double influence on Grubb, who "attempted to emulate [Pyle's] illustrated books" in his own youthful drawings.[66] One can see Pyle's vivid, well-paced storytelling—by page 4 of *The Merry Adventures of Robin Hood* (1883), Robin has won an archery contest and killed a man[67]—in the steady narrative drive of *The Night of the Hunter.* Pyle's descriptions, laden with adjectives and smoothly integrated into his eventful tales, also had a strong effect on Grubb: "Beyond these squalid huts lay the rushing, foaming river, spanned by a high, rude, stone bridge where the road from the castle crossed it, and beyond the river stretched the great, black forest, within whose gloomy depths the savage wild beasts made their lair."[68]

Grubb frequently published stories in such journals as *Collier's, Ellery Queen's Mystery Magazine, Weird Tales,* the "men's magazine" *Cavalier,* and *Woman's Home Companion.* The last two are a startling contrast that points to the diversity of Grubb's work. His stories range from comic irony—as in his first published piece, "Checker-Playing Fool" (1945), in which an arrogant sheriff is tricked into freeing a prisoner who beats him at checkers—to the "tales of suspense and the supernatural" in a 1964 collection.[69]

In 1950, Grubb wrote another story in a popular vein. He titled it "Gentleman Friend." The tale was a mystery about a killer who preys on country widows. He left the story unfinished but soon expanded it into a novel.

"Gentleman Friend"

Grubb donated the hand-corrected typescript of his story to the West Virginia University Libraries because, as he says in a prefatory note, "It seems to me that this manuscript might be of some interest to scholars who are curious about where, how and why ideas for books begin." He further explains: "The following unpublished and fragmentary story 'Gentleman Friend' is the story which—a year or so later—proved the seedling idea for my first published novel *The Night of the Hunter.* I did two drafts, abandoned it and for the next year and a half the central theme of the naive mother who is in love with a man whom only her child knows to be a mass-murderer, macerated in my head, itched my wits and finally literally drove me into the much more complex form which the novel proved to be."[70]

The idea for both story and novel is rooted in a notorious murder case in Clarksburg, West Virginia. In 1931, Harry Powers was convicted of murdering two widows, who had placed ads in lonely hearts columns, and two children. A mob tried to lynch him, but the state eventually hanged Powers in Moundsville, where Grubb was living at the time.[71] The murders in reality were far more gruesome than anything in the novel, but, as Grubb acknowledged, his work is "*loosely* based on [the

Powers case] in one way or another."[72] As if in tacit acknowledgment of the Harry Powers story, Grubb gives Preacher the name Harry Powell in *The Night of the Hunter*.

In "Gentleman Friend," however, the villain receives the bland name Mister Fielding. Young Jack Blue is distressed that his mother plans to marry Fielding, the "gentleman friend" who answered her letter to a lonely hearts club. The boy becomes convinced that her suitor is the man newspapers have called the "Mocking Bird Killer," a murderer of lonely widows, known only by the pleasant tune he has been heard whistling at the time of the killings. (The murderer's whistling harks back to Fritz Lang's film *M* [1931], in which a child killer whistles Edvard Grieg's "In the Hall of the Mountain King.") Jack is befriended by a man named Weedy. The man claims to be a detective on the trail of Mister Fielding, who is, Weedy asserts, the Mocking Bird Killer. When Weedy is killed, Jack confronts Mister Fielding with a gun. Fielding, however, explains that *he* is a detective who tried to arrest Weedy, the true killer, but had to shoot him in self-defense. Contrite and relieved, Jack goes peacefully to sleep that night. "His father was a detective," he thinks. "That would be something to tell the kids about." But downstairs the supposed detective sharpens a knife while he whistles "a tune that was haunting and gay as the fluting of a mocking bird outside somewhere in the dark."[73]

Essential elements of *The Night of the Hunter* are in place: the killer with a smooth line of talk, the naive widow, the boy who is instantly suspicious of the man his mother trusts. Specific details are also carried over to the novel. The Mocking Bird Killer's whistled tune becomes the hymn "Leaning on the Everlasting Arms." Jack's mother, like the widows whom Preacher finds, has her money hidden in a sugar bowl. During a confrontation with his nemesis, Jack fixates on the "winking link on the gold chain that laced across Mister Fielding's neat, grey vest" ("GF," 5), just as John focuses on "the gleam . . . of Preacher's watch chain against the death-gray vest" (*NH*, 116–17). In the first draft of the screenplay, James Agee seizes on the image for a striking visual effect. A dolly shot from John's point of view moves steadily toward "the fiery gleam of Preacher's watch chain."[74] The shooting script retains the effect (*AF*, 294). Yet after surviving four incarnations of the story, the watch chain disappears; it never gleams in the film.

The story is told from the boy's point of view, and Grubb starts out emphasizing its Oedipal aspect. Jack is distressed over the impending second marriage "because he and his pretty mother had had such pleasant times during that twelve month of her widowdom" ("GF," 1). His mother asks him, "Haven't we always been as close as two people could be since your—your poor father passed on?" ("GF," 2). Yet Grubb seems to lose interest in that psychological subplot. The story remains a light melodrama with an ironic and chilling (though not unexpected) twist at the end.

In expanding his work, Grubb gives it more dimension. He adds texture to the tale through descriptions that evoke a strong sense of place—a sense missing from the short story: "Soon the shantyboat people would join their fiddle and mouth-harp racket to the chorus of green frogs down under the mists in the moonlit willows. And that morning the showboat *Humpty Dumpty* had put in at the landing" (*NH*, 85). He also creates a gallery of secondary characters who add both regional color and substance to a novel about a boy trying to understand the ways of the adults around him. John Harper must contend with the bustling Icey Spoon and her meek husband, Walt; the crafty Miz Cunningham, collector of secondhand goods; and the old salt Uncle Birdie, who, in boasting that he can catch a wily gar with "mother wit—and a horse hair" and raging at the fish he calls the "meanest, suck-egg, bait-stealin' bastard between here 'n' Cairo," links himself to frontier characters of American folklore (*NH*, 137, 138). As Grubb once put it, "The brag went back to Mike Fink and those rascals who . . . would get out, click their heels in the air and say, 'I'm half alligator and half man!' And then they would launch on a tirade" (*HH*, 185).

The mother, a cipher in the story, becomes the novel's more complex Willa, a gullible, love- and sex-starved widow who is driven to replace sex with religious fervor. Overt Oedipal tensions vanish. Grubb, however, makes John's father a character in the novel and creates a situation between son and father that is reminiscent of another tale with its own Oedipal subtext: *Hamlet*. Ben Harper entrusts his son with the secret of the hidden money. John, attempting to fulfill the "oath that he had taken that day in the tall grass by the feet of his doomed and bleeding father" (*NH*, 197), is as burdened as Hamlet, who struggles to fulfill the oath taken at the feet of his own doomed and ghostly father. John and Hamlet also have to battle villainous stepfathers who are, outwardly, paragons of virtue. These echoes of Shakespearean drama add weight to John's saga and help to give it an iconic quality; it becomes a primal tale of a boy's quest through a dangerous landscape to satisfy a father's demand.

Grubb shrewdly gives the boy in the novel a younger sister, thereby adding to the protagonist's burden. That change, along with an alteration that proved central to the novel, is recorded at the end of "Gentleman Friend," in a handwritten note dated November 3, 1951: "Why not make this into two children—brother and sister—and change Mister Fielding into an itinerant preacher? Ponder this out" ("GF," 12). In pondering it out, Grubb realized that he had an opportunity to express himself on a subject of deep personal meaning: hypocrisy in the Christian church. The change of occupation for his main character led Grubb to use details from his own experience. When he was a boy, an Episcopal minister who frequently beat his son used to come to the Grubb house for dinner. "And he would say, 'Can I have a piece of your chicken, Davis?' I'd say, 'No,' and he would say, 'Aw, have a heart.' That phrase kept haunting me through the years, and I put it in Preacher's mouth when I wrote *Night of the Hunter*" (*HH*, 46). Grubb also remembered seeing a man at a bar in Clarksburg, West Virginia. More precisely, he recalled the man's fingers, on which were tattooed the words *love* and *hate*.[75] The picture comes through strongly in the novel: "The fingers. John could not take his eyes from them. They rested together on the tablecloth in pale, silent embrace like spiders entwined. The fingers with the little blue letters" (*NH*, 57).

The hands labeled *love* and *hate* express the spiritual conflict at the heart of the novel. Yet even as Grubb deepens his tale by giving it a religious dimension, he retains features typical of melodrama: a swift pace, scenes of terror and suspense, and broadly delineated characters. The ability to infuse melodrama with substance, to be both popular and literary, reveals Grubb's debt to another of his masters—Charles Dickens, the author who, along with Blake, seems to have meant the most to Grubb.[76] Simon Callow points to connections between Miz Cunningham and Mrs. Gamp, the dissolute nurse in *Martin Chuzzlewit* (1844), and between Rachel Cooper and Betsey Trotwood, David Copperfield's stalwart guardian.[77] But of all Dickens's novels, it is *Oliver Twist* (1846) that is most closely aligned with *The Night of the Hunter* in characterization, story, and theme. Oliver the orphan is an innocent adrift in a shadow world ruled by the grasping Fagin and the brutal Bill Sikes. Yet *Oliver Twist*'s gothic terrors (which, especially in the scene of Nancy's murder, are more explicit than anything in *The Night of the Hunter*) are offset by the grace and generosity of those who take Oliver in: Mr. Brownlow, Mrs. Maylie, and her niece Rose. Dickens, like Grubb, depicts good and evil in broad strokes, and he traps his young hero in a nightmare before letting him wake to the light of virtue.

Reception

In his review of Grubb's book, Walter Allen notes the Dickens influence (he, too, sees a connection with *David Copperfield* [1850], calling Miz Cooper "a hick Betsey Trotwood") but not in a wholly positive way: "The Preacher is an excellent grotesque character; but what one feels is lacking all the time is that urgent relevance of the subject to its times which is one of the great Dickensian qualities. . . . Mr. Grubb's novel does not, it seems to me, succeed in being more than an anecdotal fairy-tale about a singularly barbarous community miles off the high road of civilization."[78] Anthony West, in the *New Yorker,* also disapproves of Grubb's "moron-haunted, neo-romantic countryside."[79] In *Commonweal,* Jean Holzhauer expresses similar thoughts while revealing an even stronger urban bias: "It is hard to know Mr. Grubb's intention in writing a book populated wholly by the simple and the mad. However faithfully such portraits may reflect reality in his setting, the bottom lands of West Virginia, on paper they strain the limits of credulity and border on farce."[80]

Yet even in these negative reviews, the critics see strengths in the novel. Holzhauer writes that "the author when not indulging in a 'Pshaw, now, ma, the boy didn't mean nothin' by his loose talk' level of writing, shows considerable dramatic power."[81] West admits that one can catch "glimpses of a gift for sharp and incisive writing. . . . Three and a half pages describing a man on the staff of the penitentiary going home and sitting down to dinner after Ben Harper's execution are so brilliant as to kindle the liveliest hopes for Mr. Grubb."[82]

Indeed, Grubb's publisher, Harper and Brothers, treated the book as a "Harper Find." Congdon explains the significance of that: The novel "would get special attention from the sales force, as well as special promotion. They printed 1,000 copies of the novel even before a jacket had been designed, and sent it out to a very wide list of booksellers and authors for quotes. The 'Harper Find' meant something to booksellers because it was awarded only occasionally to a new work."[83] Grubb was also treated as a find in many periodicals. His picture, sometimes alongside those of other first novelists, accompanied notices in the *New York Times Book Review,* the *New York Herald Tribune Book Review,* and the *Chicago Tribune,* above the headline "Magic of Fine Writing."[84]

Most reviews from the time lavish praise on the novel. Harriette Arnow, whose book *The Dollmaker* would soon join *The Night of the Hunter* on the *New York Times* best-seller list, admires the way Grubb fuses the reality of his West Virginia setting with the "terrible world of fear" in the mind of his nine-year-old protagonist.[85] Herbert F. West, writing in the *New York Times Book Review,* praises "a soft-focus realism that is wholly compelling and entrancing." He also feels that young John is "a beautifully realized character" who "wins the reader's complete interest and devotion."[86] Some reviewers commend the dualities within the book. Riley Hughes in *Catholic World* writes, "This is a book of suspense and terror . . . but it is a book, above all, of human values, of decency, of compassion and of love, trusting and unashamed."[87] In the *New York Herald Tribune,* Gene Baro notes that the novel is "part idyll, part nightmare" and extols Grubb for writing with "eloquent power, and also with often singular beauty."[88] Joseph Henry Jackson in the *San Francisco Chronicle* sees a fine balance between the book's popular and literary aspects: "First of all, Mr. Grubb, having learned his trade in the magazines, makes this a fast-paced, technically admirable tale. Second, he has done this without sacrificing quality."[89]

Grubb's fast-paced narrative was not merely a critical success. Readers went out and bought the book. Grubb synthesizes various literary traditions and molds them into a compelling story that he tells in a consistent style. The various influences at play in the novel do not disorient the reader. To the contrary, echoes of, let us say, Faulkner or Wolfe or Twain lend an air of familiarity to the book. Where a poetic thriller was alien to American movie audiences of the fifties, such a work, with its mingling of the gothic and the lyrical, was understandable to the reading public. Thus, on March 14, 1954, *The Night of the Hunter* appeared on the *New York Times* best-seller list. The novel started at number 13 (out of sixteen slots), then jockeyed for position through the first week of July, several times reaching number 5. The novel was on the list for seventeen weeks.[90] Besides its inclusion in the Book-of-the-Month Club, whose newsletter promoted it in a section devoted to new books "that were particularly enjoyed or were considered important by some of our preliminary readers and judges,"[91] *The Night of the Hunter* was chosen for *Reader's Digest* condensation—perhaps the ultimate proof of a novel's popular acceptance.[92]

And then there was the film sale.

One aspect of the novel that reviewers failed to mention was of utmost importance to Paul Gregory and Charles Laughton: its filmic quality. "I make my work *from* movie images in my mind," Grubb once said. "I'm always cutting, and splicing, and everything else" (*HH*, 328). Indeed, entire scenes are ready-made for film: Preacher's sermon "Right-Hand-Left-Hand," Willa's corpse underwater in the Model T, the children's flight to the skiff, and their journey downriver. One image in particular—Preacher's tattooed fingers—seems as if it were conceived just so it could be visualized on film. The fingers are vivid enough on the page, but on screen they virtually come alive. Laughton's most famous shot—in reality a production still that approximates the scene in the movie—is of Preacher standing at Rachel's back stairs, clutching a banister with the hand marked *hate* and grasping a newel with the hand marked *love.* The picture was used on lobby cards at the time of the movie's release and has since become *The Night of the Hunter*'s chief signifier, ubiquitous in books and articles and in the lobbies of revival houses when the film is screened. Terry Sanders noted that Grubb's novel "was one of those very cinematic books. It was like *The Maltese Falcon* [1941], where Huston could tear the pages out . . . , paste them in a notebook, and start directing."[93] The comparison to John Huston and his screenplay of Dashiell Hammett's novel is a good one. Whether or not Huston truly did tear pages out of *The Maltese Falcon,* his adaptation, like the Agee-Laughton *Night of the Hunter,* adheres closely to its source. *The Night of the Hunter* on film takes most of its dialogue directly from the pages of the novel. It is a tribute to Grubb's ear that his dialogue works so well on screen. Grubb's descriptions, too, often seem like veritable directions for a motion picture, as in the scene where Preacher springs into view in Rachel's house: "And now he rocketed suddenly upward before her very eyes, his twisted mask caught for one split second in the silver moonlight like the vision in a photograph negative and she saw the knife in his fist rise swiftly as the bobbin of a sewing machine just as she began pulling the trigger while the gun bucked and boomed in her hands" (*NH*, 247).

In short, *The Night of the Hunter* is a novel that does not require an extensive overhaul to make it ready for the screen. As Sanders put it, "You have all the characters, you have the scenes, you have the story."[94] When Gregory bought the screen rights to the book, he had no intention of changing characters, scenes, or story. He would, in fact, become "a stickler" for keeping to the novel and avoiding embellishments.[95] "How many studios do you know that buy things and then the picture comes out and you wouldn't even recognize it, you wonder why they paid the price for it?" he once asked. "I *wanted* what I bought" (*HH*, 102). In this, as in so many things, Gregory and Laughton were in agreement. For them, *The Night of the Hunter* was the perfect vehicle with which to launch what they hoped would be a long and lucrative Hollywood partnership.

Three

GRUBB MEETS LAUGHTON

"My Dear Dave"

Early in April 1954, four months before the start of principal photography on the film version of Grubb's novel, Laughton made a pilgrimage to Philadelphia to spend time with the author, who was supporting himself as a copywriter at the Paul Lufton Agency.[1] In discussing the visit years later, Grubb at one time recalled that he and Laughton had barely talked about the novel. "Laughton already knew the book," said Grubb. "Now, he felt, he had to know *me* to do the kind of fanatically accurate adaptation he had in mind."[2] Another time he remembered that during Laughton's five-day visit, "We were always just talking about the book, that's all we talked about" (*HH,* 65). The contradiction is perhaps reconciled in Laughton's own hyperbolic recollection a year after the visit: "I . . . sat in his study for five straight days asking him what he'd seen in his mind while he was writing the book."[3] It is easy to imagine that conversations between the garrulous Laughton and the "flamboyant and gregarious" Grubb ranged from the novel to the writer's history and psyche.[4]

Despite all the talk, Grubb found that to satisfy Laughton's curiosity about his authorial visions "it was easier to draw the answer than tell it."[5] The few pictures he drew made a deep impression on Laughton. In a letter to Grubb, handwritten shortly after his return to Hollywood, Laughton continued the working relationship he and the novelist had established in person. As the only surviving example of Laughton's correspondence to Grubb, and as a revealing look at the way Laughton drew the novelist into preparations for the film, the letter is worth quoting in its entirety. The original note is reproduced in an article by Preston Neal Jones for a Library of Congress publication.[6] My transcription retains Laughton's stream-of-consciousness style:

My dear Dave,

The drawings are a real success people say Oh! Oh Yes of course! There would have been all sorts of battles having to be fought, preventing people from pushing it into being a gloomy looking film. I am preserving them all they are all safely in cellophane envelopes.

As I told you things are getting towards decision on sets a set designer & so forth

(Have you a pet set designer?)

I would like to know how you see the scene of Willa's testimony.

(Drawings please

I have, of course, her head in ecstasy in a couple of poses but now rather her relation to the figures round her the preacher, the congregation and perhaps an organist. Would there be flowers. Those are here round an evangelist called O. D. Jagg. Might it not be in a tent? That would be simple to do.

(*Now* the journey of the children down the river

I feel this passage must have the river behind it, every bit of it either visually or musically. It will be a brute to shoot as it will need so many more shots to the minute than dialogue scenes. Any ideas you have for varying attitudes of the children in the boat. Helicopter, long shot, close shot varying speeds of cutting (more drawings please) the kind of river music will be most gratefully received. This same river music will have to cover our whole opening sequence. I am going to write you further about that when it has jelled in my mind. I am seeing Walter Schumann tomorrow.

I am coming round to the idea of Jane Darwell for Rachel. We talked about her. You remember her in Grapes

THE NIGHT OF THE HUNTER

of Wrath. The trouble with [Ethel] Barrymore is that she is rather Hudson than Ohio River Valley.

I hope this kind of sprawling uncareful letter is going to be the right way of keeping the channel to each other clear.

Want to know all you have thought of, the best & the worst.

Charles

If you start to get nightmares or have any signs of twitching call me.

Hollywood 23509

L.

Few novelists in the history of Hollywood adaptations have had "the channel" to the director kept so "clear." It is a touching measure of Laughton's naïveté as a first-time film director that he would ask a first-time novelist with a day job in advertising whether he has a "pet set designer" and would solicit specific images to help him in the shooting and editing of the picture. Yet the letter shows that Laughton was beginning to direct the film in his mind: he was already envisioning helicopter shots.

Pleased to be sought out as a collaborator on the film, Grubb responded in a letter dated April 19. Although he opens with a formal "Dear Charles Laughton," he goes on to say, "In the informal spirit which you have already so comfortably established I am going to make this a completely impromptu correspondance [sic], without polishing or re-writing as I usually do with letters." What follows are six pages, single spaced with narrow margins, covering a range of topics: the relationship of Willa and Ben, the look of houses in Cresap's Landing, answers to queries by Walter Schumann about the use of folk music, thoughts about Jane Darwell as Rachel ("I find it difficult to hear Jane Darwell's voice here. . . . I see Jane Darwell as Icey Spoon"), and promises for more drawings. He assures Laughton, "Sketches will follow this letter but I might as well tell you now that the revival meeting was held in a little tent and NOT a church. No flowers please. No organ, either. An upright piano—twangy and out of tune." The end of his letter shows how seriously he takes the collaborative role that Laughton generously offered to him: "I am trying to think out more and more how I want this visual thing to be. I've been brushing up on theory and renewing old thinking about the translation of this kind of thing into effective visual idea. Am re-reading Moholy-Nagy's great work *Vision in Motion*. Don't worry. I won't go arty or Max Reinhardt on you. This is old stuff, long ago absorbed. I just want to refresh. It will help me get at what I *saw* while writing the book."[7]

Grubb's reassurances about not turning "arty" are ironic in light of the many reviewers who used that very word to denigrate Laughton's *Night of the Hunter*. Although Gregory once complained that Laughton "made an art film" that was difficult to sell,[8] he admits that "Charles did not set out to make this an art picture per se."[9] Laughton himself stressed that his chief concern was to "make audiences scream."[10] To help put the tale on film, and to remain true to Grubb's original rendition, Laughton decided that what he needed were more drawings, the sooner the better.

Portfolio

Grubb was already at work on his second novel, *A Dream of Kings*, when, as he recalled years later, "I began to be subjected to a daily barrage of wires, phone calls from Hollywood and letters asking me for sketches, more sketches, and yet more sketches of what this or the other scene looked like in my mind. . . . [Laughton] would even ask me to draw the expression on a character's face during certain scenes." Grubb filled every request and sent the sketches off by airmail, special delivery.[11] Anyone looking through the collection of Grubb's drawings at the Margaret Herrick Library of the Academy of Motion Picture Arts and Sciences will discover a small gallery of line drawings in a variety of styles, some in ink, some in pencil, many on oversize sheets—all of them important to Laughton's adaptation.

Grubb's realistic drawings of places are often rich in detail, complete with labels and arrows to identify such things as "Icey Spoon's confectionery," "gas lamp in yard," or "where Preacher got off train." (With a thoroughness that rivaled, or was perhaps inspired by, Laughton's own obsessive research methods, Grubb sent Laughton a booklet of maps for the Ohio Valley between Wheeling and Parkersburg, West Virginia. He annotated the maps as well: "Ben hanged at penitentiary here. Preacher's trial—the lynching," "Willa and Preacher's honeymoon here," "Miz Cooper's place.")[12] Many of the drawings, however, are roughly sketched, childlike in their simplicity. A cap and scowling eyes suggest a policeman. A few bold strokes render fat, malevolent Miz Cunningham laden with necklaces and pins. Some, particularly drawings that give Preacher a toothy, evil grin, have the look of caricature. Others, as Preston Neal Jones has pointed out, have a cartoon quality reminiscent of James Thurber's spare, evocative lines (*HH*, 121).

Given the influence of William Blake on Grubb's writing, it is little surprise that Blake's artwork seems to have inspired at least one of Grubb's drawings: a sketch of Preacher under a crescent moon advancing on the children in the foreground. Preacher, his nearly featureless face half in shadow, is armless, wrapped in something that resembles a clerical robe (see fig. 3.1). The figure's overpowering form and the drawing's dramatic play of shadow and light bring to mind Blake's *Vision of Eliphaz* from his illustrations for the book of Job (see fig. 3.2).

The image of Preacher, like much of Blake's own forward-looking art, has the stylized quality of German expressionism. Several other sketches evoke even more vividly the bold distortions of expressionist work. A drawing of Preacher in his prison cell shows him wondering, "How many widows? Eight? Ten? Twelve?" The ghosts that swarm his brain are projected above him. We see the disembodied heads—and here and there only the eyes—of the women he has murdered. A face hovering over Preacher's shoulder is composed of a Picasso-like eye and nose. On two other faces, one eye is closed and one open—a strangely disturbing effect (see fig. 3.3). Another drawing, captioned "That was dirty and hard—that other thing with Ben," depicts Willa's recollection of sex with her first husband. Her horrified face looks out from a corner of the frame. Beside her is an image of herself, nude, with downcast eyes, being embraced by Ben in front of a sign that reads TOURIST CABIN (because everyone knows—or they did in the fifties—that sex in a tourist cabin is especially dirty and hard). In two other drawings, Grubb captures more of the novel's overt sexuality, which Laughton had to suppress for the film, with grotesque imagery reminiscent of drawings by George Grosz. One sketch portrays a prostitute splayed out naked on a bed. Beneath a sign reading JESUS SAVES, she holds her legs open to Preacher, who stares with crazed eyes. The other picture is set in a burlesque house, where Preacher watches a stripper strut down a runway. Swirling lines suggest a smoky atmosphere. Faces of leering men loom over the dark image of Preacher. The stripper's heavy legs and pendulous breasts, as

Figure 3.1
Preacher approaches John and Pearl.
Sketch for *The Night of the Hunter,* 1954, Davis Grubb.

well as fat-faced men puffing on cigars, are especially strong evocations of Grosz's savage, cartoonlike images (see figs. 3.4 and 3.5).

Laughton's film may not recall the work of George Grosz, but its world of terror and sexual violence, as well as its many chiaroscuro lighting effects and stylized settings, link it to German expressionist films of the twenties and thirties. It is the unexpected use of expressionist devices in an otherwise realistic work that sets *The Night of the Hunter* apart from other films in 1955 (and helped it to fail at the box

Figure 3.2
The Vision of Eliphaz, 1825, William Blake.

office), and it is the very thing that has enhanced its reputation with later generations. Although Laughton never talked about expressionism with his crew,[13] Gregory pointed out that Laughton's "constant point of view" was to project the tale of a "very real" Preacher against a "surrealistic . . . fabric."[14] Denis Sanders remembered that Laughton talked with him about creating a film in which "each of the actions had to be larger than they would have been in life. He was not trying to achieve a realistic picture, but an impressionistic one." By the time production began, nonrealistic techniques were in the air. Hilyard Brown, for instance, felt

Figure 3.3
Preacher's memories in prison.
Sketch for *The Night of the Hunter*, 1954, Davis Grubb.

free to design stylized sets because he "thought it was more interesting than 'real' reality."[15] The question is, what prompted Laughton's desire for stylization?

Of those who have written about the film's expressionist visuals, only James R. Fultz has tried to explain in detail why the film includes such imagery. He suggests that in writing the script, Agee and Laughton devised cinematic equivalents for lighting effects in the book.[16] For instance, he cites Grubb's description of Preacher walking in a hall:

THE NIGHT OF THE HUNTER

"Now Preacher moved forward and the light from the open doorway to the parlor threw a gold bar of light across the livid line of lip and cheek and bone beneath and one eye shone like a dark, wet grape and the lid crinkled over it nervously" (*NH*, 93). That picture does indeed suggest a type of expressive lighting found in the film. Another image from the book is transferred directly to the screen: "the shadow of a man in the yellow square of light from the yard lamp: a very silent, motionless man with a narrow-brimmed hat and still, straight arms" (*NH*, 49). The novel as a whole, centered on a monstrous character whose "livid, twisted, raging oval" of a face can loom out of "moonlight, even with the mists wisping and curling against the land" (*NH*, 187), lends itself to the brooding look that Laughton and Stanley Cortez create for many scenes.

But images like the vaulted bedroom where Preacher ritualistically slits Willa's throat or the starry sky twinkling benediction over the children as they escape downriver—visuals that attempt to portray, through nonrealistic means, moods and states of mind—are not rooted in Grubb's novel. Fultz refers to "the overt expressionism of . . . momentary mental states" in the book and cites Ruby's imagining poinsettias in the torches of the lynch mob or John's fear of Preacher, which is greater than looking "'through the little bubble in the glass of the window in the upstairs hall' in which 'all of the out-of-doors stretches and twists its neck.'"[17] Literary expressionism, however, attempts to capture the reality of mental states through devices of dislocation—the "staccato sentences" mentioned by Lotte Eisner[18] or the "bent," "disjointed" elements found in "the more involved and exaggerated prose experiments of James Joyce, William Faulkner and Samuel Beckett."[19] In the moments cited, Grubb uses a realistic, not a stylized, technique to depict the perspectives of a slow-witted girl and a ten-year-old boy. Even when Grubb presents John's confused state of mind during the trial at the end of the book, he does not employ expressionistic effects. He writes a straightforward, first-person narrative that allows the reader to understand John's point of view: "I can't much figure out what any of it is about except that this fellow with the gold tooth keeps saying something about Bluebird. It seems like this Bluebird had twenty-five wives and he killed every last one of them and they been hunting him now for months and months and now they got him" (*NH*, 251). Dreams in the novel, as well as symbolic details like the "plaster stare" of Pearl's doll (*NH*, 83)

Figure 3.4
Preacher in burlesque house.
Sketch for *The Night of the Hunter*, 1954, Davis Grubb.

or false teeth in a glass that maintain a smiling, "ironic vigilance" over "innocent sleepers" (*NH*, 131), are also presented in a realistic manner. Grubb's novel is suffused with what might be called a matter-of-fact lyricism, all the better to generate a sense of horror lurking in the shadows of a leafy summer street.

We know that Laughton looked to D. W. Griffith as a model for his directing debut. Cortez and Terry Sanders, among others, recalled looking at Griffith's films in Los Angeles with Laughton.[20] The director

Figure 3.5
Ruf der Wildnis [*Call of the Wild*], 1929, George Grosz.

also traveled to New York and screened Griffith's work at the Museum of Modern Art.[21] But there is no record of his having studied German expressionist films as part of his research. At best, other silent movies he screened, such as Rex Ingram's *Four Horsemen of the Apocalypse* (1921) or Erich von Stroheim's *Greed* (1924) (*HH*, 115–16), would have shown that a film can mingle the realistic and the symbolic and still hold together. To illustrate the concept of greed in his naturalistic film, von Stroheim inserts the distorted image of hands fondling gold coins.

Ingram periodically interrupts his narrative with emblematic shots of the Four Horsemen—Conquest, War, Pestilence, and Death—riding in a smoky void. These works do not, however, point to an expressionistic approach.

It seems plausible that Grubb's several nonrealistic drawings struck a chord in Laughton and inspired him to push his work into an expressionist realm. Stylized effects on film, which are not described in the screenplay, seem like an extension of ideas planted by the novelist in various sketches. The film's burlesque-house scene, for example, combines details from the novel with aspects of Grubb's drawings. Grubb writes: "He would pay his money and go into a burlesque show and sit in the front row watching it all and rub the knife in his pocket with sweating fingers; seething in a quiet convulsion of outrage and nausea at all that ocean of undulating womanhood beyond the lights; his nose growing full of it: the choking miasma of girl smell and cheap perfume and stogie smoke and man smell and the breath of ten-cent mountain corn liquor souring in the steamy air" (NH, 22). The novel's "seething" Preacher and the knife make it to the film (with Agee's inspired addition of a switchblade flicking through the pocket and providing a symbolic orgasm for Preacher). The smoky "miasma" in Grubb's description, however, is replaced with a static, austere tableau of shadowy men isolated in the dark. Faces around Preacher, some in silhouette, looking almost like cardboard cutouts, echo the disembodied faces that surround him in Grubb's sketch (see fig. 3.4). The nonrealistic technique of the drawing also has its counterpart in the film's use of a keyhole matte to frame the dancer—a device that emphasizes Preacher's prurient view of sex even as it makes us complicit in his voyeurism. It is true, of course, that the partially clothed, gyrating woman in Laughton's film is far less George Grosz than conventional Hollywood cheesecake. The dancer, whom Jones identifies as Gloria Pall (HH, 135), was a popular pinup girl of the era who caused an uproar as Voluptua on network television the year before The Night of the Hunter was released.[22] Nevertheless, the expressionist approach to the film's sequence owes more to Grubb's drawing than to his novel.

If Grubb's nonrealistic pictures indirectly inspired an expressionistic approach to parts of The Night of the Hunter, the realistic sketches exerted a direct influence. Although forty years after the film shoot Hilyard Brown could not recall having seen Grubb's drawings,[23] it stands

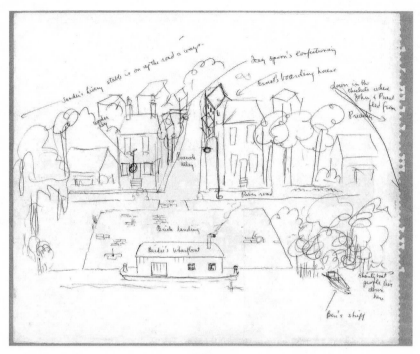

Figure 3.6
Cresap's Landing.
Sketch for *The Night of the Hunter,* 1954, Davis Grubb.

to reason that Laughton would have shown the sketches to him. We know that Laughton showed them to Cortez, who recalled that "Charles was very much involved with Grubb, and that contributed a great deal." For Cortez, the sketches "didn't contribute too much to my own thinking, they were strictly an academic outline, so to speak" (*HH,* 121). Given the evidence of the film, it seems that the drawings were more than an outline for Brown; they were a strong foundation for his own visualizations. The town of Cresap's Landing in two of Grubb's detailed sketches is recognizable as the town constructed in the San Fernando Valley at the Rowland V. Lee ranch.[24] The lane between rows of buildings, Birdie's squat wharf boat, Ben's skiff moored off to the side—everything we know from the film is there on Grubb's drawing paper (see fig. 3.6). Film interiors, such as the Harper kitchen with its potbellied stove or the cellar with its shelves full of jars and its steep flight of steps,

Figure 3.7
Preacher's shadow in children's bedroom.
Sketch for *The Night of the Hunter*, 1954, Davis Grubb.

closely resemble Grubb's drawings. "I . . . can only declare—perhaps immodestly," Grubb wrote in the introductory letter to his portfolio of drawings, "that I was not only the author of the novel from which the screenplay was adapted but was the scene designer as well."[25] It does not diminish Hilyard Brown's superb work to acknowledge the measure of truth in Grubb's statement. Some pictures are virtual storyboards for scenes in the film: the shadow of Preacher and his distinctive hat on the wall of the children's bedroom; John looking out a hayloft at Preacher on

(John)— Don't he never go to sleep?

Figure 3.8
John sees Preacher from hayloft.
Sketch for *The Night of the Hunter,* 1954, Davis Grubb.

the horizon; an overhead image of the children curled up in the floating skiff; Willa's corpse in the submerged Model T (see figs. 3.7–3.10).

Even drawings that differ from the film sometimes reveal a subtle influence. For instance, Grubb made sketches of Willa and Preacher leading a revival meeting. In one, labeled "(Revival) #1," ecstatic faces and multiple sets of applauding hands fill the foreground. (Despite Grubb's cautionary note to Laughton—"no flowers please"[26]—the author specifically identifies flowers in a vase on a piano as "calla lillies" [*sic*].) Laughton's torchlit, claustrophobic tableaux are closer in spirit to the novel's descriptions of Willa's "eyes burning in the torchlight, her face blanched and bloodless with the thrill of her Vision" (*NH,* 110) than they are to Grubb's expansive visualization of the scene. Yet the drawing displays a controlled frenzy perfectly captured in the film (see fig. 3.11). Another sketch, "(Revival) #4," may well have suggested a detail of

Figure 3.9
John and Pearl in skiff on the river.
Sketch for *The Night of the Hunter,* 1954, Davis Grubb.

Laughton's staging. Grubb depicts Willa shrieking, raising a Bible over her head, while Preacher stands staunchly behind her—a positioning (minus the Bible) used in the film.

A few drawings constitute reimaginings by Grubb, and they have no counterpart in the film. On a picture of a rambling old house, Grubb tells Laughton, "I somehow would like to consider using *this* as Miz Cunningham's second hand shop instead of the one I wrote in Night of the Hunter. It suggests *her* much more." Despite Grubb's wishes,

What Bardie saw in the river in the deep place

Figure 3.10
Willa's corpse underwater in Model T.
Sketch for *The Night of the Hunter,* 1954, Davis Grubb.

Laughton retained the novel's image of Miz Cunningham's small shop and its cluttered window "like the nest of a thieving black crow" (*NH,* 34). Grubb also changed the look of Rachel Cooper for his drawings. No longer the "gaunt" woman of the novel (and not at all the beatific Lillian Gish from the film), she has a broad, fleshy face that more nearly resembles the two actresses whom Grubb and Laughton mentioned in their correspondence: Jane Darwell and Ethel Barrymore. The most surprising pictures are those of Bart the hangman. Grubb offers no physical description in the novel, but the mundane details of his home life help the reader conjure up an ordinary man of ordinary appearance.

Figure 3.11
Preacher and Willa at revival meeting.
Sketch for *The Night of the Hunter,* 1954, Davis Grubb.

Grubb sketches him as a brawny, hulking figure with no neck and thick, hairy arms—more like a thug from a gangster film than Laughton's bowler-hatted bureaucrat (played by the mild-mannered character actor Paul Bryar [*HH,* 153]).

These exceptions only point up how closely Laughton followed most of the sketches during the casting, designing, and photographing of the film. As Grubb says in his preface to the portfolio, "Laughton assured me with considerable passion that he intended the film to resemble as nearly my mental pictures in writing the book as was possible to achieve."[27] The pictures on paper reveal just how true Laughton was to his word. In effect, he drew on two primary sources for his film: Grubb's novel and Grubb's drawings, which constitute their own visual adaptation of *The Night of the Hunter.*

four

THE SCREENPLAYS

Out of Tennessee

A few years before he met Laughton, Grubb had spent some time in Los Angeles. That sojourn among "the night crawlers . . . who went around at night looking for whatever: loneliness, or drugs, or sex" had "in a funny way" helped him to create the world of *The Night of the Hunter*.[1] But he was not inclined to return to Hollywood and re-create that world in a screenplay. Gregory, who wanted Grubb to do the adaptation, recalls that he and Laughton even tried to induce the novelist "to come to California . . . and sit in on sessions of the writing of the script and we were unable to get him to do so."[2] That was partly, Gregory believes, because Grubb was frightened by Laughton's "formidable personality."[3] Grubb, however, recalled in later years that he and Laughton had become friends during a collaboration that was, to quote Grubb's surprising description, "almost like a sexual union."[4] Nevertheless, one can imagine that the prospect of an intensive working relationship with Laughton in Hollywood would have been daunting for a writer who liked his solitude. Grubb thought it better that he "stick to his own field" and remain in Philadelphia to work on his next novel.[5] "And I've kicked my ass around the whole East Coast ever since that I didn't [go out to California]," Grubb said, "because it would have given me a screen credit, which might have led to some work" (*HH*, 59). Another time, in a more realistic mood, Grubb recognized that the film's producers needed a well-known writer to do the screenplay.[6]

Gregory once said that when he began working on *The Night of the Hunter*, he did not know a lot about James Agee.[7] Laughton, on the other hand, had probably met Agee at the salon of Salka Viertel, though how well they knew each other is unclear. According to the writer's biographer, Laurence Bergreen, Laughton "wanted his friend James Agee to write the screenplay."[8] Friend or not, Agee was a natural choice for the job of adapting *The Night of the Hunter*. Born in 1909, he spent his youth in towns of eastern Tennessee and therefore would have found himself at home in Grubb's Appalachian river town of Cresap's Landing. Jeffrey J. Folks points out that Agee was well acquainted with the fundamentalist religion in Grubb's novel and that he shared with the book a "revulsion of religious bigotry and fanaticism."[9] Other themes in *The Night of the Hunter*—coming of age, children threatened by forces beyond their control and redeemed by love—are at the core of Agee's novella *The Morning Watch* (1950) and his posthumous novel *A Death in the Family* (1957). Agee also would have felt sympathy for characters stranded by the Great Depression. In 1936, he and photographer Walker Evans lived for several weeks with three Alabama families to create the compassionate portrait of daily lives that was eventually published as the book *Let Us Now Praise Famous Men* (1941). The richly descriptive style of that book, as well as the poetic language of Agee's fiction, has much in common with Grubb's lyrical prose. Agee and Grubb are among those writers whom Thomas Wolfe once referred to as "great putter-inners"[10]— writers who most appealed to Charles Laughton. Gregory, who has said harsh things about Agee's work on *The Night of the Hunter*, nevertheless acknowledged that Agee was "a wonderful writer"[11] and said, "We went for James Agee because of the basic texture of his writing, the sensitivity of his writing."[12]

Professionally, Agee was known for the provocative film reviews he had written in *The Nation* and *Time* magazine during the 1940s. He was also respected as a screenwriter. For the CBS program *Omnibus*, he had written a five-part teleplay, *Mr. Lincoln* (directed by Norman Lloyd, November 16, 1952–February 8, 1953). For Huntington Hartford, he had written *The Blue Hotel* (1949) and *The Bride Comes to Yellow Sky* (1952), both adapted from stories by Stephen Crane. His most visible screenplay was *The African Queen* (1951), an adaptation of C. S. Forester's adventure novel. Ironically, it was the one script on which Agee had collaborated. He shared screen credit and an Academy Award nomination with the film's director, John Huston, though John Collier had also written a draft, and Peter Viertel worked on the ending after a heart attack prevented Agee from doing further work on the script.[13]

On May 31, 1954, Agee signed a contract to write *The Night of the Hunter*. His term of employment, however, began on April 7, and he agreed "to complete and deliver the first draft" of his script within ten weeks. His salary was not the $30,000 that has frequently been reported, but rather $15,000 ($1,000 a week, with a guaranteed $5,000 minimum for any revisions). He was granted an unpaid "leave of absence for one week prior to April 26, 1954, in order to complete a previous assignment."[14] Agee has been accused of many things in connection with his work on *The Night of the Hunter*, but nobody has accused him of delivering the script late. If we assume that he took the full time, with one week off to complete his "previous assignment," then he delivered the first draft on June 23. That date had important consequences for Laughton.

Screenplay by James Agee

The draft that Agee handed in, according to Terry Sanders, was "very detailed, and it was not something that you would want to go out and shoot with." Gregory said, "I read about a fourth of it and threw it out the window."[15] Out the window or not, the original script that Agee wrote soon vanished. It was replaced by a new screenplay, the one eventually published in *Agee on Film: Five Film Scripts*. Agee's first draft, however, lived on in memory and became a sort of legend. Sanders recalled that the script was "over 400 pages long." To Gregory, it was "bigger than the phone book." Mitchum remembered it looking "like a WPA project—the goddamned thing must have weighed eighteen pounds, you know."[16]

According to many reports, this Brobdingnagian production reflected Agee's "political philosophy and had no relationship to the novel under the sun."[17] In Charles Higham's words, "Agee had eliminated the few good poetic passages of the book, underplayed the drama, and introduced a whole new social background which reflected his neo-Marxist concerns as a critic. He had scenes of the WPA, the wobblies, the breadlines and soup kitchens of the Depression which were his obsession."[18] Bergreen, who pegs the script at 350 pages, notes that "Agee had not adapted the book; he had re-created a cinematic version of it in extraordinary detail. He specified use of newsreel footage to document the story's setting and added any number of elaborate, impractical montages."[19]

During those decades when descriptions of Agee's draft were passed from writer to writer, the script itself lay hidden in a letter box that had remained in Agee's house after his death. Packed into a carton of miscellaneous books, the script passed through several hands. In 2003, Paul Sprecher, trustee of the James Agee Trust, went looking for a keyboard to his son's iMac computer. He explains the result of his search: "Getting more and more frustrated at not finding [the keyboard], I ended up opening every single box in the house—and discovered the one remaining letter box containing the first draft. While many of the other papers were annotated as a result of several research projects over the years, there were no notes in this box; it is quite possible that it had not in fact been opened since the mid to late 60s."[20] Here and there on the script one finds various notations: corrections of typographical errors, brackets around lines, question marks, and signs for deletions. We may never know who made them. The notes are not Agee's because, as Sprecher says, "Agee's hand is quite distinct, and this quite certainly isn't it."[21]

The script that Agee delivered, identified as "First Draft" on the title page, turns out to be 293 pages. That is, to be sure, much longer than an average Hollywood screenplay—and twice as long as *The Night of the Hunter*'s 147-page shooting script. Still, the screenplay is not quite the "monstrosity" that it became in latter-day accounts.[22] The reported political digressions, those newsreels and breadlines and Wobblies, are nowhere to be found. It is unlikely that during his brief period of employment Agee could have written any other draft containing such digressions. Time and memory rewrote the script. Agee himself uses characters and situations organic to the story to convey the strong sense of the Depression that comes through in the book. The "montages" that Bergreen mentions are also nonexistent, although many of Agee's descriptions are indeed elaborate and impractical.

For instance, during the children's journey down the Ohio River, Agee creates short narratives about two farm wives that appear briefly in Grubb's novel. (Oddly, he makes Grubb's fat woman lean and his gaunt farm wife fat.) He devotes about a page and a half to each family. Here is a sample that reveals the observant author of *Let Us Now Praise Famous Men* at work; he could be describing people in one of Evans's photographs:

TWO-SHOT—JOHN AND PEARL
Sitting barefoot on the edge of the ragged porch, they
ravenously finish eating field-peas and chunked
fatback. . . .
FULL-SHOT—THEIR VIEWPOINT—THE OPEN DOOR
A lean farm wife stands in the doorway, dreading this
moment as she watches them; for she can't bear to send
them away; nor can she emotionally risk taking them
further into her concern. Through one more helping. At
least two of her own children are in the shot at the start—
standing very still and watching John and Pearl with that
strange cool stare of Southern country children—and now,
up to five or six more, entering the shot from inside the
house, choke up the door aperture around their mother,
all staring at John and Pearl. A baby creeps out, among
the many bare feet. (The mother is barefoot, too.) One of
them glances up questioningly at the mother, and without
looking, realizing this intuitively, she catches the little
head strongly against her hip and absently strokes the
hair—her eyes always to John and Pearl. The child looks
puzzled by her gesture and the situation, but ever so
secure. ("NH," 201)

Evidently trying to create a democratic portrait of the people living along the river, Agee devotes another page and a half to an African American family of his own invention. He describes the matriarch of that family as "an unbelievably ancient old woman, her bare feet quietly caressing each other, her rootlike hands relaxed in her lap as she sits and gently rocks, gazing dimly away into a distance as deep and mysterious as Africa" ("NH," 202). The prose writer within Agee, the "writer in love with the rhythm and force of words,"[23] has seized control of the screenwriting. That phenomenon is familiar to anyone who has read his other scripts, especially *The Blue Hotel* or *Noa Noa*, which contain passages that are "elaborately and impracticably explicit."[24] As Alfred Barson says, "Agee thinks of the scripts as integral wholes—that is, as a kind of visually rendered novel."[25]

Agee's extended descriptions find their counterparts in monologues written for characters both central and secondary. At the end of the script, as Rachel prepares for bed, snuffing out candles, closing the lid of the parlor organ, she speaks a soliloquy that covers three pages. With only minor alterations, the words are a transcription of her interior monologue in the novel: "With every child—rich or poor—no matter how warm and safe he may be, there comes this time of lonesomeness and fear, when there's no one to come or to help or to hear or to care, and dry leaves a-blowing along the ground are the whispering wings of Death's Own Angel, and the ticking of an old house in the night is the cocking of the Hunter's gun" ("NH," 290). A less important character who takes hold of Agee's poetic imagination is Miz Cunningham, owner of Cresap's Landing's secondhand shop. From descriptions in Grubb's narrative, Agee builds a two-page monologue that has nothing to do with plot and everything to do with characterization and local color: "Why I've got things here from forty years back; old party dresses, weddin-dresses (indicating); there's Jamey Hankinses ice skates; and Walt Spoon's elk's tooth; why *ever'* thing in this town, ever'thing in this whole country *round*, children, in the long run, when it ain't no good for nobody no more, it comes to old Miz Cunningham!" ("NH," 48). In his fascination with "old Miz Cunningham," Agee is of one mind with Grubb, who gave Laughton several sketches of the woman and her surroundings and who once said that he wished there had been more of her in the film (*HH*, 154). On screen, her time is cut down to a few lines that concentrate on the main issue: what Ben Harper did with the money he stole. Another character whom Grubb barely mentions, Preacher's defense attorney, is given a courtroom peroration that covers three pages of script ("NH," 267–69). Agee also gives voice to Rachel's sister, Lovey ("NH," 273–74), a silent character mentioned briefly in the novel (*NH*, 265), and he adds a character of his own—a priest named Father Scallon. Sensible, of a generous spirit, the priest is a tribute to Agee's lifelong friend, Father Flye. Father Scallon also, however, exists to state what is already implicit in the script. Rachel asks him why he comes out to see her "of a Christmas Eve," and he answers, "Because you're the truest Christian I've ever known" ("NH," 282).

Nevertheless, Agee's expansions and additions are never arbitrary. They exist to illuminate the novel's characters or to develop its conflicts. When the Harper children arrive at Rachel's farm, Agee devotes ten pages to a portrait of the safe haven that they have entered, including a charming bit in which John is transported by a bullfrog in the "cold beautiful gloom of the spring house" ("NH," 228) and an unusual bit in which John, whose clothes are being washed, has to put on a dress and spends a humiliating day "looking mighty silly in his frock" ("NH," 218). In John's predicament, Agee has found a surprising, visual way to bring out a fundamental theme of the book. John is in conflict with one female figure after another: his naive and demanding mother; his little sister, Pearl; and Icey Spoon, whose voice John cannot disobey when she calls him up from his hiding place in the cellar. Rachel, who has just bathed John and given him a sense of renewal, seems to betray him by putting him into a dress. It only heightens John's suspicion of her—and that heightening makes his ultimate acceptance of Rachel all the more momentous. Agee has not, to quote Higham again, "underplayed the drama."[26] He even intensifies the drama at certain points, as when John grabs a pitchfork and engages the knife-wielding Preacher in battle ("NH," 250–51).

Despite Agee's good intentions, his long sequences undermine his work by slowing down the story and diffusing the overall dramatic effect. Elsa Lanchester, who acknowledges that Agee "was an experienced screenwriter," suggests that he "could have been carried away working with Charles, or perhaps he just lost a practical approach."[27] Rather than straying from the book, as so many reports accuse him of doing, Agee took to heart Laughton's desire for a "fanatically accurate adaptation."[28] Every big scene, and most of the smaller ones, are in the script. Dialogue is often taken verbatim from Grubb or used with minor alterations and trims. On the wedding night, when Willa hesitantly approaches Preacher in bed, he says these words to her in the novel: "You thought, Willa, that the minute you walked in that door I'd start in to pawing and feeling you in the disgusting, abominable way men are supposed to do on their wedding nights! Eh? Ain't that right now?" (*NH,* 104). In Agee's script, he says, "You thought, Willa, that the moment you crept in that door I'd start in to pawing you and feeling you in the disgusting, abominable way men are supposed to do on their wedding nights! Eh? Did I hit the nail on the head?" ("NH," 94). The changes are small. "The minute you walked in" becomes "the moment you crept in." The rhythm of "pawing and feeling you" is altered and slowed: "pawing you and feeling you." "Ain't that right now?" becomes "Did I hit the nail on the head?" (an odd, stiff change that loses the voice of Preacher; the final screenplay returns to "Ain't that right, now?" [*AF*, 290]). Examples of this sort, in which Agee merely tinkers with the dialogue as Grubb wrote it, are found on page after page of the script.

With few exceptions, even scenes that Agee invents arise straight out of lines or situations in the novel. From suggestions found at various places in the book, for instance, Agee creates two scenes of the Harper family at breakfast before Ben commits his robbery and murders. In the first, we learn from Ben—a handyman, not a clerk in a hardware store as he is in the novel—that a fellow worker has been laid off ("NH," 4). In the second, we discover that Ben himself has been laid off. "First Jim Cudger; an' now *me*," says Ben. "Never drempt it'd hit *me*" ("NH," 15). Corrections in the margin on pages 4 and 15 turn the *C* of *Cudger* into a *G*. That makes more sense, because when Agee and Evans were researching *Let Us Now Praise Famous Men*, they lived with the family of Floyd Burroughs, whom Agee identified as George Gudger to protect his privacy. The use of the name, or even a name close to it, in *The Night of the Hunter* is Agee's private tribute to the man—and by extension to all the families—who offered him "quietness, casualness, courtesy, friendliness" in the midst of the Depression.[29] The name adds resonance to Ben Harper's anguish during his own hard times. The two scenes exist to provide motivation for Ben's robbing of the bank—and to help us get to know and sympathize with Ben and Willa. The couple may have tensions over money (Ben tells Willa they can't afford "plain luxury" ["NH," 4], and he later tells her, in words that seem difficult for an actor to deliver convincingly, "Quit naggin' me, woman! Nag nag nag. Money money money" ["NH," 16]), but we also see deep affection between them: "They lean cross-corners of the table and kiss with the full tenderness of those who are deeply well in their sexuality" ("NH," 5). Agee found those affectionate feelings in the novel, when Willa dreams about her honeymoon and first months of marriage with Ben (*NH*, 126–27).

Grubb, however, became concerned about the couple's affection. In a letter sent to Agee in New York on April 12, a few days after work on the script began, Laughton writes, "One thing Grubb said to me on the phone which I should pass on. Speaking of the early happy domestic picture of the Harpers he reminded me that the seeds of what happens to Willa would be in Willa herself—so—not to emphasise [*sic*] a too healthy picture of her."[30] A few days later, in his six-page letter to Laughton, Grubb elaborated on his thoughts:

> I do not believe that Willa and Ben's relationship was quite
> as physically and emotionally perfect as you seemed to
> feel. It was violent sexually because it had begun on such
> forbidden terms. . . . I think we must understand how
> easily Willa slipped from the physical sensuality with Ben
> to the spiritual sensuality with Preacher. . . . I simply do
> not think we can show Willa and Ben as Darby and Joan or
> as pre-snake Adam and Eve without leaving unanswered
> the question: "How could she endure such a man as
> Preacher if she had been so happy with a man like Ben?"[31]

Despite Grubb's views, to which Laughton acquiesced, Agee chose to dramatize the happiness of Ben and Willa, thereby adding dimension and pathos to the doomed couple. Whatever the merits of Agee's choice, his skillful blending of ideas from the novel to develop important characters disproves assertions that he "had not adapted the book."[32]

A still more dramatic adaptation stems from Grubb's statement that "the day they came and took Ben Harper up to the death house Preacher stood screaming after him" (*NH,* 26). Those words inspired Agee to dramatize the scene and flesh it out with other convicts taunting Preacher. He even depicts the execution, which Grubb tactfully avoids. The hangman places a hood over Ben's head. Ben cries out through the hood, "John!—Pearl!—*Children!*" Then "we hear the springing of the trap and his hooded head plummets out of sight; and with a hideous snap the rope goes rigid as an iron bar" ("NH," 38). It is no surprise that this graphic scene never made it to the shooting script. Ten years before, Billy Wilder had shot an explicit gas-chamber execution for the finale of *Double Indemnity* (1944), but it was too grim even for Wilder, and he left it on the cutting-room floor. The disturbing execution scene from *I Want to Live!* (1958) was still four years away. Hollywood was not yet ready for Agee's stark realism.

Agee's devotion to Grubb's novel is evident on every page of the script, where even his scene descriptions include details plucked from the novel, whether Bart the hangman's pipe or Rachel's jars of apple butter ("NH," 38, 241). His feelings are most apparent on the title page, notable for its unusual order of names:

> "The Night of the Hunter"
> Based on the Novel by
> Davis Grubb
> Screenplay
> by
> James Agee

Several months later, in a letter to Gregory dated January 14, 1955, Agee would reaffirm his esteem for the author: "I fully concur with Charles' suggestion; that in all reference to the initial novel we give maximal credit to Davis Grubb—who after all furnished much more of a movie story than is ordinarily done by a novelist."[33] The credits in the finished film read just as Agee typed them out in his first draft.

In a sense, Agee's screenplay represents a conversation between novelists. As such, it is a fascinating literary production. Dialogue that might be hard to sit through in a film is absorbing on the page. It is amusing to see Agee becoming so enamored of Miz Cunningham that he gives her three pages of prattle. A detailed description, not found in the novel, of John being scrubbed by Rachel until "we see a child being re-born, . . . see, once more, just a strong little boy, glowing with cleanness and, against his will, beginning to enjoy it" becomes Agee's own gloss on Grubb's character ("NH," 217). Long descriptions, of the burlesque house or Willa's corpse and slashed throat underwater ("If permissible, let the edges of the cut flesh waver in these glimpses, like the valves or fringes of a sea animal" ["NH," 151]), are vintage Agee. And because this draft of *The Night of the Hunter* is Agee's last major piece of screenwriting, it gains added significance in his body of work.

Collaboration

In June 1954, Laughton was not interested in an Agee artifact. He needed a script he could shoot. His start date for production was August 15 (*HH,* 113). Revisions began immediately and went fast. A note on July 2 from Gregory to Robert Mitchum's personal assistant reveals that 103 pages of the new draft were already completed, with "another twenty-five pages coming, approximately, which we expect to have in just a few days."[34] By July 29 the shooting script was finished. On that date Gregory sent the screenplay to Shelley Winters with a letter that said, "We think you will like the script. You will see that the part of Willa is a wonderful one."[35]

Much has been said about tensions between Agee and Laughton. Lanchester believes that "Charles finally had very little respect for Agee."[36] Sanders understood that there had been "a real tension" between the two. "I remember Laughton had this kind of black humor that he killed Agee."[37] Yet the record suggests that the two men began their partnership amicably enough. Because Laughton wanted *The Night of the Hunter* to emulate silent films, he and Agee screened the work of D. W. Griffith at the Museum of Modern Art in New York. Agee mentions the experience in his letter to Gregory and conjures up the picture of a teacher-student relationship: "I'm fascinated, and about 95 percent confident, in many things which Charles learned, and showed me, out of the Griffith films we saw."[38] In the April 12 letter to Agee in New York, Laughton says, "A couple of marked Dickens' [sic] went off to you to-day air mail and more will follow by post (I am extravagant by nature & my family holds me down)."[39] Whether the books were personal gifts or part of the research for *The Night of the Hunter,* they were sent in a spirit of camaraderie.

Once Agee was in L.A., he and Laughton worked closely together. Lanchester says that Agee came to the house on Curson Avenue "in the mornings and worked all day and every day for months, editing and carving out the story." Yet she also describes Agee as being "ill at the time. I think it was his heart; we didn't exactly know. He would sit out by the pool and look as if he were dying. He was exhausted. He wanted to drink. And we didn't know if he was drinking heavily or was on drugs or what."[40] Agee was indeed a year away from dying of a heart attack in a New York taxi. (He would never see the completed film of *The Night of the Hunter.*) Yet in the undated fragment of a letter, Agee, who was active up to the moment of his death, hardly sounds like a man ill, exhausted, or drunk. He apologizes to Laughton for a "prior obligation" that would force him to stop work on the script for a week to ten days. (This refers to the "previous assignment," which, according to the contract, was to be completed before April 26.) Agee writes: "I can only hope to assure you that it need in no way seriously worry you; that at the rate I've been going, the past couple of days, we will have a first draft ready for further anvilling, much sooner than I had estimated. . . . Nevertheless, I'm exceedingly sorry to have to report this—and fully as sorry to have to interrupt work which is going so fast and well, and which so much excites me."[41] Mitchum's biographer, Lee Server, is among those who say that Agee "refused to show anyone a page of script until he was done."[42] It may be that Laughton did not see much of the script in progress. When Agee delivered the draft, Laughton expressed surprise at its length to Grubb (*HH*, 99–100). Yet Agee was not unwilling to show pages to his director. In the letter fragment, he goes on to tell Laughton, "If it will help assure you, I'll of course be glad to send along all copy so far written, just as soon as I can get it typed. (A problem: since most people find my handwriting difficult, I am my own quickest typist.)"[43]

The very nature of Agee's work suggests a congenial relationship. The leisurely style of *The Night of the Hunter* is reminiscent of Agee's first script, *The Blue Hotel*, in which the neophyte screenwriter revels in descriptions of novelistic detail and precise instructions for camera movements. It is as though Agee were so comfortable writing for Laughton, so sure they were in accord, that he slipped into the chatty, comprehensive style of his first screenplay. It is clear that Agee himself was not expecting his draft to be drastically edited, because he delivered to Laughton (along with a letter, now unfortunately missing) a four-page annotated list of interiors and exteriors from his script. He writes in detail about scenes that were eventually dropped from the screenplay. Here, for example, he devotes several lines to his concluding aerial night shot: "A Model, centering Rachel's home, from which we pull up and away to embrace the whole world of River Country and deep starlight. The landscape in this night shot is snowed under; all glows white in the darkness except the blackness of homes & outbuildings and of woodland and of towns. There are lights in the homes, and light sheds upward from villages like shallow thistles into the darkness; the starlight is brilliant. Model could be based on a helicopter shot or, for greater scope, on aerial map photography."[44]

Agee's draft contains several scenes that speak to a creative sympathy between screenwriter and director. We know from disapproving comments by Lillian Gish that Laughton was determined to offset

Preacher's menace with lighter touches.[45] Mitchum explained, "He did it to soften the thing up. He said [imitating Laughton's voice], 'Otherwise women would drag their children from the streets at your approach.' I wanted to take it right to the max. . . . And Charles wouldn't do it, because he said he wouldn't do it to me. He said it would be much too formidable and much too frightening."[46] Laughton and Agee found one opportunity for comic shading in the basement scene, where John and Pearl escape Preacher. Grubb himself includes no comedy in the scene. He describes the children escaping while "behind them they could hear Preacher go down cursing again in another welter of crashing jars and Pearl was screaming in a high, keening wail" (*NH,* 181). In his first draft, Agee explains that the sequence "is to be designed by a comedy expert— ideally Buster Keaton," then he announces that he will "not try to detail it, but make a few suggestions." His idea of not detailing the scene is to offer almost two pages of sight gags. After bringing Mason jars crashing down on Preacher's head, he presents a nicely orchestrated sequence that has the inexorable logic of a silent comedy short:

> [Preacher] lands on a rolling jar and now he does fall—not
> a pratt-fall but flat on his face along jars, which skate him
> along.
>   Getting up, he . . . steps on a hoe-blade; the handle
> whacks him near the groin, jackknifing him over with
> an *oof;* the jackknifing protrudes his rear, which makes
> painful contact with the tines of a pitchfork; springing
> forward from this he steps on a lawnmower which, with an
> angry whirr, gives him a pratt-fall; the pratt lands on the
> tines of a rake and the rake-handle whacks him over the
> back of the head. ("NH," 179–80)

One can imagine Laughton's surprise at how enthusiastically Agee embraced his suggestions for comedy. The shooting script reduces the slapstick action to a single crash of jars and one comic slip by Preacher (*AF,* 316).

In other ways, too, Agee took to heart Laughton's desire to rekindle techniques from the silent era. Agee twice indicates the use of an iris, a favorite silent-movie device that had long been out of fashion in feature films and was, by 1954, "firmly identified with the endings of comic cartoon-films."[47] Agee uses an iris-out on the "terrible foot" of a murdered woman ("NH," 3) and an iris-out on Bart the hangman's "heavy, shamed hands" ("NH," 43). In the revival meeting, when Willa shrieks *Salvation cometh!* Agee specifies a "mouth closeup" ("NH," 103). It is the kind of shot used in silent films to intensify the sense of sound—to make the silence shout. During the picnic sequence, Agee specifies a shot of John from Preacher's point of view: "The camera catches him, for just a fraction of a second, looking straight into the lens, appalled" ("NH," 74). As Noël Burch reminds us, such glances were common practice in American films up to around 1909 and continued to be used in silent (and, one might add, sound) comedies.[48] To connect Preacher with the devilish garfish, Agee asks for "the ugliest possible close shot of a gar's cold eyes and killing jaw" to be superimposed over a freeze frame of Preacher ("NH," 122). That visual link is Agee's filmic way of conveying Grubb's simile from the novel, when John reflects that Preacher "can move . . . like the dark shadow of the gar" (*NH,* 142). Visual symbolism of Agee's sort is more common to silent films than to talkies. Abel Gance's *Napoléon* (1927), to cite but one example, includes shots of an eagle superimposed over close-ups of the future emperor.

To complement his nonrealistic visual devices, Agee uses sound in expressionistic ways. When Preacher realizes that Willa knows the truth about him, we experience visually and aurally Preacher's own shuddering realization that he will have to murder Willa: "TIGHTEN INTO A HEAD CLOSE-UP as Preacher, desperate and helpless, looks after [Willa]; and suddenly the whole film vibrates, blurring and alarming him hideously, to the deep near groaning chordlike sound of the whistle of the QUEEN CITY, and as the vibrations die, and the screen clears, we see the dying of the fright in his face and the sharpening of desperation and inevitable need" ("NH," 133). In his novel, Grubb pays tribute to the "hoarse, sweet chord" of the *Queen City*'s whistle (*NH,* 139), and in his long letter to Laughton, he devotes more than a page to a discussion of the whistle's sound, "which it seems to me is absolutely essential to the success of the river mood in this film." Grubb tracked down the whereabouts of "the great three-toned whistle" (on a condemned tugboat in Charleston) and made plans to have it recorded for the film—though in the end it seems that a stock sound effect was used.[49] Agee's prominent use of the whistle at a turning point in the story is a dramatic way to accommodate Grubb's desire for his beloved steamboat chord. Other sounds are Agee's cinematic inventions. At two points in the script we hear in voice-over John's "inner voice" as it sings the words of a taunting children's song: "Hing, hang, hung, / See what the hangman done" and "Hing, hang, hung, / Now my song is done" ("NH," 44, 46). Late in Agee's draft, the sound of a lynch mob begins as a "rustling murmur, swells to distant thunder, and still, steadily enlarges so that we begin to recognize the shouting and the feet of men. . . . (NOTE: This whole mob noise is not realistic but stylized: it is, essentially, a piece of non-instrumental music.)" ("NH," 277).

Although Laughton uses none of Agee's specific approaches to nonrealism in the film, he finds his own ways to implement some of these cinematic ideas. After Willa's murder, Preacher strides toward the house, calling for the children, and Laughton uses an iris to show the audience what Powell fails to see: John and Pearl at a basement window. "That was done on the spur of the moment, that was not done optically," said Cortez.[50] Indeed, the shooting script calls for a moving camera to "TILT DOWNWARD and CLOSE IN" on the children (AF, 307). "I happened to see an old iris in a big lamp. I said, 'That's it.' We put that in front of the lens, covered with adjustment, and that's how we did it."[51] In outtakes from the film, a widening iris also reveals Birdie's boat as the children run toward it in their flight from Preacher. Laughton, however, was not interested in a silent-film contrivance for its own sake. The iris on the boat, unlike the one on the children, serves no dramatic necessity, and it was dropped from the film. In collaboration with his editor, Robert Golden, Laughton connects the gar with Preacher by rearranging scenes in the shooting script (AF, 292–99): he dissolves from Uncle Birdie, who has just killed the rapacious gar ("There! There! You slimy, snag-toothed, bait-stealin' so-and-so!"), to the rapacious Preacher amid the flaming torches of a revival meeting. During postproduction, Laughton created his own expressionistic sound effects. When Preacher is locked in the basement, his voice is enhanced to sound like a growling wolf. He breaks down the basement door, and the sound of its crash, over an exterior shot of the children running from the house, is made unrealistically loud to convey the way John and Pearl hear the terrifying noise. As the children escape on the river, Preacher lets out an animalistic howl which then bursts into electronically created sound.

We may never know if Laughton urged Agee to create nonrealistic devices, or if such features represent the author's own experimentation with film—in which case he might implicitly have encouraged Laughton to pursue stylization within *The Night of the Hunter*. Agee, after all, brought to the *Night of the Hunter* project an interest in unusual cinematic techniques. In "Notes for a Moving Picture: the House," a 1937 surrealistic treatment about cycles of change and "the encroachment of evil on innocence,"[52] Agee specifies rhythmic editing to achieve almost musical effects. He uses the plucking of a Chekhovian violin to indicate the decadence of a changing order, and he describes a clock "burring . . . with the continuously more urgent and piercing noise of a dentist's drill."[53] In *Noa Noa*, based on the diary of Paul Gauguin, he wants the camera to be "so moved and cut as to make the sign of the Cross over Gauguin."[54] Whatever the truth in this complicated matter of influence, it is clear that Laughton and Agee shared an interest in experimenting with the film medium.

According to various reports, common interests could not prevent the relationship from souring once Agee delivered his first draft. Grubb remembered that Laughton called him "in distress, and said, 'We can't possibly use the script by Agee. It would run six hours. It's as if we had been paying $2,500. a week for a mere secretary. The man's a hack writer!' "[55] (Agee's contract actually specifies a salary of $1,000 a week even for revisions.) With few exceptions, accounts of the revision period claim that Laughton discarded the first draft, went back to the novel, and wrote his own script.

On the other hand, Simon Callow argues in a British Film Institute monograph that Laughton and Agee maintained a cordial partnership.[56] Callow's recent work revises his earlier view, stated in his 1987 biography of Laughton, that the director eventually "took on the screenwriting himself" and had "sole creative responsibility."[57] Callow credits one Peter Richards, who, in a letter of "breathtaking rudeness and arrogance" to *Sight and Sound*, prompted him to "investigate the matter [of Agee] in somewhat greater depth." Callow also acknowledges his debt to Preston Neal Jones, who let him see the as-yet-unpublished manuscript for *Heaven and Hell to Play With*.[58] Jones points out that "Laughton, at least for a time, kept Agee on the payroll and at the typewriter" (*HH*, 103).

Jones's statement is borne out by newly discovered letters from Gregory to the Paul Kohner literary agency. The letters reveal that Agee was paid for revisions over the full contractual term of five weeks.[59] A subsequent letter, sent by agent Ilse Lahn on August 23, a week after production began, offers another perspective on Agee's role: "It may interest you to hear that things on the *Hunter* set are somewhat less than happy. Especially Mitchum who feels that Laughton 'does not have the ear for this sort of thing.' I understand that Bob would like to get you back and have you on the set to sort of stand by. Would that interest you? Some deal for that could also be made if you wanted it."[60] Whether or not Gregory and Laughton would have made such a deal, Lahn's belief that Agee could return as a consultant suggests that his employers had not cast him into outer darkness.

A memo from Laughton to Agee, dated July 16, 1954, offers a glimpse of their working method. As the only surviving document from the revision period, it deserves to be reproduced in full:

> Dear Jim:
> Re: Pg. #112 CLOSE SHOT—RACHEL—CHILDREN IN B-G—:
>   At the beginning of the Pharaoh story, I feel we haven't got it clear enough that John reacts badly when he sees the Bible. I am writing you about this because a copy of the script will be going into the Breen office; and if we make it very clear that we are for religion, and not against it in this passage, we shall have an easier time with them.
>   I suggest that the first shot is of the group, with John standing to one side; close-up of John; a close-up of the Bible as she opens it; back to the group with him leaving the shot and going outside the screen door; and back to her and the Bible, where she changes her mind about the story.
>
> Re: Page #13
>   Preacher's lines: "I serve the Lord. I come not with peace, but with a sword."
>   I suggest that it read: "I come not with peace, but with a sword. I serve the Lord," as in that order it will answer the previous question about the stick-knife hid in the bed blankets, etc. ["I serve the Lord" was cut, and sometime during production, versions of lines from the first draft went back into the film.]

I understand that Mitchum is a little doubtful about talking to himself in the old Essex at the beginning. It's too bad, but I'm damned if I know how else to do it. If you see him it isn't necessary to mention this.

Best to you,

Charles[61]

The Bible-reading sequence comes from two passages in the novel that Agee wisely seizes on to dramatize (*NH*, 213–14, 215–16). Laughton's memo reworks Agee's long opening ("*NH*," 223–25) by proposing a compressed series of shots. The revised version is written up in the final screenplay exactly as Laughton outlines it in the memo (*AF*, 331). Conflict, of course, can be set aside in the name of professional courtesy, but on the surface Laughton's friendly tone does not suggest tension between the collaborators. (Neither does a cable that Laughton sent to Agee's widow on May 19, 1955: "Just heard sad news of James passing. I loved him.")[62]

Admittedly, the cordiality of Laughton's memo is somewhat offset by a different version of Grubb's story about Laughton's sneering comment: "We've got [the script] back together, with the assistance of a $2,500-a-week stenographer" (*HH*, 100). Was Laughton, then, dictating changes that Agee incorporated into a new draft? Or did Agee enter into the work and make his own suggestions?

Agee himself has something to say about the matter. On January 14, 1955, he sent a remarkable letter to Paul Gregory to accompany script-authorship forms that he had signed:

> While I'm about it, I'd like to bring up once more, a matter which I discussed at length, but inconclusively, with Charles, last summer: the whole question of proper script credit, and the verbalization of it. My feeling was, and is, that Charles had such an immense amount to do with the script, that it seems to me absurd to take solo credit, much as I'd like it. Charles' own feeling, as he can fill in (so I'll only outline it here), fell into 2 parts: 1) he doesn't like the idea of being talked of as a "genius" or a credit-hog, as he felt might happen if we split credit; 2) realizing how intricate the collaboration is, in actual practice, in crystallizing any kind of show, he felt, strongly, that the front, the

thing presented to the world, should remain ultra-simple and clear. There is such virtue in both points that I can't pretend or try to argue them out of existence. Nevertheless I'm sure you know as well as I do, or better, how embarrassed a writer should rightly feel in being given full credit, who has done a piece of work for and with Charles. It's on this basis that I feel very strongly that credit on the script should be double. At times I've even felt that it should be given him entirely; I can withdraw from that position only in realizing that I *was* useful, as a sort of combination sounding-board and counterirritant. I'll be grateful if you'll discuss this whole business with him, taking my point of view as strongly as you may happen to feel it: strongly, I hope. . . . Needless to say, I am deeply eager to see the picture, at whatever stage it's see-able.[63]

It is safe to say that few writers in any medium have requested that their credit be diminished. Agee certainly had a "leaning to self-accusation,"[64] but his abasement here is more even-tempered than the self-castigation one sees, for instance, in his letters to Father Flye. It is unlikely that even someone of Agee's temperament would invite a director to share screenwriting credit if in fact the director had not participated directly in the writing. One finds in this letter Agee's humility and deep sense of justice. For that matter, Laughton's own modesty is revealed; he felt no need to take screenwriting credit. If Agee hints at conflict with his word *counterirritant,* he is otherwise respectful of Laughton's screenwriting talents. We discover that "last summer"—that is, in the midst of the revisions—Agee was already lobbying for Laughton to share credit. His eagerness in January to see the film, and his faith in its speed and power, imply that he was satisfied with the leaner, faster-paced shooting script.

In later years, Gregory remembered that the Writers Guild had insisted Agee receive solo credit,[65] but Agee's letter and a response from Gregory himself, dated February 10, 1955, say otherwise:

Your letter of January 14th has been received, and of course I have read it, considered it and discussed it in great detail with Charles.

We do not feel, in any sense, that a change in the credit should be made where you are concerned. We feel that you made a great contribution to *The Night of the Hunter.*

I tell you very honestly if we thought the picture were bad, in order to protect you we would be more than happy to remove your name, but since we think it is great we feel that you will be happy and proud that you had something to do with it—and neither Charles nor I feel that under any circumstances should you be embarrassed over the credit, etc.[66]

Unfortunately, it remains unclear what Agee did in working both "for and with" Laughton. Agee's own description of his role during the revision process and Laughton's "stenographer" gibe suggest that he did little rewriting for the final screenplay. Still, one cannot rule out the possibility that in making "a great contribution," he took a more active role than either he or Laughton acknowledged. In any event, Agee's letter to Gregory and Laughton's memo about the Pharaoh story do point to Laughton as the driving force behind the revisions. Given Laughton's work on such pieces as *John Brown's Body* and *The Caine Mutiny Court-Martial*, it is easy to imagine him performing textual surgery on Agee's Gargantuan draft. Dwight Macdonald, writing in reference to *A Death in the Family,* says that "what Agee needed was a sympathetically severe editor who would prune him as Maxwell Perkins pruned Thomas Wolfe."[67] For *The Night of the Hunter,* Agee found his Maxwell Perkins.

Agee and Laughton on Film

Within a few weeks of its delivery, Agee's sprawling draft was transformed into a screenplay that is a model of economy. The final script is remarkably close to the final cut of the film. Descriptions now are spare and practical. Where Agee creates a page-long picture of a burlesque house, with a psychological analysis of the men in the audience and an image of Preacher's face "as shockingly out of place as the Addams cartoon of the man who giggles in a movie theatre while all others weep" ("NH," 9), the shooting script sums the scene up: "Among the members of the sad burlesque audience, he is in strong contrast: a sour and aggressive expression" (*AF,* 265).

The revised screenplay eliminates any scene that does not contribute to the forward drive of the narrative. Thus, it takes out nearly all the material that Agee added, bidding good-bye to the genial priest Father Scallon, Rachel's sister Lovey, and Preacher's loquacious defense attorney. The many scenes with the children on Rachel's farm, which delay Preacher's return for too long, are reduced to two significant moments: John being scrubbed and Rachel telling a Bible story that wins John's trust. Gone, too, are the early scenes intended to flesh out the Harper family. The shooting script picks up Ben's story in medias res, when he returns home bleeding, stolen money in hand (*AF,* 266). The script also dispenses with monologues and cuts through long passages of dialogue to seize on key lines. Willa's three-page sermon in the first draft, for example, is a nearly verbatim transcription of her speech in the novel ("NH," 101–3; *NH,* 110–12). The final screenplay cuts her monologue to several lines and still manages to maintain the essence of her religious frenzy (*AF,* 292–93).

In other places, the revision streamlines entire sections of the first draft. Agee's script introduces Preacher in four scenes:

1. He sits in the audience of a burlesque house and flicks a switchblade through his pants pocket.
2. He flees the strip show in disgust, then hurries down a street and enters a cheap hotel.
3. In his room, he talks to the Lord in a two-page monologue.
4. State troopers enter and, in another two-page scene, arrest him for the theft of an Essex touring car. ("NH," 8–14)

The shooting script presents Preacher in three scenes:

1. He drives country roads in his Essex, speaking to the Lord in a shortened version of Agee's original monologue. (This is the scene that Mitchum had doubts about, though it effectively introduces the mad Preacher to us.)
2. Cut to a stripper bumping and grinding in a burlesque house. Preacher flicks a switchblade through his coat pocket. A

state trooper claps his hand on Preacher's shoulder and, in one line, arrests him.

3. Dissolve (in the film it becomes a wipe) to the courtroom in which Preacher is sentenced to prison. (*AF,* 264–66)

Seven leisurely pages have been compressed into some two swift-moving pages. The reworking of this section also illustrates the way Laughton as director is intent on moving the story along with surprising cuts and dissolves.

Many times, the final screenplay reverts to the novel for dialogue or to restore a scene that Agee, surprisingly, left out. Grubb, for instance, includes these lines as part of a long passage about Preacher: "But the Lord sure knew what he was doing all right. He had sent him to the state penitentiary to this very cell because a man named Ben Harper was going to die. A man with a widow in the making and ten thousand dollars hidden somewhere down river" (*NH,* 25). The shooting script adapts those words for a prayer that nicely caps the prison scene between Ben and Preacher: "Lord You sure knowed what You was doin' when You brung me to this very cell at this very time. A man with ten thousand dollars hid somewheres, and a widder in the makin'" (*AF,* 271). The sound of the third-person narrative is shrewdly altered for the first-person speech. "This very cell at this very time" captures the pulpit rhythms of the fraudulent preacher. Rearranging Grubb's line, so that it ends with "a widder in the makin'," gives the prayer a chillingly gleeful climax.

Now and then the final script adds scenes not found in either the novel or Agee's draft. In both Grubb's novel and Agee's script, the scene at Bart's home ends with the hangman, who has just executed Ben Harper, washing his hands for a second time (*NH,* 30; "NH," 43). The final screenplay concludes the scene with Bart looking in on his children, asleep in their bed. Over a close-up of the executioner, we hear children's frail voices singing, "Hing, hang, hung. See what the Hangman done!" (*AF,* 273). A dissolve reveals John and Pearl listening to playmates who taunt them with the chanting rhyme. The aural transition maintains the momentum of the film, even as it suspends us in an eerie moment. The overlapping sound makes it seem as though the chant is playing in Bart's head and expressionistically portrays his feelings of shame. The offscreen chant in this scene calls to mind Agee's occasional use of the song as John's inner voice. The moment becomes, consciously or not, an adaptation of that interior voice. In a later scene, Rachel sits on her porch, waiting out Preacher in the yard. Agee's draft follows Grubb's novel: Rachel falls asleep, giving Preacher a chance to escape ("NH," 253–54). The shooting script adds a significant new action. Ruby enters with a candle, the light of which allows Preacher to slip away unseen (*AF*, 340–41). The scene strengthens Rachel by keeping her awake. It is the foolishness of a weaker character that interferes with Rachel's vigil. Thus, both Rachel and Ruby are efficiently developed. The candle also allows for a striking visual effect at the moment Preacher vanishes.

For all the differences between the two screenplays, the final version retains significant elements from the first draft. Most important, it follows Agee's structure. Where Grubb divides his novel into five sections, Agee breaks the script into six readily identifiable parts. He fades or irises out at the end of all but one section. Although the breaks in the shooting script are not as clearly defined, it, too, has six parts that closely correspond to Agee's divisions. The following chart indicates the climactic scene within each division of the novel and the scripts and gives the page number on which a section ends:

Novel (*NH*)	First Draft ("NH")	Final Screenplay (*AF*)
1. Preacher's arrival (61)	Ben's execution/Image of Bart (43)	Ben's execution/Image of Bart (273)
2. Ben hides money in doll (131)	Pearl plays with money in doll (114)	Honeymoon night of Willa and Harry (292)
3. River journey ends (205)	Children escape (189)	Children escape (320)
4. Lynching/Rachel aids Ruby (261)	River journey ends/ Time lapse: dawn (213)	River journey ends/ Dissolve: dawn (325)
5. Coda: Christmas (273)	Lynching/Rachel aids Ruby (279)	Lynch mob/Rachel aids children (351)
6.	Christmas (293)	Christmas (354)

The final screenplay also uses Agee's opening scene, which is not found in the novel. The first draft begins with Bible quotations superimposed over a helicopter shot of children playing hide-and-seek. In the midst of the game, the children discover a woman's corpse in a cellar

("NH," 1–3). Agee's Bible quotations, slightly altered, are used not as titles in the shooting script but as narration spoken by a "voice." In the film, that anonymous narrator becomes Lillian Gish. The voice-over enriches the images and establishes a comforting tone: *"Beware of false prophets . . . which come to you in sheep's clothing. . . . Ye shall know them by their fruits"* (*AF,* 263–64). At the end of the scene, Agee's iris-out on the corpse's foot is replaced by a second helicopter shot, which pulls back from the children at the "same angle and height as the last descending helicopter shot" (*AF,* 264). Visually, the scene has a formal balance that is typical of Laughton's entire film.

No doubt Laughton's sense of order impelled him to maintain the chronological flow of Agee's narrative. In the novel, the important scene in which Ben, moments before his arrest, hides his stolen money in Pearl's doll appears as a flashback midway through the story (*NH,* 119–26). Agee brings the scene forward and changes it so that the audience does not see where Ben hides the money ("NH," 17–23). The shooting script follows that plan, though it implements changes that are less cinematic than Agee's approach. In the first draft, Ben thinks about places to hide the money and says, *"There? . . . There?"* while the film cuts to various hiding places ("NH," 19). The final screenplay goes back to the scene as Grubb wrote it: Ben thinks aloud about hiding places, saying, "Under a rock in the smokehouse? Ah no. Under the bricks in the grape arbor? No, they'd dig for it" (*AF,* 267). The artificiality of that dialogue often produces snickers in the audience today. Agee's swift point-of-view shots seem more effective.

Specific lines and actions that Agee wrote can still be found, in modified form, in the revised screenplay. In Agee's draft, a state trooper asks Preacher, "What church are *you,* Mister?" to which Preacher replies, "The Church the Lord and me worked out betwixt us" ("NH," 13–14). The shooting script transfers that revealing exchange to the prison scene between Ben and Preacher and alters the wording to sharpen the lines:

> BEN: What religion do you profess, Preacher?
> PREACHER: The religion the Almighty and me worked out
>   betwixt us. (*AF,* 271)

In the burlesque-hall sequence, which comes straight from the novel (*NH,* 22–23), Agee creates his own startling moment. Preacher slips the hand tattooed with the word *love* into his pants pocket and flicks his switchblade. The knife pops out through his trousers ("NH," 9). The final screenplay retains that bit, though the description is vague: "the knife cuts through his clothes" (*AF,* 265). In the film, Preacher uses the hand tattooed with *hate,* and the knife slices up through his jacket. No doubt the pants pocket would have been a little much for the Breen Office. Laughton does, however, slip in a sexual innuendo based on Agee's first-draft description of the scene. The film cuts to a close-up of Preacher's face, which reflects what Agee calls "the moment equivalent to that of post-climax; sick, guilty, let-down in sex but tightened up in religiosity" ("NH," 10). Mitchum's priceless expression conveys the essence of that description.

Another important image that Laughton retains in his own way is the nighttime sky with which Agee concludes his script. The camera in the first draft looks up at "the most brilliant and star-filled of winter skies." While children sing the last stanza of "O Little Town of Bethlehem," the stars "blossom," as Agee puts it, into the faces of children, some smiling, some serious, "of all recognizable nations and races and peoples; a solid mosaic" ("NH," 293). The final screenplay uses the shot of a starry sky (minus the children) as a framing device to open and close the film (*AF,* 263, 354). During production, however, Laughton added a prologue to his film. He opens on the stars, but then, after an image of Gish offering a Bible lesson, he superimposes the faces of children, smiling and serious, just as Agee suggested—though they hardly represent all nationalities and races; they are little white cherubs shining out of the sky.

One sees in that night sky, as in many other details, a fascinating interchange of ideas between Agee and Laughton. It is clear that they were working toward the same goal: to render as closely as possible Grubb's novel on film. In their common pursuit, the two men complemented each other well. Laughton had never written a screenplay and needed a writer. Agee, clinging to Grubb's words, trying earnestly to give Laughton the screenplay he wanted, needed an editor. Yet however diffuse the first draft is, Agee did the initial, difficult job of "cracking the book"—finding a cinematic structure, selecting scenes to dramatize with sound and image, and drawing dialogue from Grubb's third-person narrative. Although Laughton had to make selections from Agee's mass of material, the first draft provided him with an overall plan—and many specific ideas—that guided him during revisions. Jeffrey J. Folks, writing eight years before the discovery of Agee's draft, suggests that the final script is "a composite, though hardly collaborative, effort."[68] We can now see that Agee's adaptation comes out of Grubb's novel and his story conferences with Laughton. In turn, the shooting script is derived from the novel and Agee's first draft. In their own way, Agee and Laughton did collaborate. F. X. Feeney, in a forthcoming article for *Written By*, the magazine of the Writers Guild of America, West, argues that Agee deserves his solo screen credit.[69] From the production standpoint—that is to say, from the economic and political perspective of Gregory and Laughton, who wanted to maintain a clean division of labor—it makes sense for Agee to be given sole credit. He was, after all, on the project from start to finish. From a historical perspective, however, it is impossible to ignore Laughton's work on the shooting script—work that Agee himself felt should be acknowledged. It seems only just that the two artists share the credit for which Agee vigorously argued: "Screenplay by James Agee and Charles Laughton."

In the end, the final script for *The Night of the Hunter* does honor to both of its creators. It is a testament to Laughton's skill as an editor and to his understanding of cinematic form. And, with its themes of innocence lost and its compassion for children in the midst of hard times, it is a fitting requiem for James Agee.

five

PRODUCTION AND STYLE

The Crew

The admiration for Laughton that Agee expressed in his letter about screen credit was universal among the crew with which Laughton surrounded himself. "I think he impressed me more than any director I've ever worked with," said art director Hilyard Brown (*HH*, 126). "He had a marvelous way of enthusing people and getting past the malarkey."[1] For Robert Golden, "*The Night of the Hunter* was the most exhilarating experience of my career."[2] What was most exhilarating for Golden and the other artists on the team was that Laughton did indeed treat them like artists. Brown felt that "I contributed more to *The Night of the Hunter* than I have to 90 percent of the other pictures I've done. I had a lot of freedom to do the work. I could be as creative as I wanted to be."[3] For Stanley Cortez, too, the production "was a field day for me in terms of extreme creativity that Charles appreciated."[4]

Because United Artists, in exchange for financing the film, demanded a short production schedule, Laughton was forced to begin shooting even as he continued what would normally have been preproduction work. He held nightly meetings at a restaurant on La Cienega Boulevard with Cortez, Brown, Golden, assistant director Milton Carter, and sometimes production manager Ruby Rosenberg to plan the next day's shots.[5] "We ate a lot of food, and we drank a lot of booze doing this, but—the job got done," said Golden (*HH*, 113). On the weekends the team would meet at Laughton's house, where as Brown put it, continuing the food motif that was an important feature of collaboration with Charles Laughton, "we . . . sat around and had a marvelous dinner and discussed all this stuff." At their meetings, Carter would identify the scenes to be shot the next day, and Brown would make "little rough sketches" of each camera setup.[6] "Everybody would be talking, it was a completely cooperative thing" (*HH*, 119). Cortez concurred: "It wasn't a question of outdoing each other. . . . It was a question of each one contributing for the sake of the film."[7] The production's smooth collaboration was made easier by the fact that many of the participants in *The Night of the Hunter* had worked together before. Cortez, Brown, and Golden had just finished another United Artists film, *Black Tuesday* (1954), which also featured Peter Graves, and were "transferred by the production company right over to this picture."[8] Copies of Brown's sketches were handed out on the set so that everyone from the grips to the cinematographer had a clear picture of the day's work.[9] Laughton's method was shrewdly designed for efficiency on his tight, seven-week shooting schedule. "There was no horsing around," asserted Brown. "There weren't a lot of guys off in a corner talking about last week's football game, I can assure you of that."[10]

Paul Gregory, the man who set the entire project in motion, did not participate in the nightly planning sessions. "I didn't insert myself into the business of the shots . . . and the setups," Gregory explained. "I was occupied with getting the money and creating the possibility for [the film] to happen."[11] Although Laughton and Gregory met frequently throughout the shoot, the producer rarely visited the set.[12] Brown remembered a United Artists executive asking Gregory if he was keeping close watch on Laughton, to which Gregory replied, "Look, if that fat son-of-a-bitch doesn't know what he's doing, I'm dead anyway."[13] Gregory, in conjunction with Laughton, acknowledged the creative contributions of Cortez, Brown, Golden, and Carter by giving each a 1 percent share of the profits. "Never happened to me before," marveled Brown. "Probably never will again."[14]

Even with his second-unit director, the twenty-two-year-old Terry Sanders, Laughton developed a close working relationship. Terry and his older brother Denis had made a short film called *A Time out of War*. Based on a Civil War story, "The Pickets," it had been broadcast on *Omnibus* (CBS, February 21, 1954). Sanders had photographed the drama in what he defined as a "simple and naturalistic" style patterned on the look of Mathew Brady's photographs. Laughton was impressed with footage shot along a river in the mountains near Santa Barbara, and he believed the young man would be ideal to direct a second unit for shots of the river in *The Night of the Hunter.* When Terry went over to Laughton's house, Laughton "flung open the door," and with "this very impressive bellow" said, "Brother Sanders!" He put the young man so much at ease that Sanders replied, "Brother Laughton!" Sanders and Laughton worked for several days, going over the final script scene by scene.[15] In his recollections about working with Laughton, Sanders struck a familiar note of affection for both Laughton and his gourmet food: "He was very, very gracious and warm . . . , and he was really delightful to work with. . . . He had a fabulous cook named Heidel, . . . and we had this great lunch. And then after that you'd maybe do a little more work."[16] To "keep peace in the family," as Denis Sanders put it, Laughton hired Denis as dialogue director on the film, though he also spent time talking to the young writer-director about ideas for the design of the picture and about filmmaking in general.[17] Thus, in an already collaborative medium, Laughton created a distinctly collegial atmosphere. To Cortez, "there was a feeling of camaraderie there that seldom exists in the motion picture world. . . . There's always a feeling of friendship, but not as it was on *The Night of the Hunter.*"[18]

One note of apparent disharmony, however, is sounded in the letter from Ilse Lahn, quoted in the previous chapter, about Robert Mitchum's desire to have Agee on the set because "Laughton 'does not have the ear for this sort of thing.'"[19] Mitchum had his own ideas about the adaptation. He wanted the entire film shot on location in West Virginia, and he was mildly scornful of what he called "the owls and the pussycats" in the river sequence.[20] Mitchum no doubt believed that Agee would have maintained a level of realism on the project. Nevertheless, Mitchum's own memories are of a harmonious set that centered on Laughton, "the only director I have ever encountered . . . who was really brilliant."[21] In the outtakes, one senses a mutual respect in the smooth give-and-take between director and actor. As Mitchum explained, "I sought his approbation, and I tried to please him, and he indicated his approval. I think we worked very well together."[22] In a similar vein, Lillian Gish said, "Charles was all heart. Everyone loved him and . . . worked very hard for him."[23] Yet as an actor himself, Laughton had definite ideas about what he wanted from his performers.[24] Gish recalled, "We had to stop giving him our suggestions because he became so excited and nervous about them, feeling they showed our lack of confidence in his direction. We didn't want to take him off guard or worry him, so we just kept quiet after awhile."[25]

Laughton's response to suggestions from his crew was quite different. Brown remembered that "Laughton was not like a lot of other directors. He was very open, very [receptive]."[26] At the end of the scene in which John tells Pearl a bedtime story, Laughton planned to dolly the camera in for a close-up of the children in bed while Preacher, offscreen, walks away from the house singing "Leaning on the Everlasting Arms." Such a track-in was standard Hollywood practice for heightening dramatic tension. Cortez, however, said, " 'Charles, think about it. Why don't we move back?' [Laughton] said, 'My God, why don't we do that? Because the audience will see the whole thing then.' . . . It wasn't telling him how to do it, but suggesting an idea that he could think about."[27] The shot in the film shows how wise Laughton was in taking Cortez's suggestion. The slow backward move, a reversal of what one might expect, is more emotional in its restraint than a dramatic forward movement. Viewing the children—alone in the bed in the darkened room—from a discreet distance makes them all the more vulnerable. Because Laughton was interested in serving a visualization of Grubb's novel, he could suppress his own ego and take suggestions from the experienced craftsmen around him.

Gregory pointed to another reason that Laughton was willing to listen to his crew: "Charlie was frightened."[28] As a first-time director, he felt "an enormous weight on his shoulders."[29] There had been some discussion about David Lean directing the film (Laughton had recently made *Hobson's Choice* [1954] with Lean), but Gregory told Laughton, "I bought it for you. You have to do it."[30] Laughton chose Cortez because he "would feel quite comfortable and safe working with Stanley."[31] Cortez explained that "Laughton had a very limited concept of motion pictures" in a technical sense. "Our purpose . . . was to pool our efforts to get Charles off the hook, so to speak, to help him do what he would like to do, technically speaking."[32] Golden made a similar point, stating that he was kept on the set "because of Laughton's lack of technical knowledge."[33] Awkward moments on screen attest to Laughton's inexperience. He sometimes fails to create a coherent sense of screen space. A line of children in a playground sing, "Hing, hang, hung" while the Harper children look on. But shots of John and Pearl, in their own two-shot, and of the group taunting them seem disconnected. Not until we are given a master shot of the scene can we fully understand how the characters are situated in relation to one another. Later in the film, when Preacher arrives at Rachel's house, Ruby sees him as she is crossing the screen from left to right, but a moment later she runs from right to left toward Miz Cooper. "That particular sequence wasn't covered properly," said Golden.[34] He called it "the most ad-libbed sequence in the picture" (*HH*, 295). The difficulties in the scene might also be explained by the fact that Laughton had trouble with the concept of reverse angles, wherein the director must maintain the proper positioning of characters on screen. At times during the setup of shots, Golden would intervene and tell Laughton, "You can't do that. . . . It's a reverse cut." During setup for the scene in which Preacher nearly discovers Pearl cutting the stolen money into paper dolls, Laughton, sounding to Golden like Captain Bligh from *Mutiny on the Bounty*, called out, "Bob Golden! What do I do now?" Golden remembered a subjective shot from an Alfred Hitchcock picture that had impressed him, and he suggested to Laughton that he "take [the shot] from the kids' point of view and just use the camera moving in."[35]

Golden, however, was not the only one to think of a moving point-of-view shot for the scene. In his first draft, Agee specifies a "DOLLY SHOT—CENTERING PREACHER—THROUGH ARBOR—AT CHILD'S EYE LEVEL." He also suggests a "lens which exaggerates the length of the arbor, as through the reverse of a telescope." Agee's subjective shot alternates with a "close pull shot" of John and Pearl approaching Preacher ("NH," 112–13). The final script retains the dolly shot, without any reverse angles, and adds the image of paper dolls blowing past Preacher (*AF*, 294). If Laughton called for Golden during this scene, it meant he was concerned about the editing—how best to cut together a shot of paper dolls blowing away unseen and three characters interacting at a tense moment. Golden himself, unsure whether the camera move would cut in smoothly, slipped into the editing room before screening dailies for the sequence and pieced together a few shots to make one continuous scene out of them. It looked perfect to Laughton.[36] On screen, the subjective shot effectively conveys the children's fear as they approach the looming figure of Preacher at the end of the arbor.

Laughton's technical difficulties, as well as the affection of his coworkers, are memorialized in a drawing sketched by Brown and signed by members of the cast and crew. Amid images from the film and the production are the words "Complete reverse," "What the hell do I do now?" and "I'm confused." Above the list of names are the words, "We never had it so good."[37]

At times, however, Golden did not have it so good. Keeping his editor on the set gave Laughton access to professional advice, but it also served another purpose. "He didn't want me to touch the film," said Golden. "He wanted to be in charge of [the editing]. So I had to be on the set, because if I was in the cutting room, I might be fooling around. . . . I never put a first cut together. [Laughton] was there from the word 'go.'" The director wanted to see each scene "every way" possible, so after seven months in a cement room that was "like a jail cell" (even though Laughton tried to dress it up with Japanese prints), Golden began to wear down. During one scene, as Golden remembered, "I threw the scissors up in the air and said, 'Charles, I can't please you!' And he said, 'Come with me.' He'd brought a couple of director's chairs to put out on the patio outside the cutting room. We went and sat in the chairs, and he said, 'Bob, I'm here as your guest.' So after we quieted down and smoked a cigarette, we went back in, and we went through the same routine."[38]

The story illustrates the way Laughton, despite the understandable anxiety of a novice director, retained authority during production. "Laughton had control," said Brown. "Believe me, he had control of the set." He also had a clear conception of what he wanted on screen, and he employed his own distinctive means to convey those ideas to his collaborators. At meetings with his crew, Laughton would read from the Bible or Dickens. "Or he'd read poetry—anything!" said Brown. "He would say, 'You get the idea? This is what we want on film. That's the essence of what we want in this scene.'"[39] The crew found specific ways to implement the director's general concepts. After viewing dailies from the river sequence, Laughton said to Cortez, "My God, how did you do that?" Cortez replied, "Because you used the word 'fairy tale'" (HH, 273). Brown was inspired to stylize his set designs once he understood that Laughton wanted to capture a child's point of view. "In one of our early discussions," explained Brown, "I said it might be interesting to put the audience in Johnny's place—the little boy. . . . He'd run up a street, and there would be three buildings on the street. Everything else would be blank in between, because the little kid's not paying attention to those."[40]

Brown's subjective designs also mirror the point of view of the novel, which, with its interior monologues, delves even more deeply into John's perspective. Brown and Cortez read the novel and admired it. Their sympathy for the book contributed to the "great unity" that Brown said existed between Laughton, Cortez, and himself.[41] Grubb may have been disappointed to find that pylons near Birdie's wharf boat made the waterfront seem more like a seacoast than an inlet of the Ohio River (*HH*, 115), but in other respects Brown's designs closely follow Grubb's sketches for *The Night of the Hunter*. And Cortez's cinematography often matches the lyricism of Grubb's prose.

The Baron

The final Agee-Laughton script tells a good tale, but it is the look of the film—chiaroscuro effects alternating with a rich palette of grays; stylization alternating with realism—that gives the work its peculiar power and resonance. As Stephen F. Bauer puts it, *The Night of the Hunter*'s "emotions and ideas are expressed through light and line as much as plot and action."[42] The visual eclecticism of the film can be found in the very nature of its director—in Laughton's fascination with Americana and with European art.[43] But it is also rooted in the sensibility and the varied career of Stanley Cortez.

"We used to call him the Baron," said Golden. "He was very upright and had a manner about him." As part of that "manner," he wore colorful scarves and sported a maulstick.[44] Nearly a decade after his death in 1996, he was still remembered by fellow cinematographers as "a great character"—and as "a giant in the industry."[45] Born Stanley Krantz, he took a cue from his older brother, the Rudolph Valentino–like film star Ricardo Cortez, and gave himself the more romantic surname. He began his career in New York as an assistant to still photographers, including Edward Steichen.[46] A job on a Pathé serial led him to Hollywood and a new career in motion pictures.[47] In 1926, his brother invited him to the set of *The Sorrows of Satan*, a production directed by D. W. Griffith. "I walked into that studio," Cortez recalled seventy years later, "I saw all these Cooper Hewitt lights, . . . and I saw this tremendous crowd of people, the extras, and the great orchestra, and I saw Griffith with a big megaphone. I was hooked."[48] In the thirties, he was equally proficient operating a camera on Busby Berkeley's musical extravaganzas and collaborating with Slavko Vorkapich, famous for his Hollywood montages, on an abstract two-reel film about water called *Scherzo.* "It was 'way out,' with trick lenses and false perspective," Cortez told Charles Higham. When he became a director of photography at Universal, he "was always chosen to shoot weird things." In *The Forgotten Woman* (1939), one of those "weird things" was a close-up of Sigrid Gurie's eye, over which Cortez superimposed images to portray her thoughts.[49] A few years later, Julien Duvivier directed three different tales in *Flesh and Fantasy* (1943), and Cortez shot the story based on Oscar Wilde's "Lord Arthur Savile's Crime." (Paul Ivano was cinematographer on the rest of the film.) To depict Edward G. Robinson's internal debate about committing a murder, Cortez created a series of remarkable images in which the decent Robinson converses with reflections of his devilish counterpart. In one darkly amusing shot, twin Robinsons appear in eyeglasses resting on a desk.

In 1942, Cortez teamed with Orson Welles and created a masterpiece of cinematography for *The Magnificent Ambersons.* During many scenes, he shrouds the rooms of the Amberson mansion in oppressive shadow. Faces often vanish into darkness, or characters become silhouettes, as in the scene where Tim Holt, Dolores Costello, and Anne Baxter are posed in a formal composition to say their good-byes after a party: shadow puppets conversing in a void. His effects convey the doom hanging over the Ambersons and the slow dissolution of the family—ideas that Orson Welles saw as "the whole meaning of the film."[50] Alongside symbolic shots, however, Cortez presents the Amberson mansion in a realistic manner. Long, single takes, like the scene in which Agnes Moorehead, Tim Holt, and Ray Collins hold a conversation in the Amberson kitchen, give the sense that we in the audience are eavesdropping on people as they go about their lives. In a career that mixed B pictures (*Badlands of Dakota* [1941], *Shock Corridor* [1963]) and A pictures (*Since You Went Away* [1944], *The Three Faces of Eve* [1957]), Cortez considered *Ambersons* one of his two "most exciting" experiences in film. The other was *The Night of the Hunter.*[51]

Laughton met Cortez in 1948, when the cinematographer arrived in Paris to take over on the troubled production of *The Man on the Eiffel Tower.* At a cocktail party in the hotel George V, Laughton greeted Cortez with the words, "I'm happy to meet you, you big bastard," to which

Cortez replied, "I'm very happy to meet you, you fat son-of-a-bitch."[52] Thus, in a spirit of rough affection, began a lasting friendship and a close professional partnership. There was, as Cortez put it, "tremendous *sympatico*—not a phoney veneer, but truly a *sympatico*—that existed between Charles Laughton and myself."[53]

That sympathy did not exist between Laughton and the director of *The Man on the Eiffel Tower*, Irving Allen. Eventually, Laughton refused to work with him. One of the film's stars, Burgess Meredith, ostensibly took over the direction. (Meredith receives screen credit; Allen remains credited as a producer.) In reality, Meredith directed only the scenes in which he himself did not appear. Laughton directed scenes in which he did not appear, and Simon Callow reports that when they were both in a scene, Franchot Tone took over.[54] Cortez has said in latter-day interviews that he stepped in to direct when Meredith, Laughton, and Tone acted together.[55] In any event, the film, based on Georges Simenon's 1939 detective novel *A Battle of Nerves,* is for the most part sluggishly directed and displays little of the Cortez photographic flair. Apart from several impressive tracking shots through the grid work of the Eiffel Tower, the only sequences of visual interest are those directed by Laughton. He introduces the character played by Meredith in a rapid shot that tracks along a street and ends on the image of a knife being sharpened on a wheel. Worthy of Hitchcock, the shot jolts the viewer with a sense of threat amid the bustle of a sunny Parisian street. Early in the film, Meredith enters a room slashed by ominous shadows, stumbles over a corpse, and drops his glasses, which glint at him from the floor. The striking visuals and their noirish play of light and shadow look ahead to *The Night of the Hunter*. They serve as a kind of screen test for the Laughton-Cortez team. (The pair met one more time before *Night of the Hunter,* when Cortez filmed Laughton having fun as a pirate in the negligible *Abbott and Costello Meet Captain Kidd* [1952].)

Once Cortez signed on for *The Night of the Hunter,* he gave Laughton a crash course in cinematography. "I used to go to Charles's house every Sunday for six weeks before we started and explain my camera equipment to him piece by piece," he told Higham. "I wanted to show him through the camera what these lenses would and would not do. But soon the instructor became the student."[56] Laughton helped Cortez think in new ways about "the dramaturgy, the whole structure of the script and the dramatic values" (*HH*, 86), and he offered "a great philosophy about light."[57] Indeed, Cortez stated flatly, "Of the directors I've worked with, only two have understood [light]: Orson Welles and Charles Laughton."[58]

Certain shots in the film suggest that Laughton and Cortez also had discussions about particular artworks in connection with *The Night of the Hunter*. When Cortez worked on *The Magnificent Ambersons*, he often explained his visual ideas to Welles by referring to masterworks of art—a Rembrandt portrait or a Goya "black painting," for instance. The comments annoyed Welles as pretentious.[59] Such references, however, would have been welcome to Laughton, the collector of fine art. "Charles was a great believer in the great artists: Japanese artists, French artists, German artists."[60] It is not surprising to learn from Elsa Lanchester that Laughton modeled his picnic scene on the neo-impressionist "mood" of Seurat's *Sunday on La Grande Jatte.*[61] Seurat's study in light and composition is especially well evoked by images of people seated on the riverbank under a parasol. Toward the end of the film, after John has collapsed over Preacher, Rachel picks the boy up and carries him to her house. The image is a moving replication of the Pietà. The positions of John's head and dangling arm in particular bring to mind Michelangelo's sculpture in St. Peter's Basilica in Rome. It should be noted, however, that the immediate source of the Pietà imagery is a mixture of Grubb's novel and Agee's first draft. In the novel, it is a police officer who carries the boy "back to the yard, limp and sobbing in his arms" (*NH*, 250). Agee wisely brings Rachel to the foreground: she "leads him quickly away towards the house, still sobbing" ("NH," 266). The film combines the two descriptions: Rachel carries John. The final script explicitly states, "His head hangs back over her arm" (*AF*, 347). Cortez frames the shot in such a way that as he pans with Rachel, she moves close to the camera just before she walks out of view. Her sorrowful face, briefly glimpsed at close range, deepens the pathos of the image.

Although Laughton worked closely with Cortez, he went into production with specific shots in mind. On the following pages are drawings that he created for the river sequence to guide Terry Sanders on location. In crude form, they are the very images that appear in the film. Each Laughton sketch is followed by a more detailed drawing that Sanders made on breakdown sheets in his production notebook, along with notes taken from Laughton about the specifics of the shots. In figure 5.1, a few hasty lines represent the children's boat in the wide expanse of river, and several *x*'s represent the starry sky. On the Sanders breakdown sheet (fig. 5.2), an additional scene that never appeared in the film is indicated: a medium long shot "through fireflies." Sanders did shoot doubles of John and Pearl in the skiff, though ultimately it was Cortez who filmed the spiderweb and the animals that appear along the river.[62] Figure 5.3 is Laughton's rendition of that spiderweb, which he envisioned in the foreground over an image of the skiff. On his breakdown sheet, Sanders refers to the web as "dew-jeweled" (as indeed it is in the film), and he includes another picture that ends up on screen: a "big frog profiled in f.g." (fig 5.4). In figure 5.5, the boat is seen in the distance, and looming in the foreground are two large rabbits, drawn in childlike simplicity with round bodies and large ears. The subsequent drawing that Sanders made of the rabbits is particularly close to the shot used in the film (fig. 5.6). Thanks to a drawing that Grubb had sent, Laughton also had a clear idea for the scene in which John looks out of the hayloft at Preacher on the horizon. On one page of his notebook, Sanders indicates a "process plate" with a "fairy tale quality." Sanders even shot a day-for-night scene of Mitchum's double riding a horse for use as rear projection.[63] Ultimately, however, the hayloft and the farmland beyond were constructed on stage 11 at RKO-Pathé. Brown explained, "That was a Sunday discussion: 'What are we going to do?' And I said, 'Well, we'll force perspective. We'll get a pony and put a kid on it. It's at night, so you can get away with murder.' "[64] In the end, the stand-in for Billy Chapin, who played John, rode a Shetland pony "slowly across the horizon."[65] Sketches that Sanders made of the scene include a portion of a house, which Sanders reminded himself to shoot "if available," and trees intended to "block view occasionally."[66] The image in the film retains a few trees and a portion of a fence to balance the composition, but nothing blocks the view of Preacher on his horse against a moonlit sky. Emptied of all but essentials, the stark shot heightens the terror of Preacher's unexpected appearance in the calm of the country night.

If Laughton's own visual sense informs *The Night of the Hunter,* Cortez, as the hayloft scene eloquently illustrates, re-created Laughton's mental images in his own style—a style characterized by distinctive compositions and veritable sculptures of shadow and light. For all the breadth of their conversations, Laughton and Cortez had few discussions, "if any," about the cinematographer's specific approach to *The Night of the Hunter.* "I knew that what I was about to do would fit the

Figure 5.1
Boat on river under starry sky.
Preproduction sketch for *The Night of the Hunter*, 1954, Charles Laughton.

story and would fit Charles Laughton's idea," said Cortez. "I knew it instinctively." The technical aspects of lighting and camera placement were worked out on the set.[67] On some previous films, including *The Magnificent Ambersons*, Cortez had been what Welles called a "criminally slow cameraman."[68] In the last month of production on *Ambersons*, an exasperated Welles replaced Cortez with Harry Wild.[69] Mitchum remembered that on *The Night of the Hunter* Cortez would go from place to place looking for the best camera position, only to end up at the spot where he began.[70] Yet bound by a tight schedule, Cortez moved the production along at an efficient pace: principal photography was completed in thirty-six days (*HH*, 326). (He could at times move even more rapidly; in 1962, he shot Samuel Fuller's *Shock Corridor*, with its prodigal use of shadows, in sixteen days.)[71]

Nevertheless, according to Grubb's recollection, the key sequence of Willa's corpse underwater in the Model T took three days to shoot at

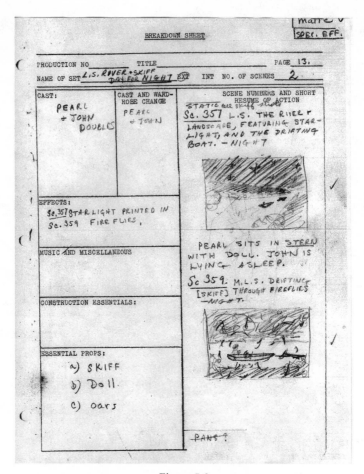

Figure 5.2
Boat on river under starry sky. Second-unit
production notebook, *The Night of the Hunter,* 1954, Terry Sanders.

an additional cost of $20,000.[72] In the novel, Uncle Birdie relates having seen Willa "just a-sittin' there in a white gown and her eyes looking at me and a great long slit under her chin just as clean as a catfish gill!—O Godamighty!—and her hair wavin' lazy and soft around her like meadow grass under flood waters" (*NH,* 172). Laughton and Cortez were intent on re-creating that verbal picture on film. Maurice Seiderman, who worked with Welles as makeup artist on *Citizen Kane* (1941), *The Magnificent Ambersons,* and *Touch of Evil* (1958), created a

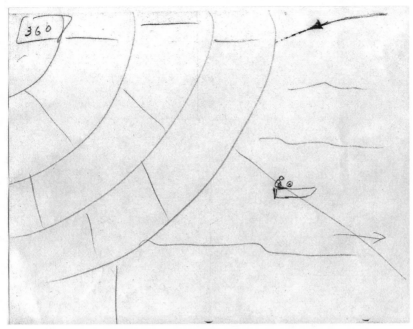

Figure 5.3
Spiderweb and boat. Preproduction sketch for
The Night of the Hunter, 1954, Charles Laughton.

wax dummy, complete with slit throat, of Willa's corpse. The car and its grisly passenger were submerged in a tank at Republic Studios. Cortez shot the scene using two cameras, one inside the tank and one outside, and huge arc lamps "to create that ethereal death-like something you had in the water."[73] Brown created current by spraying water in from a hose, and he set a fig tree upside down in the tank "so that the roots of the tree looked like water willows" (*HH*, 215, 217). The cinematic fakery resulted in images that no one who has seen the film is likely to forget. A slow pan along waving reeds picks up Willa, bound in the car, her hair flowing as though with a life of its own. In many ways, the scene defines *The Night of the Hunter*. It is at once realistic and surreal, grim and poetic. Everything about it is contradiction. The car alone is a shocking, industrial intrusion in a natural realm. The greater intrusion, though, is Willa's body, a serene picture of violent death, a floating apparition weighted to the river bottom.

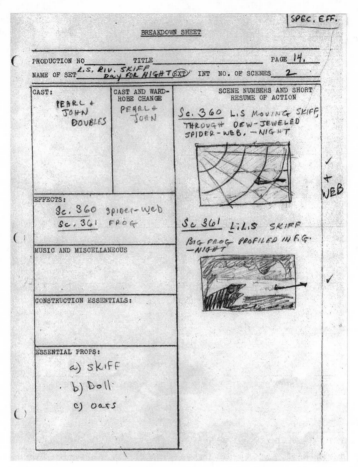

Figure 5.4
Spiderweb and boat. Second-unit production notebook,
The Night of the Hunter, 1954, Terry Sanders.

Cortez declared more than once that in crafting such shots for Laughton, he was not under any direct influences. When asked if he was inspired by any German expressionist works, he replied, "The Germanic film going back years and years had nothing to do with me on *The Night of the Hunter.* This is my own creation."[74] When asked if he had tried to emulate the look of D. W. Griffith, he replied, "No, not at all, not at all. The look of the film was strictly Stanley Cortez, that's the look of the film."[75] No one has ever claimed that Stanley Cortez lacked self-esteem.

Figure 5.5
Rabbits and boat. Preproduction sketch for
The Night of the Hunter, 1954, Charles Laughton.

Although he was determined in later years to be seen as wholly original, expressionistic and realistic influences—whether conscious or unconscious—are on display in *The Night of the Hunter.* Laughton and Cortez go beyond Grubb's novel to draw on traditions in film history as sources for their adaptation.

German American Expressionism

Parts of Laughton's film are rooted in the seminal German expressionist feature *The Cabinet of Dr. Caligari,* which does indeed go back "years and years," as Cortez put it. Directed by Robert Wiene, *Caligari* came out in 1920. Its patently artificial sets and painted backdrops find their counterparts in *The Night of the Hunter*'s river sequence. As Brown explained, "If [the sets] didn't look quite real, that's the way we wanted them, that's

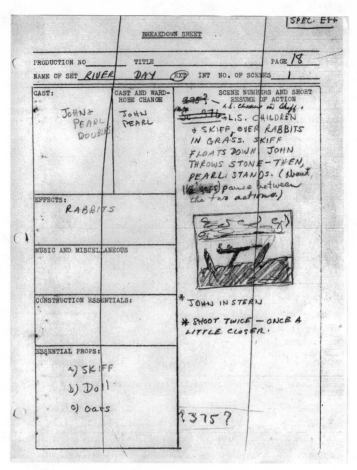

Figure 5.6
Rabbits and boat. Second-unit production notebook,
The Night of the Hunter, 1954, Terry Sanders.

exactly what we were trying to create" (*HH*, 268). When the children escape Preacher in their skiff, Laughton cuts to a long shot of the boat in the river under a sky of glimmering stars. The image is a storybook painting come to life. (Sanders copied into his script Laughton's idea for what the sequence should look like: "animal picture book.") It signals that we have entered a universe of abstracted reality. Later, an inviting farmhouse and a barn along the river look exactly like what they are—"a painting, . . . a purely scenic front, . . . no depth to it at all." A homey window with a silhouette of a bird in a cage is "just a big scenic backing with a translucent window, with the birdcage behind it and the bird jumping in there."[76] Differences between the two films are, of course, notable. The sets in *Caligari* generate a sense of madness and terror. Laughton's constructed river landscape evokes wonder and tranquillity. But each film manipulates images in a way that defines expressionism: "to destroy the external reality of a given situation and get at its 'truth' or emotional essence."[77] Laughton distorts reality to project a child's-eye view of the world. In shots created from his drawings, features of the landscape in which the children must try to survive loom with startling size. A spiderweb, a frog on a rock, or quivering rabbits are more prominent in the frame than the frail skiff floating by in the distance. Yet the oversized figures are more mysterious than frightening (the spiderweb is significantly empty). In the context of the sequence, even naturalistic shots—a turtle lumbering through mud or wisps of cattails blowing into the air—take on the aspect of something new and strange. It is the illusionist approach at a central point in the narrative that helps to lift *The Night of the Hunter* out of the realm of the ordinary. The river journey is a poetic idyll at the center of the film, bridging the first half, dominated by Preacher, and the second, dominated by Rachel Cooper.

The entire river sequence, with its mix of natural and stylized images, is in the vein of another film of self-consciously poetic visuals, Warner's *A Midsummer Night's Dream* (1935)—a film on which Cortez worked as a camera operator.[78] The production, directed by Max Reinhardt and William Dieterle, filters *Caligari* through a sensibility as romantic as the Mendelssohn score on the music track. Realistic shots of a forest in the moonlight are combined with fanciful shots of a unicorn or fairies dancing on a trail of mist. Hal Mohr's cinematography, however, is more playful and ornate than that of Cortez. He surrounds Titania with a gauzy, shimmering light, and he employs custom-made filters to create an effect of glittering stars around Oberon and other fairies.[79] Yet specific images in *The Night of the Hunter* have a kinship with shots in *A Midsummer Night's Dream*. Artificial stars over the Ohio River look back to studio-crafted stars twinkling over a Shakespearean forest. A moon in *The Night of the Hunter* travels through the night sky in a series of dissolves, and its picture-book quality matches the painted moon in *A Midsummer Night's Dream*. The Reinhardt-Dieterle film, like Laughton's work, includes beautifully crafted night shots of frogs, a spiderweb, and an owl cocking its head on a branch. Mohr's cinematography is naturally motivated by the dream imagery and the fairy world of Shakespeare's play, so its special effects, however inventive, are the sort of thing one expects in an adaptation of *A Midsummer Night's Dream*. *The Night of the Hunter* is more surprising in the way it infuses expressionism into a naturalistic murder tale.

The stylization of the river journey is all the more surprising when one looks at the novel. The only hint of otherworldliness in Grubb's river section turns up in the following mawkish sentence: "To have seen the children in that troubled time one might have supposed them to be fallen angels, or dusty woodland elves suddenly banished from the Court of the Gods of Moonlight and of faery meadows." Otherwise, Grubb's brief river journey is realistic, recounted in blunt terms: "They fell asleep, hungry and discouraged and frightened" (*NH*, 195). During the children's flight, Grubb stresses the deprivations of the Depression (ideas that Agee tried to capture in detail when he wrote his version of the river sequence). Grubb writes of "children running the woodlands and the fields without parents, without food, without love" and "children . . . roaming the big highways, sleeping in barn lofts or in old abandoned car bodies on town junk heaps" (*NH*, 193–94). The final script adapts these words when Harper explains in prison why he robbed a bank: "I got tired of seein' children roamin' the woodlands without food, . . . sleepin' in old abandoned car bodies on junk-heaps" (*AF*, 270). In his river sequence, Laughton visualizes Grubb's ideas by condensing them into a single shot. He interrupts his idyll for a scene in which John and Pearl receive potatoes from a farm woman. The composition of the image and the natural lighting on the worn mother in her doorway have the iconographic quality of a photograph like Dorothea Lange's *Migrant Mother, Nipomo, California* (1936) or the work of Walker Evans in *Let Us Now Praise Famous Men*. By stylizing most of the journey downriver, Laughton, as Mitchum shrewdly observed, did not follow "the mood of the story. He *made* it the mood of the story" (*HH*, 271).

If the river sequence employs artifice for lyrical effects, many scenes have the more typically unsettling quality of *Caligari* and other Germanic films. The most striking expressionistic sequence in *The Night of the Hunter* is the murder of Willa Harper. It is a vivid example of what Siegfried Kracauer calls "the interpenetration of realistic and expressionist style," found, for example, in Fritz Lang's *Dr. Mabuse:*

The Gambler (1922), where the set of a nightclub is made threatening by oblique, disquieting lines.[80] In an upstairs bedroom, Willa lies calmly awaiting her destruction while Preacher, her fierce judge and executioner, stands rigid beside the bed. "We elevated the set," Brown recalled, "so the camera can shoot up into Mitchum, so that he's overpowering [Winters]."[81] The room is established in a medium shot. It has a realistic appearance, although the peaked roof, emphasized by angular shadows, suggests the A-frame of a church. That suggestion is made explicit when Laughton cuts back to a longer perspective in which the bed and the room seem suspended in black space. Over the bed, shadow and light form a distinct A-frame—a cathedral shape. A doorway, recognizable and familiar in the medium shot, takes on the surprising look of an altar at the rear of a nave.

The religious imagery functions on three levels. For the audience, the visuals of this deadly scene are ironic. As Paul Hammond points out when discussing the lighting that helps to create the feel of a church, "the geometrical slivers of shadow signify Powell's splintered psyche."[82] The imagery also conveys the points of view of both Willa and Preacher. She believes that her murder will be her salvation, so to her the bedroom has become a holy place. In the novel, she thinks, "I must suffer some more and that's what he is making ready for me now: the last and total penance, and then I will be clean" (*NH*, 153). The film reinforces Willa's sense of martyrdom by surrounding her head with a halo of light. The visuals so strongly express her state of mind that Laughton left on the cutting room floor a final shot of Willa saying, "Bless us all!" (a less evangelical version of Grubb's and Agee's "Praise God!"). At the same time, because Preacher believes that his killing of Willa (and of women in general) is a religious act, the cathedral look renders his righteous viewpoint. Listening to the voice of his demonic god, Preacher tilts his head (a detail taken from the novel, where we are told that "his head was cocked a little toward the light" [*NH*, 152]) and, in a gesture as stylized as the balletic movements of the somnambulist in *Caligari*, lifts his arm at an unnatural angle to align it with the slant of the roof and become one with the "church."

A scene that graphically renders the children's point of view recalls a moment from another work by Lang, his first sound film, *M* (1931). As John tells Pearl a bedtime story, Preacher's shadow, huge in a wide, flat hat, looms up on the wall. The sudden appearance is not in Grubb's novel, where John opens his eyes while he lies in bed and discovers the shadow already in place (*NH*, 49). The final script calls for John's shadow to move away, leaving "the shadow of PREACHER, motionless" (*AF*, 277)—an idea held over from Agee's draft ("NH," 55). On the set, however, Laughton and Cortez discovered that it was impossible for the boy's small shadow to cover the larger one. "So we had Mitchum's enormous shadow enter the scene," explained Cortez. "It made more sense, and it was very effective dramatically" (*HH*, 158). The solution to a technical problem resulted in an image that echoes the entrance of the child killer in *M*. As a little girl bounces her ball against a reward poster for the murderer, Peter Lorre's shadow—also huge, also wearing a hat—glides across the poster and looks down on the offscreen girl.

Cortez himself teamed with Lang on *Secret Beyond the Door* (1948). Several scenes in that film prefigure images in *The Night of the Hunter*. During a daydream sequence, Michael Redgrave imagines himself on trial. The full courtroom is never seen. Redgrave, against a diffused background, sits isolated in the witness chair much the way John, framed against a wall, sits during Preacher's trial. The faces of Lang's judge and jury, completely obscured in shadow, look ahead to the faceless figures around Preacher in Laughton's burlesque house. It is notable that the stylized cinematography for the trial in *Secret Beyond the Door* reflects a subjective point of view; we are inside a character's dream. Stylization in *The Night of the Hunter* may suggest a state of mind (Preacher's intense focus on a stripper or John's sense of dislocation at the trial), but it remains part of a third-person presentation. Because Laughton's nonrealistic effects are unexpected, not obviously prompted by a dream, a hallucination (as in *Caligari*), or supernatural elements (as in F. W. Murnau's *Faust* [1926]), they are all the more disorienting for the viewer.

With its interplay of light and shadow, *The Night of the Hunter* also calls to mind a series of horror films from Universal in the thirties and forties. In movies that have since become classics, like *Dracula* (1931), *Frankenstein* (1931), and *The Mummy* (1932), Universal's creative teams adapted the nightmarish designs and exaggerated shadows of such German films as Paul Wegener's *Golem* (1920) and Murnau's *Nosferatu* (1922) to create a veritable house style. Indeed, Karl Freund, who was cinematographer on *The Golem,* also shot *Dracula* and directed *The Mummy.* Along with a general atmosphere of terror, *The Night of the Hunter* contains specific scenes that parallel images in Universal films.

As Willa walks down a lamplit street on the night of her murder, she is engulfed by a swirling fog. That scene may recall any number of previous films, including *Secret Beyond the Door,* but in the way it prefigures Willa's death, it has a particular affinity with *Dracula,* where mist often signals the arrival of the vampire, and *The Wolf Man* (1941), in which every murder scene is shrouded in fog. Typical of Laughton's film, however, the menacing mist of the horror film takes on an added, ironic dimension. Willa tells Icey that she is "needed to keep peace and harmony" between John and Preacher. "It's my burden and I'm proud of it, Icey!" she says, exuding the "radiant Christian faith" that Laughton can be heard requesting in the outtakes for the scene. A low camera angle reinforces the sense of her elevated spirit. Walking off in rapture, her hair edged in a luminous glow, Willa seems almost to float into an ethereal fog as though being transported to a realm of heavenly peace. Another, less complicated image is that of the lynch mob out for Preacher's blood. Carrying torches, advancing toward the camera, the crowd looks like the torch-bearing mob that marches straight toward us in James Whale's *Frankenstein.* In *Dracula,* a narrow, shadowed staircase in the vampire's final lair looks back to "the obsession with staircases" in German expressionist films,[83] even as it looks ahead to the dark basement stairs in *The Night of the Hunter.* While chasing John and Pearl up those stairs, Preacher stiffly extends his arms in a way that recalls the outstretched arms of Bela Lugosi's Frankenstein monster in *Frankenstein Meets the Wolf Man* (1943)—a look indelibly associated with the monster by generations of children acting out the part.

Cortez contributed to the Universal horror legacy when he photographed Albert S. Rogell's seriocomic *The Black Cat* (1941), so it is not surprising that the Universal style would find its way into *The Night of the Hunter.* In *The Black Cat,* the studio's mists and shadows are all in place, though given the particular sharp-edged look that is characteristic of Cortez's cinematography. (Rogell's film is not to be confused with Universal's more familiar 1934 *Black Cat,* which starred Boris Karloff and Lugosi. That earlier work, directed by Edgar G. Ulmer and featuring Bauhaus set designs from Charles D. Hall, contains high-contrast cinematography by John J. Mescall that is, in its stark beauty, worthy of Cortez.)

The look of the Universal films was devised to maintain a sense of horror, but it also allowed the studio to cut costs by, for instance, constructing "only the portion of a set that would be visible through the shadows or fog."[84] Such cost considerations made sense for *The Night of the Hunter* as well, budgeted in the range of $600,000.[85] It is true that Cortez and Brown both stated that while they were naturally aware of the picture's cost, they were not driven by budgetary constraints. "I did what I wanted to, the way I wanted to," said Brown. Cortez agreed: "[The budget] did not determine what I was doing. This was not a low-budget picture in the accepted sense. It was a picture that made good sense in terms of [the techniques] we used."[86] Nevertheless, aesthetics and economics often fuse. When Willa unknowingly walks home to her death, the luminous fog adds emotional resonance, but it also helps make "a small street on a small stage" appear to be a long street.[87]

The Night of the Hunter's disturbing narrative and its inventive, economical use of film ties the work to another American form that derives, in part, from German expressionism: film noir. Although critics like James Damico see noir as a genre of film,[88] others find that noir crosses too many genres to be considered one of its own. Raymond Borde and Étienne Chaumeton point out in their seminal study "Towards a Definition of Film Noir" that elements of the form can turn up within "a character, a scene, a setting" in any film.[89] Thus it is that qualities of noir appear unexpectedly in a Depression-era drama about a false preacher.

A noir crime film tends to look at criminal psychology "from within, from the point of view of the criminals."[90] *The Night of the Hunter,* with its omniscient stance, shifts point of view from character to character, but the first half of the film frequently offers up the perspective of Harry Powell—in the burlesque house or during Willa's murder, for example. Among eleven categories of film noir suggested by Raymond Durgnat are "Sexual Pathology" and "Psychopaths."[91] Laughton's film has a place in both categories. The violent, sexual dimension of Preacher's hatred for women is visualized by his orgasmic release during the strip show, when his switchblade flicks through his coat pocket, and by the way he stretches his body across Willa on the bed just before he slits her throat. Durgnat writes, "Slim knives horrify but fascinate the paranoid '40s,"[92] and that noirish fascination is carried over to *The Night of the Hunter* in the mid-fifties.

Low-key lighting also links *Night of the Hunter* stylistically to film noir and its landscape of shadows. The shot of Preacher's black figure beside the streetlamp outside Willa's house contains echoes of the opening scene in *The Killers* (1946), in which the silhouettes of two hit men flank a lamp of the same general shape as the one in *The Night of the Hunter*. On another night, the room in which Preacher waits to attack Rachel and the children is as ominous as the living room in which Barbara Stanwyck waits to kill Fred MacMurray in *Double Indemnity* (1944)—"perhaps the central *film noir*."[93]

There is, however, a difference between noir and *The Night of the Hunter*. At the moment MacMurray, with his own murderous plans, enters Stanwyck's darkened living room, his shadow precedes him into the house and falls across a rear wall. MacMurray's shadow is dramatic but not entirely unrealistic. Indeed, noir "as a general rule . . . is realistic."[94] In the scene described previously, in which Preacher's silhouette appears on the wall of the children's bedroom, the shadow is unnaturally large. It gives Preacher, who is after all a stand-in for the devil, a mythical dimension. The oversized shadow adds to the irony of John's line after he has seen Preacher's distant form standing by the gas lamp outside their house: "Just a man."

Double Indemnity, based on James M. Cain's novel, points up the fact that a sizable percentage of noir films derive from fiction by American writers like Cain, Dashiell Hammett, Raymond Chandler, and Cornell Woolrich.[95] Here is another difference between film noir and *The Night of the Hunter*. The blunt, world-weary style of such hard-boiled authors is a long way from the ambling prose of Grubb's novel. Tough-guy fictions and their film adaptations also frequently present characters alienated from themselves and others, driven to their doom by their own actions and forces beyond their control. In the world of noir, even an apparently happy ending (the solving of the Swede's murder in *The Killers,* for example) does not necessarily restore a sense of perfect order. Moral ambiguity reigns, because "good and evil go hand in hand to the point of being indistinguishable."[96] John in *The Night of the Hunter* may in some ways fit Robert G. Porfirio's picture of a film noir hero: "Set down in a violent and incoherent world, [he] tries to deal with it in the best way he can, attempting to create some order out of chaos, to make some sense of his world." But as Porfirio goes on to say, "the attempt is seldom totally successful."[97] In the world of Grubb, Laughton, and Agee, good and evil, in the form of Preacher and Rachel, are sharply defined in Manichaean opposition. In the next chapter I will discuss a musical tag that possibly undercuts the film's happy ending, but the visuals and the dialogue at the conclusion generate an overall mood of happiness and harmony that is alien to film noir.

Still, just as Laughton bent expressionist techniques to lyrical purposes, he took elements of film noir, generally an urban, contemporary form, and set them in a rural drama of the thirties. Even noir films in less urban surroundings—*On Dangerous Ground* (1952), *Cape Fear* (1962)—do not revel in the bucolic the way *The Night of the Hunter* does. The film may be the only example in American cinema of a pastoral noir.

Griffith-Laughton Realism

Daytime sequences in Cresap's Landing, on Rachel's farm, and in the West Virginia countryside place *The Night of the Hunter* in a realistic, plein-air tradition that reaches back to the beginnings of cinema. At least two writers, in different ways, connect the pastoral side of the work with Scandinavian films. François Truffaut, in a 1956 review of *The Night of the Hunter,* states that "the production flounders between the Scandinavian and the German styles, touching expressionism but forgetting to keep on Griffith's track."[98] In a tribute to the film written a few years later, Ian Johnson sees a Scandinavian quality in the film's "love for the rural."[99] The Scandinavian manner, which David Robinson defines as "a feeling for the drama of the setting itself, for man seen against the background of natural forces," is best located in silent films, especially those from Sweden, during a "brief golden age" from about 1913 to 1921.[100] In Victor Sjöström's *Terje Vigen* (1917), for example, the sea becomes a virtual extension of the vengeful main character, and in *The Outlaw and His Wife* (1918), a doomed couple meet their tragic end in a blizzard.

An intimate, and sometimes ironic, connection between characters and landscape is a significant feature of Laughton's film. When Ben commands John to swear that he "won't never tell about the money," John stands ramrod straight between fir trees. It's as though John's resolve is as sturdy and deeply rooted as the trees in his yard. During the picnic sequence, Willa is dressed in a flowered, filmy dress. It makes her part of a natural world, which on that particular sunny day is presented, for nearly everyone but John, as innocent and carefree. And then there is Preacher, who strides through the idyllic world of the picnickers in a black suit, black tie, and black hat. He is a stark contrast to the soft grays and whites of the riverside woods. The setting for the picnic is a kind of Eden, in which Preacher becomes the serpent, ever at odds with nature. His chief antagonist, the angelic Rachel Cooper, is in harmony with the land. She dresses in various shades of gray that blend with the landscape around her. On her farm John and Pearl seem to rediscover Eden—until the devil, in his suit of black, rides in. He appears on a white horse, which, with its traditional connotations of virtue, magnifies the disjunction between the bright countryside and the dark figure intruding on it. In addition, Preacher sits awkwardly astride his animal. (Mitchum himself seemed to have trouble with the nag. In the outtakes, Milton Carter calls to the offscreen actor: "Come on, Bob. Okay, Bob. Come on!" Mitchum, still offscreen, replies, "Don't hold your breath.") Laughton, who developed a strong affection for the American landscape during his cross-country reading tours, displays a sensitive feel for the West Virginia farmland—even if he was re-creating it in the San Fernando Valley.

Laughton reserves his deepest emotions for the river. To Grubb, "Laughton matched the movie I'd had in my head in this one way: He seized upon the real hero of the story, which is the river itself. And he did it in a way which grabbed that whole river in his film" (*HH,* 259). Although the novel, replete with phrases such as "mists from the river," the "river cold," the "river dusk," and "river ghosts," keeps the Ohio in our minds, the film is able to keep the river literally in view throughout. Therefore, it has an even stronger presence on screen than it has in the novel. As a virtual character in the film, the river has many moods. It is benevolent, part of a Tom Sawyer boyhood, when John and Uncle Birdie spend time on it together. When they fish, they even manage to catch the evil gar and end his reign of terror in the water. Yet the river can be indifferent to human life, flowing placidly by the bound corpse of Willa Harper. Once the children escape on the river, they enter Huck Finn's world, where the river reveals, as it does for Huck and Jim, even more dimensions. Far from human passions, it can be a temporary source of comfort. On the evening John decides to spend the night on land, the river is calm. After he discovers that Preacher is nearby, stalking them in the night, he returns to a river bubbling with turbulent water. Thus, as in the work of Sjöström and other Scandinavians, the river becomes "an expressive element in the action."[101]

Like many Russian filmmakers, Scandinavian directors built on lessons they learned from Griffith,[102] so in a sense, if one sees Scandinavian attributes in *The Night of the Hunter,* one is looking obliquely at the work of Griffith, the man Laughton called "the Old Master."[103] For despite Truffaut's feeling that Laughton veered away from "Griffith's track" and despite Cortez's assertion that Griffith did not influence the look of the film, the spirit of D. W. Griffith hovers insistently over *The Night of the Hunter.* Lillian Gish herself, in the role of Rachel Cooper, conjures up that spirit. Between 1912 and 1921, Gish made thirty-eight films with Griffith, including the features that made her famous: *The Birth of a Nation* (1915), *Broken Blossoms* (1919), *Way Down East* (1920), and *Orphans of the Storm* (1921). She was so closely associated with Griffith that at least one writer believes the director eventually came "to resent the fact that the audiences as well as the critics now thought Lillian Gish was essential to him."[104] In technical ways, too, *The Night of the Hunter* evokes Griffith. Laughton asked the Museum of Modern Art to send prints of Griffith's films to Los Angeles so that he could use them as yet another way to show his crew what he had in mind for his adaptation.[105] Cortez, who said that "Laughton was a great fan, a great disciple of Griffith,"[106] went so far as to acknowledge that "the pictorial concept of Griffith's films influenced Charles in the structure . . . of the film. . . . If you'll notice in *The Night of the Hunter,* there were many times where Charles would go back to the exact same shot or the exact same angle to serve as a sort of psychological reminder for the audience, which is what Griffith did" (*HH,* 316).

Griffith was not the only silent filmmaker who cut back to the master shot, but he used the technique with dramatic flair. After Lillian Gish has been kidnapped in *Orphans of the Storm,* Griffith goes back to a full view of the street to show that the blind sister, played by Dorothy Gish, is now utterly and frantically alone. Laughton uses a repeated master shot for quiet emotional effect in the scene where Willa returns to her house at night. She stands outside, overhearing Preacher try to worm the secret of the hidden money from Pearl. Both versions of the script remain in close-up on Willa after her face registers disbelief at what she is hearing. In Agee's first draft, she even moves forward, "straight INTO CAMERA" ("NH," 132). The film, however, goes to the other extreme and cuts unexpectedly back to the master—a long shot of the yard and the house. Its windows aglow in the night, the house is an inviting picture. Yet the picture is made ironic by an enveloping fog and the offscreen sound of Preacher's words to Pearl: "Tell me, you little wretch, or I'll *tear your arm off!*" His line, once again recorded for unsettling effect at a volume that does not match the long shot, is followed by Pearl's scream. With effective reserve, the shot makes us contemplate the unseen terror within the walls of the cozy house and lets us see Willa enter her home for what we know will be her last time.

Although Cortez felt that Griffith's influence on *The Night of the Hunter* was purely structural, Terry Sanders pointed out that Laughton wanted to duplicate an important aspect of Griffith's cinematography— its "sharpness of detail."[107] Sanders remembered seeing one of the films that the Museum of Modern Art had sent out to Los Angeles: a 35mm, hand-colored print of *Intolerance* (1916). Having watched only bad 16mm dupes at UCLA film school, he was astonished by what he saw. "It was the sharpest, clearest, most beautiful photography I'd ever seen in my life, much sharper than anything that you see today. The nitrate film and those lenses were just really incredible."[108] Griffith's chief cameraman, Billy Bitzer, recalled, "We got the best photographic results in early morning, without shadows. It is then the light sharpens the distant hills and accentuates the blackness of objects in the foreground."[109] Laughton reinforced the Griffith look he wanted with words that Sanders copied into his script: "Always sunshine—*crisp* and *light* nursery feeling—clear, see everything." Laughton himself, in the tradition of his mentor, "didn't shoot on cloudy days, he shot when the sun was high and things were really bright." Sanders had been hired because his cinematography in *A Time out of War* was "exactly what [Laughton] wanted." The young man saw his job as "essentially to somehow capture D. W. Griffith's spirit and . . . make sure that all the scenes along the river with the children and the scenes with Mitchum's double evoked that D. W. Griffith sensibility."[110]

Sanders spent a few days scouting the Mississippi and Ohio rivers before settling on a stretch of the Ohio near Wheeling, West Virginia. Because of union regulations, Sanders was not allowed to operate the camera for the scenes he directed in *The Night of the Hunter*. Although he could no longer recall the name of the operator, he did remember that when it came time for the shot, "his arm came up, and it was like a piece of machinery. . . . He could do an incredibly smooth pan." With the help of his meticulous camera operator, Sanders lived up to Laughton's expectations ("He was very pleased," said Sanders)—and to the Griffith ideal. After three weeks on location, he returned to Los Angeles with his own sharply etched shots along winding roads and helicopter vistas of the Ohio River countryside.[111]

The helicopter shot that begins the story, by descending on children at play, is another scene reminiscent of *M*. In Lang's film, however, a high-angle shot of children, placed on gray pavement in a formal arrangement, has a disturbing quality that matches the nature of their game, a version of Eeny, Meeny, Miney, Mo played to the words, "Just you wait a little while, the nasty man in black will come. With his littler chopper, he will chop you up." The sunny location shot that Sanders made reflects Laughton's instructions, which Sanders recorded in his script, to capture a "healthy point of view." Yet the picture of noon light and children's games becomes ironic when the youngsters discover a woman's corpse in a cellar. By starting his story with a bucolic image out of Griffith's America, Laughton makes all the more potent the intrusion of violent death.

Part of the Griffith "sensibility" that Sanders spoke of—and captured in his location footage—is a palpable delight in landscape. That pleasure is evident in the picturesque woods and winding stream of Griffith's first film, *The Adventures of Dollie* (1908). He later made periodic sojourns with his Biograph players to Cuddebackville, New York, where he could take advantage of "scenic features that would add unusual touches to the backgrounds: the old canal; the Neversink River passing through the hills; impressive rocky cliffs."[112] A strong feeling for the outdoors in silent films is, of course, not unique to Griffith. It is prominent in cinema's first actualities and is notable throughout the silent era in dramas like *Rebecca of Sunnybrook Farm* (1917) and *Sunrise* (1927), as well as in comedies like Harold Lloyd's *Grandma's Boy* (1922) or Buster Keaton's *Steamboat Bill, Jr.* (1928). But Griffith, who offered innumerable ideas for the visualization of each scene,[113] suffused most of his landscapes with a distinctive, lyrical affection, bred into him no doubt by the rolling acres of Kentucky farmland on which he grew up. Years before he worked on *The Night of the Hunter*, Agee wrote percep-tively about Griffith: "He was capable of realism that has never been beaten and he might, if he had been able to appreciate his powers as a realist, have found therein his growth and salvation. But he seems to have been a realist only by accident, hit-and-run; essentially, he was a poet. . . . [I]n epic and lyrical and narrative visual poetry, I can think of nobody who has surpassed him."[114] Richard Schickel agrees that "mere realism was never enough for him; it was not poetic enough and not spectacular enough."[115]

A film like Henry King's *Tol'able David* (1921) provides an instructive comparison that helps clarify the Griffith, and *The Night of the Hunter,* method. King shot the film on location in Virginia, not far from Davis Grubb territory, and his cinematographer, Henry Cronjager, sought the most natural light possible.[116] The viewer seems to experience the interiors and exteriors firsthand, almost as though a camera were not intervening. One can virtually feel the texture of wood on a farmhouse or the warmth of the sun falling through a window onto a mother nursing her baby. The cinematography in a Griffith film can have a blunt reality: scenes in a trench during *The Birth of a Nation,* particularly a close-up of parched corn being scraped out of a pan, have a documentary look. Yet the film's battle scenes and shots of the dead are more than naturalistic pictures of slaughter; they contain, as Agee suggested, the grandeur and solemnity of epic poetry. On a more intimate scale, when two lovers stroll by a lake on a sloping hillside of trees and placid cows, the water gleams, and the entire scene is cast in a misty light that abstracts the image to a realm of romantic perfection—an effect heightened by an iris that frames the shot as an icon of the idyllic. Even a field of cotton, where slaves, in Griffith's warped history, smile as they labor in the sun, fills the frame with an abstract beauty. A sun-dappled close-up of hands picking cotton is a delicate, romanticized study in light and shade.

The Night of the Hunter has a few realistic images in the vein of *Tol'able David.* Tracking shots of wooden houses, used for rear projection behind Preacher's touring car, and head-on shots of country roads have the same photojournalist quality as Conjager's imagery. They call to mind the documentary work of photographers such as Walker Evans, Russell Lee, or Ben Shahn. Although these second-unit shots are smoothly integrated into the film, another one seems out of place. It is a long shot of the skiff in the middle of the river under luminous puffs of clouds. Laughton, once again keeping Griffith in mind, had instructed Sanders to concentrate whenever he could on "foreground foliage"— words that Sanders copied into his script—and the shot contains leaves and blossoms that frame the tiny boat. The scene is an arresting image of the children adrift in vast spaces, but its bright realism comes as a jolt in the midst of the dreamlike river sequence. It is a throwback to Agee's all-encompassing approach to the river journey, in which, as he stated on his list of interiors and exteriors, shots were to be taken "at various times of day and night and with richest feasible variety of light and weather."[117] The inclusion of the scene points up how little room there is for thoroughly realistic imagery in *The Night of the Hunter*.

Laughton's type of poetic realism is on subtle display in the picnic scene. In one low-angle shot, the reflected glow of the river ripples across Preacher's face as he looks down to straighten John's tie. That supposedly friendly, even fatherly, act comes across as a threat and a brutal reminder of how John's real father was executed. The impressionistic beauty of the light dancing on the face of the murderer makes his gesture all the more chilling. Staging within the frame intensifies the irony of the shot. The right foreground is dominated by Preacher's dark figure. In a pool of sunshine on the left side of the frame, Willa, certain that Preacher's love for her is pure, runs in girlish excitement to Icey, and the two women embrace. The lighting and the framing create a virtual split screen and emphasize that the characters are living at the moment on two separate planes. Poetic effects, then, stylize even Laughton's pastoral scenes. The re-creation of West Virginia settings on the Rowland V. Lee Ranch also contributes to that stylization. The town built at the ranch is, as Brown noted, clearly the construct of a river town. In the same way, the shop run by Walt and Icey Spoon is built up, in a sort of visual synecdoche, from selected images—the counter, a popcorn machine—to create the model of a classic ice-cream parlor.

One Griffith work in particular would have offered Laughton inspiration in his quest for poetic realism: the idiosyncratic *Broken Blossoms*, which stars Richard Barthelmess and Lillian Gish. In the tale of a Chinese immigrant who falls in love with the fifteen-year-old daughter of an abusive father, the film, like *The Night of the Hunter*, mingles tenderness and violence. Also like *Hunter*, the film uses conflicting styles to portray its unstable world. Soft focus and strong backlighting are used to idealize the girl. "Griffith opposes this to the stark, clear photography of the violent scenes."[118]

Along with such lessons in overall tone and style, *Broken Blossoms* contains a specific image that relates to a shot in *The Night of the Hunter*. In the harrowing climax of Griffith's film, the girl is locked inside a closet while her enraged father batters down the door. A similarly narrow space and a similar sense of entrapment, though without the overt violence, is found in *Night of the Hunter* at the moment Preacher blocks John's path in the front hallway of the Harper house to explain that he and Willa are getting married. Twice during the closet scene in *Broken Blossoms,* Griffith darkens the sides of the frame so that the space closes in even more on the terrified girl. *The Night of the Hunter's* shooting script calls for just that sort of masking at the start of the hallway scene, when John approaches the front door: "A tall, narrow shooting-frame; right and left thirds of screen are black" (*AF,* 287). Although that particular image does not appear in the film, Laughton does approach it by opening the scene with a high-angle shot of the hallway, in which arched, foreground shadows on either side of the frame help to compress the space.

The claustrophobic setting is also emphasized by close shots of Preacher seated on a bulky piece of furniture—a mirrored umbrella stand and hat rack—and leaning in toward John. The rack is mentioned in Grubb's novel and Agee's draft of the script (*NH,* 92; "NH," 84). Left out of the final screenplay, the hat rack vividly reappears in the film to reinforce Powell's devilish nature: its knobs, jutting out near Preacher's head, suggest horns. This is the second time such a prop has appeared in the frame with Preacher. A smaller hat rack hangs behind him on the wall of Spoon's ice-cream parlor when he first encounters John. Neither the novel nor the two screenplays mention the rack in this scene. The film alone displays the prop in two different settings. In Spoon's, the hat rack remains at a distance, across the room. In the hallway, when Preacher becomes more of a threat in the confined space, the projections of the rack are more prominent—and more sinister. The careful use of setting, prop, and camera angle to tell the story and to define character further illustrates how Laughton, as he explained to Denis Sanders, was trying to "construct [*The Night of the Hunter*] like a silent picture of the Griffith era."[119]

Silent Talkie

Laughton chose to emulate an older type of filmmaking because he felt it would have the paradoxical effect of refreshing the cinema of his day. "When I first went to the movies," Laughton told Gish, "they sat in their seats straight and leaned forward. Now they slump down, with their heads back or eat candy and popcorn. I want them to sit up straight again."[120] In the letter that Agee wrote to Gregory, he mentioned "many things" that Laughton had learned from the Griffith films they watched together, and he said, "If they do work, and I think they will, they're going to make movie story-telling faster, and more genuinely movie, than they've been in many years."[121]

Agee never identified the "things Charles learned," but Griffith's visual economy is one element that fits Agee's category. Near the start of *Intolerance*, a long film of multiple narratives, two shots of geese and chickens are enough to establish the garden belonging to "The little Dear One" (Mae Marsh) and her father (Fred Turner). Two more shots establish the girl herself: a medium long shot, in which she runs into frame to hand her father his lunch and bid him good-bye with frisky dance steps, and a medium close-up in which she waves and blows playful kisses. To reinforce the girl's loving, innocent character, Griffith cuts in a shot of goslings apparently kissing each other. In the film's Huguenot story, an early two-shot of Catherine de Medici (Josephine Crowell) leaning over her son (Frank Bennett) tells us all we need to know of her malevolent influence at court.

Laughton also uses as few shots as possible at every stage of his story. In the sequence in which the children run from Preacher, the final script indicates eighteen shots from the appearance of Preacher on the horizon to the escape of the children on the river. The film uses only ten. The script's shots include close-ups of John pushing on the oar of the skiff to free the boat from mud. In a holdover from Agee's draft, there is even an insert of John's hands "straining" (*AF*, 319–20). Laughton shot at least two close-ups of John in the boat (they remain in the outtakes at the UCLA Film and Television Archive), but he chose not to use them in the film. Just as Griffith frequently lets action play out in a wide shot, Laughton keeps his camera at a short distance from the children to watch them pick their way through mud or to see John push the boat away from shore. These scenes are intercut with medium shots of Preacher hacking through brush. To heighten the suspense, Laughton has John struggling to get Pearl into the boat, not, as the script has it, simply throwing her in. Thus tension is created through the mise-en-scène and in cutting between master shots of the children and Preacher. Laughton does not build suspense by cutting in close-ups and extending the time of the sequence. "You don't need all that," declared Cortez. "When we see Mitchum coming out after the kids in the boat, there's no need for . . . all the different cuts."[122] To further condense the sequence, Laughton cut out dialogue from the shooting script ("Get in the skiff, Pearl, goodness, goodness, *hurry! . . . Wait! Wait! I'll slit your guts!*" [*AF*, 319–20]). All we hear spoken, two different times, is the offscreen shout from Preacher: "Children!" Although we hear music and sound effects, the lack of dialogue makes this section of *The Night of the Hunter* feel even more like a silent film. Preacher's final approach and the children's escape are viewed in a single medium long shot. Preacher slips and stumbles in the mud, but it is obvious from the master shot that he could still reach the children. While tense music rises toward release as in a conventional scene of cinematic suspense, the climax of the sequence becomes one of Laughton's stylized images: a symbolic tableau of innocence eluding evil.

The logical conclusion of Laughton's silent technique is to convey a dramatic moment in a single shot without words. He does just that after Ben's arrest. In Grubb's novel and Agee's first draft, the scene belongs to John and Pearl; their mother is absent (*NH,* 126; "NH," 23). The final script includes Willa in the scene, thereby bringing the family together at the very moment the family is breaking apart. While the children stand watching Ben, who is riding away offscreen in a police car, Willa runs into the shot, carrying a bag of groceries (so we know where she has been). This is Willa Harper's entrance, and the shooting script includes the expected "close shot" of her, which tells us that "she has a rich body" (*AF,* 269). Once again, however, Laughton made the shot but chose not to use it. After a final image of the car driving away, the film returns to the three-shot of Pearl, Willa, and John. The simple actions that follow are charged with conflict and emotion. Willa scoops up Pearl and her doll. John looks at the two women, turns, and strides off. Willa turns to watch him, then looks back at the offscreen car. She stands with Pearl in her arms while John breaks into a run in the distance. The audience understands Pearl's fright, John's suspicion of the women (in the script he is "laden with his oath" to keep the secret of the hidden money [*AF,* 269]), and Willa's helpless bewilderment—all without the benefit of dialogue or analytical editing.

As the foregoing descriptions suggest, Laughton uses close-ups judiciously throughout *The Night of the Hunter.* Griffith himself, along with many other silent filmmakers, uses close-ups only when necessary to reveal an important detail or to heighten the drama. The enraged face of Battling Burrows (Donald Crisp) coming straight at the camera in *Broken Blossoms* is a significant example. Joyce E. Jesionowski speaks of "Griffith's regard for the long shot as a structural unit."[123] Laughton displays a similar regard in shots of Rachel and the children that were, according to Sanders, "somehow in [Laughton's] mind . . . the way D. W. would have done it."[124] When John and Pearl first meet Rachel Cooper, she is seen at a distance, on the other side of an inlet that runs by her farm. She picks up a switch and drives the children along in front of her. The camera remains across the inlet for three successive shots of the group, each image slightly farther down the path. In staging that harks back to the early days of cinema, the camera never pans with the characters; it remains stationary, waiting for the three figures to enter the frame to the right and watching them leave the frame to the left. Laughton's use of the immobile camera, typical of Griffith, whose camera movements, despite notable tracking shots in *Intolerance* and *The Birth of a Nation,* were highly "circumscribed,"[125] helps to fix the characters in a realm of old tales. "They move across the meadow like a nursery frieze," says the shooting script (*AF,* 326). In her floppy hat, herding two goslings, so to speak, with a switch, Rachel does indeed have the traditional appearance of Mother Goose. (Laughton echoes this shot later in the film, when Rachel and the children hurry out of town. This time, however, Rachel is at the head of her gaggle, and the camera, in medium long shot, tracks beside the moving group. In outtakes of this scene, Laughton emphasizes the fairy-tale aspect of the shot when he says to Gish, "Mother Goose triumphant, Lillian. All right, come on.")

Laughton cuts to an even longer shot across the water when he reveals Rachel's picturesque farm for the first time (complete with real geese in her yard). Rachel's other orphans, Ruby, Mary, and Clary, are not introduced in close-ups. Rather, Laughton uses a "full shot" of "three crouching figures" and has each girl pop her head up "like a rifle-target" (*AF,* 326). The first close-up in the sequence is granted to Rachel. In a shot from John's point of view, the camera tilts up slowly from Rachel's worn boots and comes to rest on her face, tender with question and concern. The close-up is all the more effective for having been so long delayed. Its use now, when John "feels he has come home" (*AF,* 327), deepens the emotion of the moment.

The Night of the Hunter's revival of silent-film techniques extends to Laughton's working method on the set. Outtakes from the film reveal that Laughton slates a shot once, then keeps the camera rolling through multiple takes. For Peter Graves, the continuous filming was "a wonderful way to work," because "'cut' always means adjustments, . . . and so you're taken away from your scene for a few minutes."[126] At least once, however, the method unsettles a performer. During the picnic, Laughton counsels Evelyn Varden, "Quietly, darling. Calm yourself down. This is your philosophy of life," to which Varden says with a nervous laugh, "I'll never get calm if you keep talking to me." In another outtake, in which Billy Chapin and Sally Jane Bruce, who played Pearl, are at the skiff trying to escape Preacher, Laughton's continuous direction reinforces pace and mood:

> Now then, Billy, as fast as you can. Ah-ah, Sally! Start
> again. Sally, don't anticipate that. Don't expect to go
> through the mud. Let Billy take you. You stay there. Go on,
> Billy, undo [the rope]. Stay there, Sally—still. Undo it now.
> Undo it. No, don't look. . . . Sally, you put your hand out to
> him, sweetheart. It spoils it. . . . All right, look back again,
> it doesn't matter. . . . Don't put your hand out to him. Let
> him take you. That's it, Billy, take it off now. Fine. Now
> take Sally's hand. Now lift Sally into the boat as gently as
> you can. Whoopsy-daisy. Whoop. Mind you don't hurt
> her. Now get her into the boat, fella. Whoopee.

At times Laughton interrupts his actors to request a new approach:

> GISH [*to children in her house while waiting for Preacher to
>   attack*]: Now, there was this sneaking, no-account,
>   ornery King Herod—
> LAUGHTON: Do it again, Lillian. That wasn't quite begin-
>   ning the story. Any story. I don't want to know
>   what the story is at all.

Between takes, Laughton can be incisive (to Varden, matchmaking at the picnic: "All right, Evelyn, your mind is already on the baby shower") or harsh (in the honeymoon scene: "For God's sake, cut it, that was terrible") or encouraging (to Gloria Castilo, as Ruby, outside Rachel's barn: "All right, sweetheart, relax. Come on. And shout—and don't twist your face up. You're too pretty").

This directorial method made sense in silent films, where the director did not have to worry about the sound recorder, but it was an unusual technique in the talkie era. "Never before or since have I seen it," said Graves.[127] For the creators of a 1952 musical, *Singin' in the Rain,* the technique lent itself to a nostalgic parody of directors from a bygone age shouting instructions to their actors. For Laughton, the method remained a contemporary tool of filmmaking. Without losing the mood of the moment, he could stay directly involved in the creative process even as he let his actors try out new effects on the spot.

Laughton's directing style points up again that *The Night of the Hunter,* for all the camaraderie and collaboration of cast and crew, bears the personal stamp of Charles Laughton. To Cortez, Laughton's individualistic film "was way ahead of its time" (*HH,* 218). The statement is true in the sense that it took several years before critics and audiences fully appreciated the film's artistry. *The Night of the Hunter* is not, however, "ahead of its time" in the revolutionary sense of breaking new artistic ground. Its expressionism, its pastoral imagery, even its mingling of realism and stylization, are all ingrained in film history. Nevertheless, the work is unique. For one thing, whatever conscious or unconscious influences are evident in the film, the cinematography retains a distinctive quality. The contrast of blacks and whites is a Cortez contrast. Painterly and sculptural styles are unmistakably his. Even within Cortez's body of work, the film stands apart. *The Night of the Hunter* looks like no other film in American cinema. Laughton, too, shapes cinematic traditions to suit his needs, and in doing so he creates a blend of forms that is all his own: a lyrical horror film, an expressionistic period piece, a realistic fairy tale. Yet the mixture is not what one critic calls "a clattering eclecticism."[128] Surprisingly, it all holds together.

The next chapter looks at ways in which *The Night of the Hunter* keeps from flying apart at the seams.

COHERENT
CONTRADICTIONS

A Unified Picture

Moylan C. Mills speaks of Laughton's "unsettling mix of clashing
elements," yet he points out that such influences as "Griffith, Welles,
and the German expressionists, as well as the Biblical stories and the
fairy tales of childhood . . . have then been compellingly reworked into
an idiosyncratic whole."[1] Indeed, Laughton and his team, particularly
Cortez, Brown, and Schumann, synthesize the diverse aspects of the
film to create unifying visual and aural patterns. "I tell you," said Brown,
"there's hardly anything on this picture which is accidental."[2]

One carefully crafted element in the film is its dreamlike quality.
The idea of a dream comes from the novel. Midway through his book,
using the refrain "it is a night for dreams," Grubb looks in on the sleep
of John and Willa. Their dreams provide flashbacks that flesh out the
story while creating a sense of loss for a happy time (NH, 119–28).
For John, life becomes a nightmare once Preacher arrives in Cresap's
Landing. By the end of the story, when the prosecuting attorney cross-
examines John, the boy can no longer picture a clear reality: "The blue
men came. I remember that part of the dream. And they took him away.
Who? Well, I'm not so sure about that part" (NH, 250).

The film dispenses with literal dreams. Rather, Laughton uses
dream imagery as a motif in his adaptation. Over the initial credits,

a children's chorus announces the subject by singing, "Fear is only a dream, / So dream, little one, dream." Gish and the faces of rapt children are then superimposed over a starry sky. That surreal image gives way to Sanders's location shot high above a river town. The shift to a naturalistic scene and a godlike perspective begins a restless series of shots in which space has the instability of a dream. We glide down to children playing and discovering a corpse; we pull back and are whisked away on another overhead shot to the road where Harry Powell is driving his touring car; we are not on the road long before we are dropped into a burlesque house, peering through a matte in the shape of a keyhole. In the dark theater, human figures blend into shadow, and we feel more than ever that we are part of a waking dream. A shift in place and visual style is also a shift in point of view. The multiple viewpoints derive from Grubb's omniscient technique, but where Grubb moves in a leisurely fashion between his characters, the film's compressed narrative often prevents the viewer from resting in any one point of view for long. The changing perspectives contribute to a sense of disorientation at the heart of the film. (For an argument that the film is consistently presented through John's eyes and thereby maintains a "fairy tale structure," see Stephen F. Bauer's psychoanalytic reading, "Oedipus Again.") In speaking of the scenes on the river, in which the scale of animals to humans is reversed, Laughton is explicit about his purpose: "We tried to surround the children with creatures they might have observed, and that might have seemed part of the dream. It was, in a way, a dream for them."[3] The most surreal visions of the film, however, are in the murder scene and its aftermath. Willa's bedroom, designed and lit to look like a cubist church, has the off-kilter feel of a dream space. A short time later, we are introduced to the preeminent dream image of the film: Willa's corpse in the Model T, her hair waving in sun-streaked waters.

Those two scenes illustrate another important unifying element in the film. Just as Cortez's short film *Scherzo* was an abstract study of water, *The Night of the Hunter* is, on one level, "about the beauty and the drama of light."[4] On *Black Tuesday*, which Cortez shot just before *Night of the Hunter*, he experimented with what was then a new film stock— Tri-X, a high-speed film that provides sharp contrast between blacks and whites. He even shot a close-up by the glow of one candle.[5] Cortez occasionally used Tri-X on *The Night of the Hunter*, not for its speed but for its "dramatic value." He explained, "By that I mean the blacks. They had the luminous, phosphorescent light I wanted in certain sequences." Thus, when John looks out from a hayloft to see Preacher on a horse crossing the horizon, the blacks, as Cortez puts it, "go *black*."[6] Houses lit up against the night and Harry Powell's dark-suited figure beside a streetlamp are studies in the art of chiaroscuro. Even in more unexpected details, Cortez brings out a striking contrast. Preacher stands in shadow behind the children in the grape arbor while they scramble to stuff the money back into Pearl's doll, and his white shirt glows against the blackness of his vest. The depth of the black and the strange luminosity of the white combine to make Preacher's tall figure especially eerie and threatening. Although Cortez's apprenticeship with New York photographers was long behind him, the spirit of a still portrait artist is alive in *The Night of the Hunter*. Witness, in addition to the scenes just described, Harry Powell's psychopathic face transformed into a mask of half shadow and half light as he listens to an inner voice telling him to kill, or the shot of the hangman's two children asleep in bed, their angelic faces brushed by moonlight.

Jack Ravage, reviewing the 1988 release of the film on videotape, speaks of a "diamond-shaped pattern of growing darkness (peaking at the river-chase sequence) followed by increasing lightness (as Rachel enters the story)."[7] That may describe an emotional pattern in the film (the nightmare does darken psychologically, then gradually lighten once the children reach Miz Cooper's farm), but the visual pattern is not as schematic as Ravage would have us believe. Light and dark alternate throughout—until the final sequence, which Laughton saw as a sort of coda, separate in tone from the rest of the film. He told Cortez, "Stanley, I want to get the feeling here that this is a Christmas party wrapped up in a beautiful package and off they go."[8] In other daylight scenes, bare or sparsely decorated walls behind characters are lit with a gray diffusion. That empty look reinforces the sense of a stark and hollow world. It is not until Christmas day at Rachel's, when the world has grown safe, that backgrounds become rich with cheerful detail—Christmas decorations, kitchen furnishings, snow falling outside a window. For the homey setting, Cortez created a soft light and muted, morning shadows very different from the ominous shadows in the rest of the film. Except for the closing sequence, then, the relationship between light and goodness, between dark and evil, is complicated. Contrasting ideas do not simply follow each other in slack rotation; they are interwoven in a way that knits the film together.

The pastoral world, for example, is not merely a haven of purity. The festive picnic is marred by the figure of Harry Powell, an unctuous devil suited in black. When Walt and Icey Spoon read the postcard from Preacher, the letters from their outdoor shop sign cast shadows that read backward on the wall behind them. The hovering shadows—on the surface, a realistic touch in the setting—lend a vaguely sinister air to the folksy picture of the ice-cream parlor. Considering the hatred and vengeance that will pour forth from the Spoons at the end of the film, the shadows are a reminder of darkness lurking even within apparent decency.

By the same token, darkness in the film is not simply a shroud of evil. Once the children are on the river, the night, which until now has been a threat, turns comforting. Pearl sings a lullaby to her doll, and John falls asleep in a fetal position. Later, as the children drift by a flock of sheep, the camera pans along a fence in a composition of formal and soothing regularity. At that moment, John feels secure enough to leave the river and spend the night on land, nestled in a hayloft. Then John wakes in the middle of the night to hear Preacher in the distance singing "Leaning on the Everlasting Arms," and the night once more belongs to the hunter.

The song's chilling effect is heightened by the fact that we have heard Harry Powell sing the melody twice before. Later in the chapter, I will look more closely at the use of the hymn. It is enough for now to say that the echoing of the song, heard at key points in the story, is one of many repetitions that tie together the disparate parts of the film.

One significant visual repetition occurs in courtroom scenes where first Preacher and then Harper are sentenced. When Powell is sentenced to jail for car theft, the courtroom is presented in a spare, expression-istic manner. The entire scene is a single shot. Preacher stands in the foreground, his back to the camera. In the close distance, the judge sits on his bench and a court reporter types at a desk below him. The relative sizes of Powell and the judge create a sense of perspective, yet the camera lens flattens the distance between the characters; the image seems oddly foreshortened. That disorienting sense of space, along with harsh light that casts deep shadows, generates a Kafkaesque quality that gives authority an intimidating power. Images of that authority—a flag and a framed picture of Abraham Lincoln—are all that adorn a gray wall behind the bench. (To reinforce the judge's power, Laughton takes a line from the arrest scene in Agee's draft of the script, transfers it here to the courtroom, and expands on it. The arresting trooper in Agee's draft says, "Your name Harry Powell?" to which Preacher responds, "The *Reverend* Harry Powell, Brother" ["NH," 13]. In the shooting script, Powell tells the judge his name is "*Preacher* Harry Powell," and the judge says, "A car thief! Picked up where *you* were! A man of God? (to Clerk) Harry Powell" [*AF*, 266].) A few minutes later, when Ben is sentenced to hang for the murder of two bank guards, the identical setup is used. The duplication of the shot establishes the two men as John's fathers—well before Preacher becomes the boy's stepfather.

Later, during Preacher's trial for murder, the courtroom is once more created with spare means. In a medium close-up, John sits glumly on the witness stand, and though we hear the prosecuting attorney, all we see are his hands in the frame as he points past John at the unseen preacher. Behind the boy is another gray wall and the portion of another framed picture. The disembodied attorney suggests John's disassociation from the adult world; it is as if the boy sees neither the attorney nor the preacher. This is Laughton's visual adaptation of John's fear and denial during Preacher's trial in the book: "There is a certain place on that stage where I cannot look because I know if I look something terrible will happen like I think it did in that dream and every time they tell me to look over there at this place I get all out of breath and start to shake like I had a cold and then they stop" (*NH*, 251). On screen, John's resolute silence suggests that the boy refuses to cooperate with authority. The look of the shot, reminiscent of the courtroom scenes in which each of his fathers appeared, implies that in some way John has confused the two men and will not condemn his sometime father, Harry Powell.

That confusion is made explicit in another of the film's repetitions. Early in the film, just after Ben has hidden the $10,000 and sworn his children to secrecy, John watches as the police grab his father's gun, throw the man to the ground, and handcuff him. Near the end, he looks on as other police grab Preacher's knife, throw him to the ground, and handcuff him. The two sequences employ an identical series of shots: cuts between John in anguish and the police manhandling their prisoner. When Laughton filmed the two scenes, according to Golden, he "deliberately used the word 'choreographed.'"[9] Both Peter Graves, as Ben, and Robert Mitchum move with stiff, stylized gestures that look like part of a modern dance. In outtakes from the scenes, Laughton calls out numbers for the four segments of the "dance," so that Graves and Mitchum can move with the same rhythms. Watching the replay of his father's arrest is too much for John. He drops to his knees over Preacher, beating the doll with its hidden money against his back, crying, "Here! Here! Take it back! Dad, take it back! I don't want it, Dad! It's too much! Here! Here!" John seems not merely to be talking to his dead father. Harry Powell and Ben Harper have become one for him—each, in his own way, hounding him, demanding too much of him. By flinging the money at Preacher and symbolically returning the money to Ben, John breaks free of his fathers. Rejecting them both, he releases himself from the money's oppressive secret and clears the way for a less shadowed, independent future.

The scenes of sentencing and arrest, like other moments discussed in chapter 5, play out in master shots. Such scenes form a pattern of tableaux in the film. The studied way that Laughton composed his single shots is evident in the outtakes for the scene in which Rachel, standing in front of the children, phones for troopers to come arrest Preacher. Before the take begins, each child carefully assumes the pose assigned by Laughton: Mary Ellen Clemons, playing Clary, folds her hands under her chin, Gloria Castilo places a sorrowful hand over her eyes, and Billy Chapin puts on a delighted grin. Only when the children are set in their attitudes behind Gish does Laughton begin the scene. The many tableaux in *The Night of the Hunter* remind us that the film is meant to be viewed as both realistic drama and a kind of morality play. In the revival sequence, Willa and Preacher are posed on a stage lit by torches. The emblematic scene might be titled "Vice and Hysteria Preach to the Multitudes." Those multitudes, actually a small group on benches in a corner of the tent, are presented in another tableau of flickering shadows and light. At the rear of the tent, silhouetted worshippers echo the silhouetted men in the burlesque house. The visual link between the two scenes points up the way religion and sex are intertwined in both Grubb's novel and Laughton's film. (When Grubb suggested an older actor to play Preacher, Laughton told him, "People who sell God, Davis, must be sexy.")[10] Laughton and Mitchum make the connection explicit in the outtakes for the scene:

LAUGHTON [*to congregation*]: Do it again now. Wild as hell.

Remember, this is a substitution for—

MITCHUM: Poontang.

LAUGHTON: Poontang. Exactly.

Just as important as visual echoes are repetitions built into the text. Stories are told and retold throughout *The Night of the Hunter*. The use of narrative once more displays Laughton's faithfulness to the novel, in which, as Paul Hammond puts it, "story-telling provides a running commentary on events."[11] In both the book and the film, John transforms the events of his own life into a bedtime tale about an African king with a son and daughter. "Bad men" took the king away, but he managed to tell his son to "kill anyone that tried to steal their gold" (*NH*, 47). When John and Pearl float away on the river, Pearl tells a story to her doll (in the film, she sings the story) about a "pretty fly" with "two pretty children" who flew away "into the sky—into the moon" (*NH*, 189). Both Hammond and Bauer relate the children's stories to the Freudian concept of the "family romance," in which a child imagines that his parent is not his true mother or father and that the real, noble parent will one day return.[12] Rachel reinforces the family romance by turning the story of Moses in the bulrushes into a parable about John and Pearl. She also tells the children the story of Herod when they themselves are threatened by a killer. In Hammond's perceptive analysis, the stories within the larger narrative of both novel and film signal a progression in John's development: "John's dawning awareness that he is characterized in Rachel's stories, that he can be part of a fabled but known moral universe rather than a dislocated phantasmagoric one, heralds his impending liberation from the family romance, from the nightmare of Harry Powell."[13]

In relation to the novel, however, Hammond's statement needs to be qualified. In the interior monologue that concludes the book, John recounts part of the Christmas story but cannot decide whether it is true or not: "You never know what they tell you. You never find out if it's real or a story." His doubt reflects both a religious skepticism—having heard the false words of Preacher, he may never accept the Word of the Gospel, even if it comes through Miz Cooper—and continued confusion about what has been real in his own life: "I wish I could remember stuff. It all gets mixed up inside you" (*NH*, 272). Grubb depicts John, charged with the protection of his sister and the stolen money, taking his first steps into adulthood, but he also shows the boy still groping through the thickets of falsity and truth.

Because the film does not include John's interior monologues, it loses the nuances of his struggles with story—that is to say, with his questions about appearance and reality or the nature of faith. On the other hand, the film, compacting Grubb's book into ninety minutes of screen time, gains momentum and thematic cohesion by moving forward on a series of tales. The narrative is driven by Preacher, whose entire life is a lie and who is, therefore, forever spinning yarns. In prison, he pleads with Ben to tell him where the $10,000 is hidden so that he can build "a tabernacle make that Wheeling Island tabernacle look like a chicken house." At Spoon's, he claims that he was employed by the prison to counsel condemned men. After he has murdered Willa, he spins a fiction about her having turned him out of bed on their honeymoon night (projecting his own sexual revulsion onto Willa).

Preacher, of course, tells his stories to manipulate his listeners and gain his selfish ends. That strategy points to a central idea implicit in *The Night of the Hunter:* power belongs to the one who controls the story. For Preacher, his sermon on love and hate is the most important tale in his repertoire. It is a way to prove his righteousness and to charm those he needs for one reason or another. It is also a way of finding out who will fall for his line. In Spoon's ice-cream parlor, Preacher displays his tattooed hands for the folks he has just met. "Ah, little lad," he says to John, "you're starin' at my fingers. Would you like me to tell you the little story of Right-Hand-Left-Hand—the story of Good and Evil?" As he delivers his sermon, he clasps his hands and presents a hard-fought wrestling match. "Hot dog!" he cries finally. "It's Love that won! And old Left Hand Hate is down for the count!" He slams his left hand to the counter of the ice-cream shop. "I never heard it better told," says Icey Spoon. Willa is starry eyed, and little Pearl runs over to sit in this storyteller's lap. Even Walt Spoon, who has his suspicions later in the film, seems hypnotized. John alone is not taken in by the tale. The final script calls for a close-up of Preacher to let us see his reaction to the boy's attitude. The script tells us, "Something new enters his eyes; a game has begun between them" (*AF,* 281). In the film, Laughton exercises restraint by not cutting to a revealing close-up. He maintains a medium shot of Preacher, Pearl, Willa, and John. Yet even in the wider view, one can see an ironic glint in Preacher's eye. A silent battle of wills has begun, and for Preacher it is indeed a kind of game. For John, it is the beginning of his nightmare.

Later in the film, when Preacher has tracked the children to Rachel's farm, he again displays his fingers and utters familiar words (only slightly altered): "Ah, madam, I see you're lookin' at my hands. Would you like me to tell you the little story of Left-Hand-Right-Hand—the tale of Good and Evil?" He starts in with the very words we heard before, spoken a bit mechanically this time. That tone is Mitchum's interpretation of Laughton's laconic directions: "Don't forget yours is a routine, Mitch" and "Medicine man!" Preacher barely gets under way with his sermon when Rachel cuts him short to probe him with suspicious questions. By uncovering the lie in his tale about where the children came from ("Right funny, ain't it, how they rowed all the way *up* river in a ten-foot john-boat?"), Miz Cooper wrenches the story from Preacher. The effect of Preacher's sermon this time around is emphasized by camera angles different from those in Spoon's ice-cream parlor. At Spoon's, the camera is level with the preacher as he rises from his stool and assumes a commanding position in the room. Laughton, following his principle of limited close-ups, cuts twice to a shot of Willa, Walt, and Icey looking on, spellbound. Keeping the three of them together in the frame emphasizes the fact that Preacher can achieve a sort of mass hypnosis. Laughton took, but did not use, a shot from behind Preacher, showing his hands grappling in front of his three listeners. He reserves such a shot to express the central conflict between Preacher and John. In the midst of the sermon, Laughton cuts to a slight high angle. Preacher's interlocked hands are seen in the foreground. In the background, as though under the weight of those powerful hands, John stands beside his sister, looking on helplessly. When confronting Miz Cooper, Preacher stands at the bottom of her porch steps, and high angle shots from Rachel's perspective keep him in an inferior position. She, in turn, is seen in low angle, glowering down at the man. The transfer of power from Preacher to Miz Cooper signals the beginning of the end for Harry Powell.

In finally destroying Powell's fiction, Rachel receives help from John. If later, while violently returning the stolen money, the boy melds Preacher and Ben into one father, at this point in the story John is not in the least confused. Confronted with Preacher, John says, enunciating each word in a level tone, "He ain't my dad." Rachel responds with the equally emphatic and laconic, "No, and he ain't no preacher, neither."

Their exchange is perhaps the finest example of the film's skillful adaptation. In the novel, the scene never reaches the biting climax found in the film. After John says, "He ain't my Dad," Preacher tries to persuade Rachel that John is lying, and Pearl enters to declare that Preacher is "Daddy" (*NH*, 236). In his first draft, Agee retains Grubb's scene and adds several exchanges of his own. He also gives voice to words that Grubb put into Rachel's head: "Mister, you ain't no rightful preacher. I've seen a peck o' preachers in my day and some was saints on earth and some was crooked as a dog's hind leg, but you've got 'em *all* beat for badness" ("NH," 249). The shooting script retains the speech, though with changes that Laughton explained in a letter to Geoffrey Shurlock, who had recently replaced Joseph Breen as head of the Production Code Administration:[14] "There was something about the speech that disturbed me. That is why I asked you about it; and I find, upon thinking it over, that the speech seemed to imply that there was an equal quantity of good and bad preachers—which indeed, in fact, is not so, and I altered it as you will see. I think this is reasonable and correct, and I don't think it would offend any religious body."[15] In the following quotation from the shooting script, I have italicized Laughton's subtle alteration: "He ain't no preacher neither. I've seen Preachers in my time, an' some of 'em was saints on earth. *A few* was crookeder'n a dog's hind leg, but this 'un's got 'em all beat for badness" (*AF*, 339). Whether because of further religious scruples or for aesthetic reasons, Laughton eventually, to the great benefit of the scene, pared the moment down and left only the essential lines between John and Rachel. Their brief exchange is highly effective as an ironic finish to Preacher's storytelling career. After all the false words that Preacher has spun, two simple statements of truth defeat him. In the outtakes, Laughton even reminds Billy Chapin to "look as if you're telling the absolute, clear truth, so keep your head quite, quite steady."

Rachel's triumph, which also becomes John's triumph, is all the more satisfying because throughout the film, John has been powerless—that is to say, he is without a story. The novel makes this plain when Preacher tries to make John sing a hymn during a storm, and John cries out, "I don't know no words! . . . I don't know no words!" (*NH*, 84). Although the film leaves out that symbolic statement, John's lack of voice is revealed in other ways. When he tells Pearl the fairy tale about a rich king and his son charged with protecting the man's gold, the story is cut off by the startling appearance of Preacher's shadow on the wall. In the novel and Agee's draft, John stops the story himself by telling Pearl that he has forgotten the rest of the tale. The expressionist visuals in the film show us that John, even before he has met Preacher, is outmatched in a conflict of opposing stories. From that point on, he has no words with which to defeat the charismatic preacher. John has only the truth, and in the world of Cresap's Landing, that is not enough. When he tells his mother that Preacher has been trying to learn the secret of the money, she says, "John, you always make up that lie." It is not until a woman wiser than Willa truly listens to John that his words finally gain power and shatter Preacher's myth.

Rendered helpless by Rachel and John, Powell (his suggestive name, hinting at the word *power,* now made ironic) finds himself looking up the barrel of Rachel's shotgun and is forced to retreat. When he later makes one more attempt to invade the house, Rachel pulls the trigger of her gun and reduces the man of glib words to a squealing animal who runs wounded into her barn. The yipping sounds that Preacher makes are the final noises in a pattern of animalistic sounds—growls at the cellar door, a rising howl in the river—that Laughton uses to characterize Preacher over the course of the film. Laughton wanted the moment played in a comic way. The novel and the two screenplays treat the scene seriously. In the final script, Preacher "runs yelping with pain into the barn" (*AF,* 344). Agee in his draft even compares the feeling of the scene to "the kind of nausea you get from crushing a millipede" ("NH," 262). On screen, Preacher is reduced to a ludicrous figure, almost cartoonlike in his frenzied exit. Laughton told Sanders, "The audience is going to laugh, they're going to love it."[16]

After Preacher is captured, Rachel and her surrogate family celebrate Christmas. She has a special gift for John: a pocket watch. In the film, even more than in the book, the watch ties in with the theme of storytelling and language. The novel emphasizes the watch as a source of new life and strength for John. It cost Rachel a dollar, but the boy is certain "she paid a lot of money for it because it is gold or something like that" (*NH,* 271). Grubb refers to the watch's "magic heart beating against [John's] own" (*NH,* 270). In his final monologue, the boy speaks to the shadows in his bedroom—similar to those that had frightened him on the night Preacher arrived in Cresap's Landing: "'I ain't afraid of you!' he whispered to the shadows. 'I got a watch that ticks! I got a watch that shines in the dark!'" (*NH,* 273). Those lines are part of the shooting script, but

Laughton eliminates them in the film. The power of the watch, precious as gold, is clear from John's awe as he stares at it and listens to it tick. By keeping words to a minimum, Laughton stresses that the watch is a silent acknowledgment of the understanding shared by Rachel and John. As the director explains to Chapin in the outtakes of the scene, "These are two people that don't want to show they love each other." The film retains lines from the novel that express deep affection in an indirect way:

> RACHEL: Be nice to have someone around the house who
>   can give me the right time of day.
> JOHN: This watch is the nicest watch I ever had.
> RACHEL: Well, a feller just can't go around with rundown,
>   busted watches.

Even if John delights in a childlike way in his gift, the watch represents a rite of passage—a step into adulthood. John is now the man around the house who can give the family the correct time. Near the beginning of the story, John coveted just such a watch in the window of Miz Cunningham's secondhand shop. Here at the end, having fulfilled his obligation to his father and his sister, John receives his reward. And it is Miz Cooper who fulfills his desire, bestowing on him a mark of growth within his own personal narrative.

By the end of the film, we can look back to the opening and realize that Rachel Cooper has been in control of more than John's narrative. When at the start of the film Laughton superimposes an unnamed woman delivering a Bible lesson, we might assume that she will have a place in the story, or we might accept her as a framing device—a narrator putting the story in motion. However the woman is perceived, Laughton uses her to draw the audience into the circle of the storyteller. She begins in medias res: "Now you remember, children, how I told you last Sunday about the good Lord going up into the mountain and talking to the people?" At first, she seems to be speaking directly to us, her captive listeners. Even after children's faces appear and reveal her true audience, it is hard to escape the sense of the woman offering us in the darkened theater (or living room) a moral tale. She speaks into the camera one more time and then opens her Bible to read, "Beware of false prophets which come to you in sheep's clothing." With a dissolve to the Ohio River valley, the story proper—a film about a false prophet in sheep's clothing—begins. Later in the film, when the skiff in which John and Pearl have escaped drifts into reeds along the shore, the camera tilts up to a shot of a starry sky. It is an echo of the film's opening shot, over which the storyteller's benign image appeared. The repeated shot suggests that the children have come to rest, that goodness and hope are at hand. Twittering woodwinds add to the impression, which is confirmed by a dissolve to sun breaking through clouds. With the coming of dawn, the children—and we in the audience—seem to wake from a dream. A female voice calls to the children, and the dreamlike imagery of the river sequence gives way to the realistic scenes of Miz Cooper's world. When the owner of the voice appears, we realize that we have come full circle: the heavenly storyteller has returned. As a character who both participates in and frames *The Night of the Hunter,* Miz Cooper holds what amounts to supernatural sway over evil forces. She is the guardian of "little things" in the world—and the keeper of the story.

Thus, to the end, she spins tales and points morals. At the conclusion, as the final script tells us, she stands at her stove, "praying as she works, which is the best way to pray." She says, "Lord save little children! The wind blows and the rain is cold. Yet, *they abide*" (*AF,* 353). (In at least two outtakes Gish says, "the rain's a-cold," and it sounds as if she uses that phrasing in the film. The words bring to mind the refrain of Edgar in *King Lear:* "Poor Tom's a-cold"—a resonant echo from a character who suffers yet manages to "abide" and "endure.") The final screenplay retains several lines of the long monologue that Agee transplanted from the novel: "For every child, rich or poor, there's a time of running through a dark place. . . . And when that child sleeps, it's a Tiger's sleep, and a Tiger's night, and a Tiger's breathing on the windowpane" (*AF,* 353). In the outtakes one can hear Gish gracefully delivering the speech. Yet her final musings—her benediction—are more effective for being less verbose. Rachel speaks to herself in the final moments of the film, though she seems also to be indirectly addressing us in the audience. In one take not used, Gish looks into the camera on the line "You'd think the world would be ashamed to name such a day as Christmas for one of them and then go on in the same old way." Laughton, however, reserves the effect of breaking the frame for the penultimate shot of the film. When Rachel says, "They abide, and they endure," she looks up and appears to be speaking to the audience. The shooting script, in fact, includes the stage direction "telling us" (*AF,* 354). In the outtakes for this shot, one finds a take in which Rachel does not look into the camera. Laughton was apparently testing when precisely he wanted Rachel to bring the audience into her confidence. Although the novel ends with John's interior monologue, Agee's first draft leaves the screen to Rachel and her reflections on children. Laughton retains that change and deepens its significance within the structure of the final film. He gives *The Night of the Hunter* symmetry by opening and closing with Rachel speaking to the camera in her role as storyteller.

In the novel, John and Pearl go to bed under a quilt stitched with Bible scenes, and Grubb concludes with these lines: "And so John pulled the gospel quilt snug around his ear and fell into a dreamless winter sleep, curled up beneath the quaint, stiff calico figures of the world's forgotten kings, and the strong, gentle shepherds of that fallen, ancient time who had guarded their small lambs against the night" (*NH,* 273). John and Pearl—and Rachel, "gentle shepherd"—are taken out of their private story and elevated to a realm of myth. Agee's conclusion in the first draft, the shot of stars blossoming into "a solid mosaic" of children's faces, is an attempt to visualize Grubb's apotheosis of his characters. Laughton reverses Grubb's and Agee's mythologizing. He sets his film up as a mythical tale, then chooses to end on a simpler note. He concludes with a shot of snow falling on Rachel's house. No longer under threat, the house becomes part of an idealized Christmas scene—a cozy picture of peace. In its studied perfection, the image reinforces the film's fairy-tale quality. The shot is, in a sense, a declarative statement: "And they all lived happily ever after."

Cortez admired the final image because it repeated the shot with which Laughton began the sequence. He felt that the repetition "became a symphonic concept, because, in great pieces of music, you start with the main theme and you invariably end with that theme" (*HH,* 316). Laughton's patterns throughout the film do have the repetitive, emotional quality associated with music. It is, therefore, not surprising that the music track itself employs motifs that help knit the film together.

Laughton's "Right Hand"

The score was of such prime importance to Laughton that he had only one choice for composer: Walter Schumann, the man with whom he had collaborated so successfully on *John Brown's Body.*[17] "That was [Laughton's] closest association," said Golden. "They knew each other like a book. . . . They had an understanding about the music."[18] Schumann's widow, Sonia Goodman, confirms Golden's impression: "When they worked on the *a cappella* chorus for the stage production of *John Brown's Body,* Mr. Laughton would just say, for example, 'I want them to sing fire sounds here.' My husband would sit down at the piano and play some music, or hum the vocal texture, and Mr. Laughton would say, 'Yes, exactly like that'" (*HH,* 28). Schumann and Laughton did not work together in an orthodox Hollywood way. In an article published in *Film Music* at the time of the picture's release, Schumann states that he and the director discussed "pre-scored themes" for the film even before shooting began.[19] And Laughton kept Schumann involved at every phase of production. On the weekends, the composer sometimes joined the crew at Laughton's house, where, Brown recalled, "he would play what he hoped to have for [a particular] scene. It was interesting because it set the mood of what we were going to do and how we were going to do it."[20] For much of the shoot, the composer could be found on the set. Although it may be an exaggeration that Schumann was, as he says, at "all of the editing sessions with Mr. Laughton and our editor" (Golden recalled that Schumann did not sit in on the day-to-day editing[21]), he still helped shape the film in postproduction (*FM,* 15). Schumann explains: "We decided upon the scenes where music would be of primary importance. As Mr. Laughton put it, 'In these scenes you are the right hand and I am the left.' So in the shooting of these scenes he purposely went far over footage. This, of course, is a composer's dream; to have flexibility and not be tied to exact timings. In actuality, to edit the film to the music. . . . A rough cut was completed with all of the 'music' sequences left overlength until the score was finished" (*FM,* 15).

Laughton's concern with a tight overall structure led him to suggest "a technique which he called 'long muscles.'" The music was divided into six segments. The director asked Schumann to compose music not for individual scenes but for a segment as a whole. Six becomes an important number in the organization of Laughton's work. The six musical segments, as defined by Schumann, correspond roughly to the six-part structures found in both drafts of the screenplay: (1) "main title and establishing scenes"—apparently through Ben's execution, (2) "courtship by Preacher, through the marriage to the murder scene," (3) "the beginning of the chase," (4) "the river sequence," (5) "completely devoted to Rachel Cooper," and (6) "the lynching scene and the Christmas scene" (*FM*, 15–17). Laughton, unlike many Hollywood directors (then and now), does not carpet his film with wall-to-wall music. Therefore, when themes enter and reappear, they gain in dramatic significance and emotional weight.

Walter Schumann's Musical Sermon

"In our preliminary discussions," Schumann writes, "Mr. Laughton and I agreed that since melodrama was ever-present in the plot, that photography and music would be used to capture the lyric quality of Davis Grubb's writing" (*FM*, 13). The music, however, captures and even heightens the melodramatic oppositions at the heart of the film. Schumann provides a musical equivalent for Preacher's arm wrestle between love and hate.

In considering a theme for Preacher, Schumann rejected an ironic lyrical melody. Several times in the novel Preacher sings "Leaning on the Everlasting Arms," but Schumann felt that using the hymn as under-scoring "would dignify and create sympathy for [Preacher's] psychopathic religious beliefs." Instead, he wrote what he thought of as "a pagan motif, consisting of clashing fifths in the lower register" (*FM*, 13):[22]

Example 6.1
Preacher's theme, Walter Schumann.

A low, sustained G, a crescendoing roll of the timpani, and four dark chords sounded by heavy brass—the first part of Preacher's "pagan motif"—begin the film with a sense of threat. Those menacing open fifths are followed in the violins and woodwinds by an agitated figure of danger and suspense. It is drawn from the following passage, written for the children's flight from Preacher:

Example 6.2
"Danger" motif, Walter Schumann.

The brass return but this time descend to a final, unstable chord—the last part of Preacher's theme. The agitated figure makes its reappearance, and then the two themes are combined in what promises to be a full symphonic development. Within two bars, however, the disquieting themes give way to a serenity created by shimmering strings and the liquid notes of a celeste. (The superb orchestrations are by Arthur Morton, uncredited in the film, though identified by Schumann in his article as a man "whose good taste and understanding contributed much more than pure orchestration" [*FM,* 17].)

Schumann's opening illustrates the way *The Night of the Hunter*'s music track, in common with other film scores, makes use of musical codes that carry "cultural associations" that "have been further codified and exploited by the music industry."[23] Certain harmonies and orchestrations suggest peril; others suggest tranquillity; still others tip us off to the appearance of a comic character, and so forth. The title sequence, which Schumann rightly compares to an overture (*FM,* 15), offers up a musical preview of the film's struggle between evil and good.

A children's chorus enters with a lullaby whose words, written by Grubb, comment directly on the sinister music we have just heard:

Dream, Lit-tle One, Dream,____ Dream, my Lit-tle One, Dream.____

Though the hun-ter in the night___ fills your child-ish heart___ with fright,___

Fear is on-ly a dream,_____ so Dream, Lit-tle One Dream.

Example 6.3
"Lullaby," Walter Schumann.

The music plays over a black sky dotted with stars. In a textbook example of the way music alters one's perception of an image, the sky looks ominous when the foreboding themes sound, but when the lullaby enters, the sky takes on a quality of enchantment. The interplay of music and image immediately establishes night as a source of both terror and comfort.

When the image of Rachel Cooper appears in the sky, she speaks directly to the audience in soothing tones that blend naturally with the music. Harp and strings characterize Rachel as an angelic force. In the moments following the credits, the music continues to pit sanctity and malice against each other. An instrumental development of the "dream" lullaby accompanies our descent from Rachel's heavenly point of view to children at play. When a woman's twisted corpse is revealed, the music track blares the film's opening chords (see ex. 6.1). Rachel's musical voice reading homilies from the Bible comes in again over a helicopter shot of Preacher in his touring car. With the first medium shot of the preacher, Rachel's voice-over narration (along with the lullaby) ends, and we hear no more of Preacher's antagonist until the last half hour of the film. Wickedness, for a time, moves forward unimpeded. The chief sign of hope in the film comes from the music track, which now and then offers, through a serene or cheerful melody, the promise of virtue triumphant.

Over the initial shot of Preacher's face, however, evil announces itself with the last four chords of Schumann's "pagan motif" (see ex. 6.1). The music identifies Preacher as the murderer of the woman whom we have just seen. Several scenes later, Icey Spoon and Willa discuss the possibility of a second marriage. Willa says, "Icey, I just don't want a husband," to which Icey eventually responds, "It's a *man* you need in the house, Willa Harper." After each line, the film cuts to a low-angle shot of a fast-moving locomotive, accompanied by the sudden blast of Preacher's theme. The cutaway to the locomotive is not in Agee's draft, and in the shooting script the train appears only once, after Icey's line about "a man in the house." It is described as "a short, lighted, toy-like train" leaving town along the river (*AF*, 276). Laughton replaced that picturesque, storybook image with a train charging powerfully toward the viewer. In context of the dialogue about a husband, the train crosses the screen on both narrative and symbolic tracks. The narrative logic is that Harry Powell is on the train, coming closer and closer to Cresap's Landing. Symbolically, the train takes on a masculine, libidinal power—the power by which Preacher, who ironically is revolted by sex, seduces his female victims. By cutting not once but twice to the train and its musical jolt, Laughton turns what would otherwise be a moment of cheap theatrics into an effect so bold and operatic that it becomes something more—the very sound and image of approaching fate. It is the music in particular that puts that fate on screen. The music has become Harry Powell. His theme, whether in a four-chord or eight-chord version, is used relentlessly in different keys and at different tempos throughout the first two-thirds of the film as a dramatic stinger announcing the presence of the preacher. For example, when Preacher's shadow on the wall interrupts John's bedtime story, the music breaks into the swift progression of the first four chords in Preacher's motif.

John looks out the window and sees Powell under a streetlamp in front of the house. While the preacher moves away, he sings "Leaning on the Everlasting Arms." The use of the hymn in this scene signals that it will function as a secondary theme associated ironically with evil. Preacher's singing continues over a shot of John climbing into bed beside Pearl. The children are then sung to sleep by the distant, hollow sound of the hymn: "Lean-ing, lean-ing, safe and secure from all alarm." Coming from the mouth of Harry Powell, the song is a false benediction, a hymn sung by the devil. Yet because it is a hymn—and because it plays over an image, beautifully sculpted in shadow and light, of the unsuspecting children nestled in bed—it holds out a possibility for genuine peace and security. The effect of the music at this point is to mingle hope and fear in a subtle and complex manner.

That paradoxical effect is followed by a musical moment of pure happiness. A steamboat is passing Cresap's Landing. Sanders shot the boat on location, and it was matted into footage of water taken at the Rowland V. Lee Ranch to create a spacious image that releases the tension of the previous, claustrophobic night scenes.[24] The music track, too, opens up to give us a lighthearted melody and jaunty rhythms, which, in terms of Gorbman's "musical codes," have a naval sound that would not be out of place in *Captain Blood* (1935) or *The Sea Hawk* (1940). The tune is a sort of shanty cast in the form of a round. The music accompanies John's visit to Uncle Birdie, an old salt living on a houseboat—a man who, for a time, acts as a surrogate father to John. The music associated with Birdie (although in 2/4) has a rhythmic affinity with a 6/8 theme that Schumann called "The Hen and the Chicks" (*FM*, 16), associated with John's other surrogate parent, Rachel Cooper:[25]

Example 6.4
Uncle Birdie's theme, Walter Schumann.

Example 6.5
Rachel Cooper's theme, Walter Schumann.

Yet apart from that loose connection, Birdie's music does not interweave with any other themes, and the seafaring melody receives no extensive development. We hear it only at the beginning and end of this scene between John and Birdie. Later, Birdie strums a banjo as he sings a short ballad, for which Grubb wrote lyrics, about "Uncle Birdie and the times that ere gone by" (*HH*, 173). That song, too, stands alone in the film. The old man's music, then, is something of a dead end in the story. It is an apt reflection of Birdie himself. When Preacher marries Willa, Birdie senses trouble at home and urges John to come to him in time of need. But when Preacher is chasing the children, John runs to Birdie for help and finds him in a drunken stupor. Like Preacher's hymn, Birdie's cheerful music offers a false hope of security. John is forced to run from his useless companion (one of several adults, including his own mother, who let the boy down) and make for the river.

During the chase sequence, the score weaves together variations on Preacher's theme and the agitated motif heard in the opening of the film (see exs. 6.1 and 6.2). Now in its proper narrative context, that second, "danger" motif takes on the connotation of flight. Parts of it will be heard again at the end of the film, when the lynch mob is gathering, and Miz Cooper has to hurry her charges out of town ahead of the angry crowd. Adding to the complicated musical texture in this chase sequence are two other themes. One is a delicate motif associated with children and innocence. By this point, we have already heard the music twice. Four bars of it came in when John and Pearl were introduced, and more of it played when John told his sister the bedtime story. Pearl will eventually sing words about a pretty fly to this melody, which Schumann identifies as "the main theme of the picture" (*FM*, 14). Here is the theme, with Grubb's lyrics included:

Example 6.6
"Pretty Fly," Walter Schumann.

When the children are on the run from Preacher, variations on the once-peaceful theme, now played at a faster tempo on soaring strings, take on an urgent quality: innocence threatened. When the preacher comes within view of the children at the river, Schumann adds another theme—a menacing figure in the bass, wonderfully Wagnerian in its chromaticism and heavy brass:[26]

Example 6.7
Secondary Preacher theme, Walter Schumann.

By adding a complementary theme of evil near the climax of the chase sequence, Schumann intensifies the terror. Throughout the chase, the music track emphasizes the endless grapple of "Right-Hand-Left-Hand." Themes of evil and innocence circle around each other, never resolving, ever repeating. The unsettled nature of the music helps to create tension and suspense: will the children escape, or will evil triumph?

The tension is released as the children push off into the river, out of Preacher's grasp. Suspense music gives way to a rising, animalistic howl from the preacher, which dissolves into a burst of electronically created sound. "I don't know what they did in postproduction," Gregory said, "but they worked on that, they just had a ball doing that particular thing. I know, because Laughton would tell me, 'We've got a sound that's going to knock you right out of your seat, old boy!'" (*HH*, 248). The unnerving sound gives way to tremolo strings and the ethereal tinkling of a celeste. Otherworldly evil fades away before otherworldly goodness. The children drift downriver, and the complex layering of musical themes resolves into simplicity as the score returns to the film's main theme (see ex. 6.6). This motif, having passed successfully through danger, now settles into its full, serene statement. Accompanied only by an orchestral shimmer, Pearl sings the childlike melody to her doll—and by extension to John, who has fallen asleep from exhaustion in the bow of the skiff.

In the two drafts of the screenplay, as in the novel, Pearl speaks her story about the pretty fly. During preproduction, it was decided that she should sing. Grubb recalled that Schumann phoned and asked

THE NIGHT OF THE HUNTER

for lyrics to the lullaby that would be used later in the river sequence. "I don't remember why they were in such a hurry, but he needed [the lullaby] right away, so I said, 'Call me back in twenty minutes.' . . . I think we worked on the little girl's song the same day" (*HH*, 262–63). In the outtakes, Sally Jane Bruce sings a slightly revised version of the lyrics that Grubb dashed off for Schumann.[27] Her unaccompanied voice has the frail, unsteady quality one might expect from a five-year-old. Charming in its unaffected authenticity, Bruce's voice was nevertheless replaced by that of a professional singer. "I have a feeling that it was . . . a young woman named Betty Benson, who had sung Melora's song in *John Brown's Body*," said Schumann's widow (*HH*, 252). Laughton made certain that the singer emulated the little girl's sound. The result is an eerie, though affecting, voice that is at once childlike and adult. The "Pretty Fly" song, like the music accompanying cutaways to the locomotive, makes *The Night of the Hunter* a melodrama in the original sense of the word—a drama whose story is told through music. Like a musical or an opera, the film sets a key emotional moment to song. The unexpected lullaby lifts the scene into the stylized reality of musical theater and is therefore a fitting start to the river sequence, the most stylized sequence in the film.

When Grubb wrote about the river journey in his letter to Laughton, he did not mention stylization, but he did offer these reflections:

> I agree that the passage down the river must be lyric and
> *flowing*. It seems to me that the chaos of exodus is the place
> where quick fast cutting must occur. The early part of the
> passage down the river must be a blessed and lyric moment
> of dramatic relief. I want the audience to feel the river as
> the womb of safety—as the flowing breast of succor. They
> must love the river as I do—as the children did. It must
> envelop and embrace this sequence warmly and richly.
> And yet I think we must keep the quick, bright edge of
> danger sharply at the corners of this sequence. The quick
> water running. The preacher on the shore. The snags and
> sawyers and sandbars. But *some* of this river sequence must
> flow gently and lead sweetly to Rachel on the bluff in the
> green, gentle morning under the willows. I will provide
> sketches for this.[28]

To convey the feelings that Grubb describes, Laughton slows down the pace of the film as the river journey begins. He told Golden that the lyrical opening shot of the sequence should be "extended as long as it could possibly hold on the screen. As l-o-n-g as it could possibly hold" (*HH*, 248). Subsequent shots of the skiff gliding smoothly along the river are also held for several seconds. Yet it is the music that creates the deepest sense of the river as "the womb of safety." We are in a realm of legato strings and calming woodwinds. "Here I had complete musical freedom," Schumann says, "and wrote a twelve minute tone poem based on the 'Pretty Fly' and 'Lullaby' themes" (*FM*, 16).

Still, just as Grubb suggested, Harry Powell is not forgotten. The idyll on the river is interrupted twice to show his progress on the chase. The first time he is seen on the children's trail, he is riding his white horse—a visual irony equivalent to accompanying his presence with a hymn. The music track, however, is not ironic at this point. The shot of Preacher is accompanied by a recapitulation of his eight-chord motif (see ex. 6.1). His next appearance is one of the film's strikingly lit tableaux. He preaches around a campfire to a group of migrant workers about the abominations of "impudent youngins." His sermon is met with glum silence and a raspberry of sorts: one of the workers spits tobacco juice into the fire at the end of Preacher's harangue. The scene tells us how Preacher lives as he hunts the children and what others on the road think of him—information conveyed over four pages in the novel (*NH*, 192–95) and packed into a single shot for the film. The music for the tableau is a descent in the brass (a figure we have heard before as occasional punctuation in scenes with the preacher) but not the original theme of evil. Indeed, Preacher's theme disappears from the film until near the end, when police officers hustle Powell away from a lynch mob. The prolonged absence of Preacher's main theme suggests the weakening of evil's hold on the children, who find sanctuary on the river and who will soon come under the protection of Rachel Cooper.

When John decides to spend a night on land, and the children glide into shore, the music segues into a familiar melody: the dream lullaby from the film's credit sequence (see ex. 6.3). The song, however, is given a new set of lyrics to fit a new situation. As the children approach the farmhouse and stand gazing at the silhouette of a birdcage in a window, a throaty female voice from inside the house sings:

Hush, little one, hush.

Hush, my little one, hush.

Morning soon shall light your pillow,

Birds will sing in yonder willow.

Hush, my little one, hush.[29]

The unseen woman (Kitty White, a singer whom Schumann had heard in a nightclub and who was, coincidentally, a friend of Davis Grubb's [*HH*, 262]) seems almost to be singing to Pearl and John, though with poignant irony: they have no pillow to rest on, no mother to sing them to sleep. ("Are we going home now, John?" Pearl asks.) The children take refuge in a hayloft. While they sleep, a whip-poor-will accompanies woodwinds on the music track. For the moment, the night is free of fear.

In the film's troubled world, however, peace does not last long. The "quick, bright edge of danger" that Grubb believed was essential to the river sequence is felt when John wakes up to look out across the meadow. The serene music ends, and dogs begin barking. Suddenly even that sound changes. The barking is closer, more urgent. And then music resumes: the voice of the preacher singing, "Lean-ing, lean-ing." More insidious than the preacher's theme would be at this moment, the hymn, distant and thin but cutting clearly across the silence of the summer night, produces a memorable cinematic frisson. This is the third time we have heard the hymn. Preacher sings it first on the night John sees him outside his house. He sings it again, offscreen, over the final shot of Willa's corpse in the river. A prayer of dark irony ("safe and secure from all alarms"), the hymn is all the more disorienting in this underwater scene because we do not yet know where the voice is coming from. Harry Powell seems a supernatural presence. In the next shot, we discover the source of the hymn: Preacher's all-too-human figure leans nonchalantly against a tree outside the children's house as he sings. It is broad daylight now. With Willa gone, Powell has no more need to move stealthily in the dark. "Leaning," at that moment, becomes a song of triumph. We are witness to another game of hide-and-seek, and the song is Preacher's way of saying, "Ready or not, here I come." He follows the hymn with a drawn-out, musical call—"Chill-*dren*"—that is at once playful and frighteningly confident (see ex. 1.1). Thus, by the third appearance of the song in the hayloft scene, the hymn is the sound of terror. Where once it sang the children to sleep, it now rouses them from sleep and sends them running back to the river. As John and Pearl descend the ladder of the barn, the music track subtly picks up the hymn. The entrance of the orchestra is barely perceptible—a furtive accompaniment to the sleepless hunter stalking the night. The other two renditions of the song were a cappella. This time, the nondiegetic accompaniment adds sinister weight to the hymn.

The music then marks time as the children run to the skiff and once more prepare to flee. The orchestra offers tantalizing hints of the "Pretty Fly" theme, skirting the edges of the melody, as though refusing to land on a recognizable motif until the children are safely on their way. Grubb suggested "quick water running" as a way to keep alive a sense of danger, and Laughton provides just that image. Waters that were placid on the children's arrival at the farmhouse are now churning, as though all of nature is in upheaval. When finally the skiff is in the current of the river, the music breaks into a flowing, symphonic statement of the "Pretty Fly" melody (see ex. 6.6). The motif is heard in a swift incarnation—the theme of threatened innocence—and we understand, through the ease with which the lullaby is altered, just how tenuous a child's peace can be. In this recapitulation, however, the theme's emotional resonance is still more complex. It is urgent, yes, but suffused with both a yearning and a surprising sense of exhilaration. The surge of the music matches the children's triumphant escape through turbulent waters.

Within a few bars, agitation drains away in a slower rendering of "Pretty Fly" and a return to the woodwind figures of the peaceful hayloft scene. The skiff drifts slowly into reeds along the shore, where Miz Cooper will find John and Pearl. Music and image combine to bring us to Grubb's "green, gentle morning under the willows." When Rachel calls out brusquely to the children, lighthearted music by bassoon and clarinet tells us that her bark is benign. She uses a switch to hurry the children along, yet the melody that now attaches itself to her confirms her benevolence. Clarinet, flute, and pizzicato strings offer up a bouncing, comic theme (see ex. 6.5). That motif is followed by a restatement of the film's lullaby, last heard by the mother in the farmhouse along the river (see ex. 6.3). The children, so the music suggests, have found their new mother.

When danger returns, which is to say, when Powell reappears and asks Ruby questions about John and Pearl, the music track does not sound any of the obviously threatening motifs associated with Preacher. Instead, it offers a subtler threat by way of a theme associated with Willa Harper. To explain the use of that theme, I will need to backtrack and trace the use of Willa's music in *The Night of the Hunter*.

A preliminary version of Willa's theme enters when she and Preacher drive off to be married in Sistersville. The orchestra swells in a quick-stepping waltz, music that would not be out of place in a ballroom scene. Its high spirits, however, are woefully ironic, because we know that the marriage is a fraud. The bride's naive susceptibility to Preacher's charm is underscored in a dissolve from the doting Pearl, who has just told her brother, "I love Mr. Powell lots and lots, John," to Willa preparing for her wedding night. Pearl's frilly dress is echoed by Willa's lacy nightgown, and the mother, primping herself in front of a bathroom mirror, moves with an awkward, girlish quality. In short, daughter and mother become one in their blind adoration. And with the shift in scene to the young bride on her wedding night, the waltz theme finds its essential form. Slower now, flowing on strings, the melody is romantic and wistful:

Example 6.8
"Willa's Waltz," Walter Schumann.

As Willa turns to the door to join her husband in the next room, she moves gracefully in time to the music track and even takes a subtle waltz step to the side. It is as though she is hearing the music in her head. That impression is reinforced a few seconds later when she steps up to her new husband, who is lying with his back to her. Not looking at her, he reaches out with his hand. In the words of the final screenplay, "she puts out her own, expecting a loving hand-clasp; but PREACHER points to the window." He says, "Fix that window shade" (*AF*, 290). The music trails away, as though his unromantic request turns the music off in Willa's head. For the rest of the scene, during which Harry refuses to make love with his bride, no music plays—a superb example of the restraint Laughton and Schumann display in the film. The contrast of the lilting waltz and a musical void is more effective than a modulation into "dark" chords or the introduction of a new theme to convey Willa's grief.

Surprisingly, the waltz was first conceived as accompaniment to Willa's murder. Cortez, who said, "I have always used music as a key to many of my interpretations," heard Jean Sibelius's "Valse triste" in his mind during setup for the murder sequence.[30] Laughton could see that he was lost in thought and, as Cortez recalled, asked, " 'What in hell are you thinking of right now?' I said, 'None of your God-damned business,' in the nicest way." He did finally tell Laughton what music he was hearing. " 'My God,' [Laughton] said, 'how right you are. This whole sequence needs a waltz tempo.' "[31] The director sent for Schumann. With understandable pride, Cortez claimed, "This had never happened before, or since, where the composer comes on the set to look at the photography so he can interpret it in musical terms."[32] Schumann first intended "to use an emotional and tense musical treatment" for scenes involving Willa and Preacher. Laughton, however, said to him, "If the actors and I have stated it properly on the screen, then you don't have to re-state it with music." Schumann created what he called "a very simple waltz." For the murder scene, he set the waltz against Preacher's motif in dramatic counterpoint (*FM*, 15):

Example 6.9
"Willa's Waltz" and Preacher's theme combined, Walter Schumann.

Just as the design and lighting for the murder sequence convey multiple points of view, the music presents different viewpoints through its complex weaving of themes. From the viewer's perspective, the tristesse of Schumann's own waltz is emphasized. The theme is recognizable from the honeymoon sequence, but the melody's romantic wistfulness is now ironic—even tragic. Preacher looms over Willa on the bed, accuses her of spying on him, and slaps her hard. Yet if we hear the music from Willa's point of view, its association with a wedding night is not ironic. She believes that she will soon be in the embrace of a loving God. Although Preacher's theme enters early in the sequence, the score does not offer Powell's point of view. He thinks of himself as righteous, lifting his arm as though reaching for heaven, while the music tells us that he is psychopathic. In the outtakes, Laughton carefully choreographs Preacher's movement: "Uh, Mitch, would you do that gesture once more? And don't speed it up at the end." Powell's slow, disturbing gesture is accompanied by an undercurrent of the preacher's theme (see ex. 6.1) and what I call a B section of the waltz that is darker than the flowing B section from the wedding night. Here are the two B parts, with the original, wedding-night melody first:[33]

Example 6.10

"Willa's Waltz," B part, wedding night, Walter Schumann.

Example 6.11

"Willa's Waltz," B part, murder scene, Walter Schumann.

The new B part has a more ominous sound, partly because it is set in a minor key to meld with Preacher's theme and partly because it is obsessively repeated. In a scene of misguided beliefs and conflicting personalities, where Willa's naive faith opposes the dark drives of Harry Powell, the love music and the hate music achieve a troubling fusion.

The published sheet music has yet a third version of the B section. In an attempt to draw a hit tune out of the movie, Schumann's music was published as "Willa's Waltz (the Theme from *The Night of the Hunter*)." As part of a promotional packet from the public relations firm Arthur P. Jacobs, an anonymous idea person had written, "It is suggested that a composer such as Sammy Cahn be engaged to write a haunting ballad which can be recorded by Frankie Laine, etc., to be called *The Night of the Hunter*."[34] Someone evidently pointed out that Schumann had written a "haunting ballad" of his own, and "Willa's Waltz" took the place of a Sammy Cahn tune. Schumann's theme, stripped of all ironic overtones, comes complete with Tin Pan Alley lyrics by Paul Francis Webster:

> The humming birds are humming in the willow tree,
> My lady love is coming down the lane to me.
> This is my love,
> Her name is Willa . . .[35]

And so forth. As one might expect, the B section of the waltz published for home enjoyment is more commonplace than anything we hear in the film—someone's idea of a more "commercial" progression in the melody (see ex. 6.12).

The published version points up how evocative and complex the waltz-theme variations are in the film. As the preacher pulls down the bedroom shade and readies his knife, the tempo of the waltz accelerates and becomes a kind of *danse macabre*. The preacher slowly strides to the pulsing rhythm, stretches himself over Willa, and raises his knife. All the while the music crescendos and climbs the scale, but before it can resolve it is cut off by a change in scene, made through a wipe that suggests the motion of the knife across Willa's throat and a sonic dissolve to the cough and chug of a car engine: Powell is driving off to dispose of the corpse.[36] When we are finally granted a view of the car and Willa's corpse submerged in the river, the waltz theme plays again, the irony of its lyricism more tragic than ever. The thin, unearthly resonance of the waltz,

Example 6.12
"Willa's Waltz," B part, published version, Walter Schumann.

muted on high strings, matches the dreamlike quality of the image. The music, echoing with earlier associations, is at once a waltz of hopeful love and a dance of death. The sublimity of this eerie cinematic moment is marred only by a bit of "mickey-mousing" when Uncle Birdie's descending fish hook is given a comic presence through turns in the bassoon.[37] The amusing figure will be used more wisely on Rachel's entrance later in the film—another musical linking of John's two surrogate parents.

Willa's theme is not heard again until Ruby goes into town for an assignation with one of the local boys. The music ties Ruby, naive and easily infatuated by Harry Powell, to Willa. In this incarnation, however, the theme is a sultry fox-trot played on saxophone and muted trumpets—instruments that connote urban decadence. Grubb's novel makes it explicit that Ruby goes into town to engage in sex: "Miz Cooper, I done it with men! Yes, ma'am, I done what they asked me to!" (*NH*, 228). The Hollywood adaptation necessarily keeps her activities vague. In a letter to Harry Cohn, Joseph Breen cites violations of the Production Code that he discovered in a synopsis of Grubb's novel. In Breen's sensitive understanding of the material, he objects to "certain . . . questionable items, such as the portrayal of the thirteen-year-old girl, Ruby, as a juvenile sex delinquent."[38] The film, therefore, bowdlerizes Ruby's confession to Miz Cooper. She says vaguely, "I've been out with men." (Hollywood hypocrisy is amusingly on display in a promotional report about the actress playing Ruby: "Extensive cheesecake has been shot and planted on Gloria Castilo with the wire services.")[39] If we have any doubts about what Ruby is up to, the truth is told in the instrumentation and syncopation—a Hollywood code for lust—that accompanies her as she ventures into town. Thus the simple yearning of Willa's original theme takes on a jaded, worldly aspect. Willa's theme by this time is also charged with threat and therefore works as an effective accompaniment to Preacher's reappearance. It was Willa who helped put the children in danger by marrying Powell, and now Ruby, heir to Willa's motif, tells Preacher where John and Pearl are. With its reminiscence of Willa's murder, the waltz theme reminds us that Ruby herself could be in danger.

That possibility is emphasized visually when Ruby hears the preacher singing outside Rachel's house and rises from bed to investigate. In another example of the film's artful repetitions, A-frame lighting effects over Ruby's bed re-create the cathedral look of Willa's room in the murder scene and tell us that Ruby is another potential victim of the misogynist preacher. "Women," Rachel says, "is such durn fools," and the film, in its portrayal of Willa-become-Ruby (and of Icey Spoon, who helps push Willa into Preacher's bed), seems to say the same—at least about some women. For it is the down-to-earth Miz Cooper who is not fooled by Powell. The music reminds us just how powerful an antagonist she is. Preacher, waiting outside a darkened house as he did on his first night in Cresap's Landing, once again sings "Leaning on the Everlasting Arms." The woman inside, however, is not the gullible Willa Harper, charmed by the preacher's song. It is Rachel Cooper. And she sits on her porch with a shotgun across her lap. Yet she is armed with more than a gun. She is armed with faith. If the image of Ruby in the A-frame bedroom suggests the grim prospect of an unchanging universe, the image of Rachel, illuminated by a subtle halo, represents the hope that the cycle of evil can be broken. She joins the devil in song, engaging him in quiet battle by adding the word—that is, to say, the Word—that Harry Powell has left out: "Leaning on *Jesus*." It was Gregory who told Laughton about the contrapuntal element in the hymn. He remembered it from childhood Sundays at a Baptist church in Iowa (*HH*, 304). Indeed, a thirties hymnal of the sort with which Miz Cooper might have been familiar prints the music and lyrics of the refrain in two parts:

Example 6.13
"Leaning on the Everlasting Arms," 1887,
Elisha A. Hoffman and Anthony J. Showalter.

When Rachel's voice enters, Preacher's dwindles to accompaniment. Miz Cooper has appropriated his song and thereby reduced his power, just as earlier she cut short his normally surefire sermon "Right-Hand-Left-Hand" and stole his capacity to charm.

The hymn as Rachel sings it stands in contrast not only to Preacher's devilish use of "Leaning" but also to the communal rendition of "Bringing in the Sheaves" at the start of the picnic sequence. In the bucolic, riverside setting, the song rings with joy—the sound of a harmonious community. Preacher's booming participation, which we know to be devious, only heightens the sense of the townsfolk's innocent faith. Laughton's own voice in the outtakes reveals how sincere he wants the song to be. He calls out over the singing of the group: "Edna, come 'round! Margaret, come on! . . . Betsy, get in the world!" Later in the film, when we see a vengeful Icey and Walt Spoon whipping a lynch mob into a frenzy, the picnic hymn no longer seems so innocent. The apparently decent folk of the town are revealed to be as hateful as Preacher himself, and their song is merely the veneer of Christian civility that can be stripped away in a moment of fury.

The film's ironic use of hymns is rooted in Grubb's novel. His choice of a hymn for the picnickers is "Shall We Gather at the River?" (*NH*, 76). Later they sing "Let the Lower Lights Be Burning" on a boat in a storm, a song that becomes sinister when Preacher attempts to exert power over John by forcing him to sing with the group (*NH*, 84–85). In the first draft of the script, Agee retains "Shall We Gather at the River?" ("NH," 67). The final screenplay changes it to "Brighten the Corner Where You Are" (identifying it as "Brighten the Corner" [*AF*, 282]). The film eventually settles on "Bringing in the Sheaves"—an inspired choice. Its repetitive music and words make the hymn seem, at least in retrospect, mechanical and hollow, an aural commentary on the nature of religion in Cresap's Landing.

If Laughton and Schumann had followed Agee's script more closely, there would have been even more religious songs in the film. Agee's Christmas sequence includes "O Come, All Ye Faithful" and "O Little Town of Bethlehem." In the scene after Willa's death, when Preacher tries to draw the secret of the money from the children, he cajoles Pearl into singing a duet:

> Jesus Gentle Shepherd hear me,
> Bless Thy little lambs tonight.
> In the darkness be thou near me,
> Keep me safe till morning light.
> Ahhh-Men. ("NH," 172)

It could have been a marvelously eerie moment, though it makes dramatic sense to cut the song and allow only the one duet between Miz Cooper and Preacher. Another hymn might also have increased difficulties with the Production Code Administration.

Joseph Breen, ever cooperative with religious organizations, had submitted *The Night of the Hunter* script to the Broadcasting and Film Commission of the National Council of the Churches of Christ.[40] Shortly after production on the film began, the commission's West Coast director, George A. Heimrich, wrote Gregory a four-page letter detailing the script's many offenses against the Christian religion. His chief complaint is that Harry Powell "is a villain portraying a minister, who definitely states that he is a man of God, and furthermore he leaves the impression that he is a minister." Heimrich helpfully suggests deleting several scenes and bits of dialogue so that "the character in question ('Preacher') becomes a person not portrayed as a preacher, who murders, lies and deceives to obtain money, etc. for his own personal use." He is also unhappy that "two well-known hymns, 'Brighten the Corner' and 'Leaning on the Everlasting Arms', are sung or hummed by Preacher. Undoubtedly the association of Preacher with these songs will be offensive to millions of Protestants, as these hymns have a deep spiritual significance."[41] A later memo written by Geoffrey Shurlock states, "The two hymns [Preacher] sings will be changed to other songs not identifiable as standard hymns."[42] No such change, of course, was made. Schumann and Laughton may have been concerned about a misuse of "Leaning" in the underscoring for Preacher, but they clearly had no doubts about the ironic power of his singing the hymn, especially because Rachel ultimately uses the song in holy struggle against Preacher.

At the moment Ruby steps onto the porch, the duet between Miz Cooper and Harry Powell breaks off. Here again, as in the honeymoon sequence, silence proves more alarming than a shift to new music. Preacher stops singing, and we know he is gone. He must be in the house. Yet because Miz Cooper has defeated Preacher in song, it is a foregone conclusion that she will triumph. Rachel's victory with her shotgun is almost anticlimactic in the wake of the remarkable musical duel. Aware that nothing more need be said musically, Laughton has Schumann score neither Powell's flight from the house nor his arrest by state troopers.

When music does resume, it is in a more conventional capacity than is usual for the film: an underscoring of excitement while the town pours out for a lynching. Nevertheless, there are distinctive touches. As Rachel and the children flee ahead of the mob, Schumann uses brass instead of woodwinds to work dark variations on "The Hen and the Chicks" theme (see ex. 6.5). When the crowd goes after Preacher, we hear, in ironic turnabout, bits of the "danger" motif that once accompanied his deadly pursuit of the children (see ex. 6.2). Also, in the midst of the action music, there is a brief, startling statement of "Willa's Waltz." We hear its first four notes over an image of Ruby in anguish outside the police station, pining for the imprisoned Harry Powell. No longer jazzed up, played swiftly on a solo violin, the theme reverts to its original yearning quality and gives to Ruby's folly a note of pathos (see ex. 6.8). Her romantic longings are swept away as Miz Cooper grabs Ruby and drags her off. Ultimately, it is Rachel's comic, skipping theme that sets the world right. She puts the chaos of the town behind her and leads her adopted family along streets decorated for Christmas.

Jingling sleigh bells under Miz Cooper's theme provide a transition into the final sequence of the film—Christmas day in Rachel's house.

This epilogue weaves together "The Hen and the Chicks" (ex. 6.5), the lullaby (ex. 6.3), and the "Pretty Fly" melody (ex. 6.6) to tell us that the world has grown safe. But has it really? Two musical echoes, "Willa's Waltz" and Preacher's theme, cast doubt on the apparent certainty of the ending.

The waltz, in its original, legato form, plays as Rachel gives Ruby her Christmas present: a small brooch (see ex. 6.8). Earlier in the film, Rachel sternly referred to such jewelry as a "geegaw." Her action now, a touching acknowledgment of Ruby's femininity, reveals her essential tenderness. But what are we to make of the music that accompanies Rachel's gesture? It may be that in context of the serene melodies surrounding it, this theme is to be taken, for the first time in the film, at face value: the sound of romance, of young, innocent womanhood. Perhaps Miz Cooper, in defeating Harry Powell, has purged the waltz of its ironic overtones. Perhaps Ruby has learned the difference between lust and love. Perhaps. The theme, however, cannot easily shed its associations with woman's folly. Indeed, the waltz seems to draw the normally shrewd Miz Cooper into the circle of gullible women. It links her to Ruby and Willa (and to Pearl, who, as a child incapable of assessing Preacher's evil, is a symbol of the susceptible female) and implies that, in the end, women are "durn fools." Despite its new context, the waltz still resonates with Willa's murder, and it therefore shadows Rachel's well-intended gesture toward Ruby.

Soon after this, however, another theme dispels dark thoughts and, at least momentarily, allows us to accept Rachel's wisdom on the subject of children. She speaks her final words, as she does those in her first appearance, to the camera: "They abide, and they endure." The underlying music is the same melody we heard in the opening credit sequence: the lullaby, which is especially pertinent here at the end, with its reminiscence of the lyrics "fear is only a dream" and "rest, little one, rest" (see ex. 6.3). Music and image together provide a sense of closure.

The music track brings us full circle in another way, with disconcerting results. Over the Christmas-card shot of Rachel's house in snow, the orchestra swells to a resonant close and sounds four chords in the brass that unmistakably echo Preacher's theme from the start of the film (see ex. 6.1). This time the chords are major, and in the world of movie music (as in Western music generally), a major key connotes brightness and hope. The transformation of the motif implies that evil has been vanquished. "The sweetly sentimental Hollywood ending assures us that all is right with the world," states David Ashley King. "Yet the questions persist. The ominous tone will not fade. One comes away from the film unsettled, distressed, edgy."[43] The music contributes to the feelings that King describes. We might remember Miz Cooper's biblical warning in the film's prelude: "Beware of false prophets in sheep's clothing." The final major chords could be a kind of sheep's clothing, hiding something evil. Doubt lingers because even in the major, the sequence of chords carries strong associations of Preacher and his wickedness.

The film contains many themes associated with goodness: the two lullabies and their variations, "The Hen and the Chicks" theme, Uncle Birdie's music—even Willa's theme, for her illusions are pathetic rather than wicked. But apart from some minor brass figures, there is only one main theme of evil. I do not include "Leaning on the Everlasting Arms," because the preacher has perverted a religious melody and because Miz Cooper ultimately reclaims the hymn. That musical imbalance is a testament to the power of hate: it has a strength that requires an array of forces to bring it down. The fact that Preacher's theme, disguised though it may be, returns to conclude the film is a telling reminder that evil, too, abides and endures. This is not to say that the music track obliterates the victory within the narrative. Rather, it offers a worldview as realistic as that of Miz Cooper, who knows that "it's a hard world for little things." The music offers a sense of triumph in its harmonic resolution, even as it reminds us of the hunters who roam by night and day.

In a work as dialectical as *The Night of the Hunter,* it is only fitting that the score conclude with conflicting ideas suspended in dramatic tension. The film's balance of opposing forces, maintained through repetitions in the music, the visuals, and the narrative, further illustrates the way Laughton, though a first-time director, exhibits sophisticated control of cinematic elements. It is no surprise that while directing his performers, he creates patterns of contrasting acting styles that are consistent with other patterns in the film. It is surprising, however, that as an actor-turned-director, Laughton has occasional lapses in the control of his performers. The next chapter, which draws on the hours of outtakes held by the UCLA Film and Television Archive, looks at Laughton and his cast on the set and on location in the latter months of 1954.

Seven

THE DIRECTOR AND HIS
ACTING COMPANY

Mitchum and Gish

Willa has been murdered, and Preacher has told Walt and Icey that she ran off in the night. Sobbing theatrical sobs, he lays his head down on the counter of Spoon's ice-cream parlor. Walt says, "Oh, she'll come draggin' her tail back home," to which Preacher replies, "She'll not be back." He looks up with one eye, the more to savor the devilish irony of his next words: "I reckon I'm safe in promisin' you that." His sly manner proclaims his hypocrisy.

In one of the outtakes for the scene, Robert Mitchum delivers his line in a matter-of-fact tone that does not point to the double meaning of his words. But it was the more flagrant reading that Laughton wanted from Mitchum.

Later in the film Rachel prepares to hustle her children out of a restaurant, ahead of the lynch mob seeking Preacher's blood. "Where's Ruby?" she asks. "She went," says Clary. Rachel gasps.

In the first take of this scene, Lillian Gish responds with broad pantomime. Her eyes widen, her mouth gapes open, and her hand flies up in a gesture of fear. The silent screen actress is on display, albeit an actress playing in a broad style that Gish rarely embraced. Offscreen, Laughton says, "Uh, Lillian, do it again, please. . . . The eyes are just a flicker too wild." Gish displays her consummate skill by instantly performing a second take in the restrained style that was a hallmark of her career.

The choices Laughton made reveal how consciously he sought a stylized, exaggerated performance from Mitchum and a naturalistic, unadorned performance from Gish. Each style of acting becomes a code in itself: Mitchum's affected manner signals Preacher's deceitful nature, and Gish's straightforward approach identifies Rachel as direct and honest.

To Mitchum, his broad technique in the film was "fairly implicit in the book."[1] Grubb does mention Preacher's "grand manner," which captivates the people of Cresap's Landing, and he describes a "rolling, booming voice" in the pulpit (*NH*, 65). He also links Preacher to the devil, giving him a mythic quality. On film, Laughton crafts images that at times make Preacher seem other than human: his looming shadow on the children's wall or his head appearing upside down ("snake-like," says the final screenplay [*AF*, 270]) from an upper bunk in his prison cell. It is, however, chiefly Mitchum's heightened performance that gives Harry Powell a larger-than-life dimension. Ultimately, Mitchum's incarnation is more hyperbolic than Grubb's Preacher. In the book, the man is capable of folding his hands in "tranquil piety" (*NH*, 56). When presenting Preacher's dialogue, Grubb does not specify a tone of self-conscious artifice: "'I was with Brother Harper almost to the end,' he said in his clear voice. 'And I 'lowed as how it would cheer the soul of this poor child to know how brave her husband was—how humble in the face of Eternity and the final judgment'" (*NH*, 56).

Mitchum's performance, then, is not the only possible interpretation for Grubb's character. Preacher could be portrayed with the easy charm of, say, Joseph Cotten as the adored Uncle Charley, with his own history of murdering widows, in Alfred Hitchcock's *Shadow of a Doubt* (1943). For a time, Gregory and Laughton considered Laurence Olivier for Preacher because the film, in Gregory's words, "would be much more menacing with this figure, that kind of texture that Larry has. Mitchum looks evil." Gregory even toyed with the idea of Jack Lemmon in the role. Difficult as it is to picture Lemmon as a serial killer, he illustrates the sort of nonthreatening persona that Gregory had in mind. (Gregory did finally give Lemmon a villainous role when he cast him as John Wilkes Booth in a television production of *The Day Lincoln Was Shot* [1956].)[2]

For that matter, Mitchum himself could have played Preacher differently. In the Western *Rachel and the Stranger* (1948), he is Jim Fairways, an affable hunter who entertains himself and others with a guitar and a selection of pleasant songs. In a reversal of the hayloft scene from *The Night of the Hunter*, Fairways at one point is heard singing offscreen, and the sound of his familiar voice brings delight to a boy (Gary Gray) and his young stepmother (Loretta Young). He later gives up his hunter's garb and appears in a store-bought outfit that his rival Davey (William Holden) laughingly refers to as "parson's clothes." The suit, with its black coat, tie, and hat, is a surprising prototype of Preacher's costume in *The Night of the Hunter*. Seeing Powell's black suit in a comic context, worn by a character with a gracious, captivating manner, one realizes that Mitchum could have portrayed Preacher with a seemingly genuine, low-key charm instead of an unctuous theatricality.

There is a nice symmetry to the fact that in Laughton's unique film, Mitchum gives a performance that is unique in his body of work. Whatever type of picture he appears in, Mitchum moves across the screen in a reserved, even somnolent, manner. Several years before James Agee wrote a film for Mitchum, he wrote this comment about the star's performance in the film noir *Out of the Past* (1947): "Bob Mitchum is so very sleepily self-confident with the women that when he slopes into clinches you expect him to snore in their faces."[3] Even Mitchum's villainous roles before and after *The Night of the Hunter* are notably understated. Slouched at a poker table in *False Colors* (1943), one of several Hopalong Cassidy Westerns with which Mitchum began his career, he exudes a sense of coiled threat. When Andy Clyde inadvertently reveals Mitchum's poker hand, Mitchum grabs him and says, "I'll break every bone in your body," not with rage but as a level statement of fact. Two decades later, as the vengeful Max Cady in *Cape Fear* (1962), he speaks in a languid, conversational tone when he tells a lawyer who sent him to prison (Gregory Peck) that killing him with his bare hands would be "too easy" and "too fast." Cady and Preacher are Mitchum's most vicious characterizations, yet Cady's simmering malice is the opposite of Preacher's florid rage ("Tell me, you little wretch, or I'll *tear* your arm off!"). The humor within Mitchum's portrayal of Preacher also differs from that in his other performances. In the caper film *The Big Steal* (1949), he and Jane Greer have the following exchange:

GREER: Look, stop calling me "Chiquita." You don't say
that to girls you don't even know.
MITCHUM: Where *I* learned Spanish you do.

He utters the gag in a dry, offhand manner worthy of Bing Crosby. Even in a bit of slapstick during *Rachel and the Stranger,* when Mitchum splashes in a river to retrieve clothes that are floating away, he downplays the physical comedy and keeps gesture to a minimum. In *The Night of the Hunter,* on the other hand, a basement shelf crashes down on him, and he pulls on his cheeks to make a broadly funny face. When Rachel shoots him in her darkened house, he runs out the door in a wild gallop, yelping and flailing his arms.

According to Mitchum, he and Laughton never discussed a particular approach to the role of Preacher. As he explained, "I did it, and Charles approved of it, that's all."[4] The director whose approval he sought, of course, was also an actor known for his outsized performances. In *The Old Dark House* (1932), the first feature that Laughton shot in America, he bursts onto the screen, chattering loudly and braying an obnoxious laugh. The large vocal and gestural effects, and the exuberant delight in performing that shines through the characterization, set the pattern for a series of portraits that made Laughton an instantly recognizable subject for impressionists and caricaturists: Nero in *The Sign of the Cross* (1932), Henry VIII in *The Private Life of Henry VIII* (1933), and Captain Bligh in *Mutiny on the Bounty* (1935). Laughton somehow infuses even small actions—combing his mustache and beard in *Henry VIII,* a habitual scratching of his nose in *Mutiny on the Bounty*—with a larger-than-life quality. He also has a knack for infusing such nefarious characters as Nero or Henry VIII with a broad humor. Simon Callow refers to Laughton's acting technique as "Brechtian" and points out that Bertolt Brecht admired the way Laughton both performed a role and pointed to himself as the performer.[5] Mitchum, a man not prone to talking about the technique of acting ("I'm never conscious of acting *styles,*" he once said[6]) and certainly not likely to invoke Brecht in connection with his craft, never said explicitly that Laughton's method influenced his own performance. Yet it seems more than a coincidence that the one time Laughton directed him he gave the one Laughtonesque performance in his career. As Gregory put it, "I think Laughton shaped everybody and everything he ever worked with in his own style."[7] Callow notes the

Brechtian aspect of Mitchum's *Night of the Hunter* performance, in which "both the actor and the character seem to be giving conscious performances."[8] What Preacher and Mitchum are doing is aptly described by Martin Esslin's definition of the Brechtian style: "acting in quotation marks."[9] When Preacher sits in front of Willa and her friends for the first time in Spoon's ice-cream parlor and says about his supposed job at the prison, "The heart-rendin' spectacle of them poor men was just too much for me," he plays at being sincere. He is on a stage of his own making, and he enjoys watching both his gullible audience and his own performance. Later in the scene he realizes that John sees through him, and his eyes glitter with enjoyment. It seems to amuse Preacher that someone recognizes his falsity, and it amuses him all the more that John is alone in his perception. "It's me your mother believes," he tells John later in the film with smug triumph.

Behind Preacher's delight in his performance, one senses the delight of Mitchum himself in seeing how far he can exaggerate his character and still make him believable. In the scene where Preacher traps Billy in a narrow hallway, Mitchum leans forward and widens his eyes in a crazed manner. It is a tribute to the control that is so much a part of the Mitchum persona that the actor keeps even his excess in check; the exaggerated facial expression remains just this side of melodrama. When Preacher plops down on a bench in the cellar and laughs at Ben's hiding the money in Pearl's doll, the extravagant guffawing becomes an image of the actor delighting in hyperbole. In its stylization, Mitchum's performance is linked to those stylized, noirish elements in Laughton's design that call attention to their cinematic artifice and keep the viewer on edge. When Mitchum stands apart from his role and virtually announces that he is an actor playing a part, the result is disorienting because the actor we are watching is not the actor of films past. The grandiose performer on screen is all the more frightening for being strange to us.

At the other end of the performing spectrum, the naturalistic turn from Gish is tied to the film's pastoral sphere, in which cinematic effects immerse the viewer in the reality of the drama. Gish's acting attempts to efface the actor and leave only a character on screen. As far back as 1927, Edward Wagenknecht praised Gish for being "the profoundest kind of actress: that is to say she does not 'act' at all; she *is*."[10] Ironically, Laughton himself calls attention to the actress by placing her in a decidedly nonrealistic prologue. When a woman appears on screen in a star-filled sky, we do not yet know her as Miz Cooper. But we do know her as what Roland Barthes calls a "face-object" from "that moment in cinema when capturing the human face still plunged audiences into the deepest ecstasy."[11] The face of 1954 is, naturally, older, but its features are still those of a Lillian Gish familiar from nearly forty films.

At the height of Gish's fame in the silent era, Marion Davies performed parodies of Gish, Mae Murray, and Pola Negri in the 1928 feature *The Patsy*. Her impressions of Murray (pouting lips, batting eyes) and Negri (vamping with a knife clenched in her teeth) are broad and funny. To portray Gish, however, Davies throws a shawl around her shoulders and offers a portrait of Gish's motherly, saintly quality that is more of a heartfelt tribute than a spoof. For there is little about Gish that one can parody. Her acting is, for the most part, restrained. When she does give way to emotion, as in *Broken Blossoms* when trapped in the closet while her father breaks down the door, her acting is too real-istically anguished to be parodied and held up to even gentle ridicule. In her impersonation of a sweet, timid Lillian Gish, Davies brings out an essential aspect of Gish's screen character. Whether embodying the abused and fearful daughter in *Broken Blossoms,* the virginal young woman in *Orphans of the Storm,* or the naive country girl deceived and betrayed by a libertine in *Way Down East,* Gish is an image of frailty and innocence. Her essential goodness made her a natural choice for the role of the fallen yet angelic Hester Prynne in *The Scarlet Letter* (1926) and for the role of the nun in *The White Sister* (1923). Yet Davies, in her vignette, cannot encompass the complete personality. Gish's dainti-ness is offset by fierce resolve: desperately baptizing her dead baby in *Way Down East,* searching for her blind sister in *Orphans of the Storm,* or battling relentless wind and sand in *The Wind* (1928). Slight, child-like, of delicate features, she radiates a spiritual intensity that manifests itself in physical strength. As Richard Dyer says, "Gish's face and body have characteristics that suggest both the steeliness and the simplicity of virtue."[12] Gregory's appellation, in the greeting of a letter to Gish, is fitting: "Dear Little Iron Butterfly."[13]

If Gish's roles in sound films up to *The Night of the Hunter* are more limiting in their scope, they nevertheless allow her to adapt the youthful persona established in silent films to more mature characters. In *Duel in the Sun* (1946), she is the tough but tender matriarch, fighting not to give in to the consumption that finally overtakes her. In *Portrait of*

Jennie (1948), she once more dons a habit for a brief appearance as a gracious nun. (Gish was cast against type only once, in Vincente Minnelli's *Cobweb* [1955], where she plays the imperious head of a psychiatric clinic.) Other actresses whom Laughton considered for the part of Rachel included Ethel Barrymore and Jane Darwell. Barrymore, however, as Laughton wrote to both Grubb and Agee, is the wrong type for a West Virginia setting.[14] Darwell, a memorable Ma Joad in *The Grapes of Wrath* (1940), lacks the qualities of inner grace and purity that are essential to Rachel. Those very qualities in Gish create the sense that she, as Dyer puts it, "appears to be the source of light" within her films.[15] The presence of Gish at the start of *The Night of the Hunter* tells the viewer that the character on screen, though yet unknown, is a woman of fundamental decency, of spiritual force. When the children's skiff later comes to rest amid waterweeds, we hear offscreen, "You two youngsters get up here to me this instant!" The voice-over is in Agee's first draft ("NH," 213) but then vanishes in the final screenplay, where Miz Cooper says the line on camera (*AF*, 326). Laughton wisely returned to Agee's first idea. The voice-over entrance of the character in this scene aurally balances her visual entrance at the start of the film. We do not yet know what character in the story is speaking. But we recognize the voice, liquid yet commanding. Even before we see the speaker, we know that the children are safe, because we have heard the voice of Gish.

When at last the speaker is seen, Laughton keeps the camera at a distance from her. In a medium long shot, we watch her grab a switch and herd the children along the water's edge. Unlike the film's opening scene, this one does not allow us to engage with Gish the star. Enveloped in a shapeless dress and floppy hat, she more or less disappears into the character of the farm woman. When Laughton does grant us a close-up of the woman, we see her from John's point of view. The subjective camera, following John's eyes, tilts up from the woman's shoes, past her worn clothes to her face. It is, of course, the familiar and comforting face of Lillian Gish. Yet she is no longer strictly Barthes's face-object. Because we now gaze at her through John's eyes, Gish melds into the character in the drama, the children's newfound protector, Rachel Cooper. From here to the end of the film, Rachel is in the forefront. She is, however, served by the actress who infuses Rachel with warmth and toughness. Gish also serves Rachel (not to mention Grubb and Laughton) by using her mellifluous voice and sure sense of rhythm to deliver in the most natural way lines that might seem ponderous in the mouth of another actress: "It did seem like it was a plagued time for little ones—them olden days, them hard, hard times." That line from both the novel and Agee's draft is omitted in the final script (*NH*, 244; "NH," 259). It is fortunate that Laughton put the line back in during production, because the musical reading of the words becomes one of Gish's finest moments.

In the last seconds of the film, at the end of Rachel's monologue about children, the character lifts her eyes and seems to speak into the camera. In that reminiscence of her first appearance in the film, Gish emerges from behind Rachel. "They abide, and they endure," she says. The words are all the more reassuring because they are spoken not only by the Rachel we have come to know and admire, but by Gish, the essence of fortitude.

Supporting Cast

The split in the acting styles of Mitchum and Gish is mirrored in performances by the rest of the cast. Laughton had specific ideas for the way each character should be played. His direction in the outtakes makes it plain that he wanted Uncle Birdie, for example, to be natural and untheatrical. It is surprising, then, that he initially cast Emmett Lynn as Birdie. Credited in some early films as Emmett "Pappy" Lynn, the actor played some version of "the old coot" in more than a hundred films. In his cowboy movies—at RKO, for instance, where he rode first with Tim Holt and then with Holt's wartime replacement, Robert Mitchum (in *Nevada* [1944])—Lynn was noted for the farcical humor typical of Western sidekicks.[16] He is the butt of a practical joke in *Wagon Train* (1940) and runs shirtless, skinny arms flapping, through an encampment of wagons. In *Dead Man's Gulch* (1943), laden with a chair and an armful of bedding, he stumbles through a narrow doorway, somersaults off a porch, and does a pratfall in the dirt. Lynn's portrayal of Birdie, however, is notable for its lack of humor. In the outtakes for *The Night of the Hunter*, Lynn and Billy Chapin perform the scene in the skiff, where they fish for "Mister Gar" and Birdie offers his protection to John. With his rough-hewn face and outcropping of whiskers, Lynn certainly looks the part of the weathered riverman. His performance, however, is mannered in the extreme. Laughton says to Lynn, "I don't want to take the fun out of you"—a comment that suggests the director, looking for less histrionic acting in this scene, had tried to tone down Lynn's natural exuberance. Tactfully, he continues, "You're doing it very quietly, and it's gone very well, but don't take the fun out of you." Lynn, however, trying to adjust his usual clownish technique, never captures the fun, the lively spirit, of Birdie. He drawls his lines in halting, unnatural rhythms. One is conscious only of the actor and his studied delivery, not of a character named Uncle Birdie. Laughton can be heard offscreen between takes, saying, "If you can inhabit the world of the little boy, you'll come off a thousand percent. You've got to live in the world of the little boy. . . . Just a little bit more of the little boy's world from you, Emmett. Remember. Go ahead."

Laughton had to fire Lynn. The replacement was an inspired choice: James Gleason. One of the dependable, ubiquitous figures in the roster of classical Hollywood's character actors, Gleason brings to *The Night of the Hunter* the hard-boiled but likable persona from such films as *Here Comes Mr. Jordan* (1941), *Arsenic and Old Lace* (1944), and *The Clock* (1945). An essentially urban (specifically Brooklyn) type, he makes himself at home in the West Virginia landscape. Gleason's screen personality fuses with Grubb's character, whom Laughton carried over intact into his film. Gleason conveys the outward strength of a protector for John, yet reveals, without descending into bathos, the inner weakness of a man who needs his snort in the morning and who passes out drunk at the very moment John needs him. In the film's outtakes, Laughton has little to say when Gleason performs. His direction to the actor is summed up by his telegraphic comment during Birdie's first scene with John in the wharf boat: "Jimmy, all the charm in the world, Mark Twain, go!" (*HH*, 161). (Grubb also implicitly linked his character and Mark Twain when he sent Laughton a drawing of Uncle Birdie with thick mustache and cigar that is the very image of Twain.)[17] In the fishing scene where Lynn struggled, Gleason fully embodies Uncle Birdie. At once rough and tender, folksy and wise, Gleason's Birdie does "inhabit the world of the little boy." Although Gleason's performance is more expansive than Lynn's lifeless turn, it never becomes so exaggerated that it calls attention to itself. Even when Uncle Birdie curses the gar and beats it with his oar, Gleason keeps the man's rage in check and does not overplay the humor of the moment, thereby making it that much funnier. Other supporting players who match Gleason in their restraint are Peter Graves as Ben Harper, Don Beddoe as Walt Spoon, and Paul Bryar as the hangman.

Graves exhibits a touching earnestness that makes Ben, despite his crime, a sympathetic figure. A year before, in *Stalag 17* (1953), Billy Wilder used that same ingenuous quality to hide the fact that Graves is a Nazi agent pretending to be an American. Laughton employs Graves in a less complicated way, though a sense that the likable actor is putting on a facade of toughness adds to the idea that Ben Harper is a good man driven to act against his nature.

Beddoe also made a career of ingenuous character parts. An affable type whose open face and easygoing manner are equally at home in urban and Western settings (in *The Best Years of Our Lives* [1946], he plays the insurance man Mr. Cameron; in *Wyoming Renegades* [1954], he plays the banker Horace Warren), he is perfectly cast as the henpecked Walt of Cresap's Landing. He plays the man's constant befuddlement in a simple fashion, with no fussy mannerisms. During outtakes for the picnic sequence, in fact, Laughton cautions him, "Too much," after Beddoe reacts to Icey's public comment about their sex life ("I just lie there thinkin' about my canning"). Even Beddoe's comic swig from a bottle of brandy is performed so swiftly and smoothly that it seems utterly natural—the willful guzzling of a child.

Bryar, in the role of the hangman, has less screen time than either Graves or Beddoe—barely five minutes in the sad aftermath of Ben's execution—but his monotone delivery and unsmiling face make such a deep impression that it is unsettling near the end of the film to see him grinning in pleasure at the prospect of executing Preacher (though Grubb himself thought the man's cheerful return was an "excellent" idea [*HH*, 328]). A police officer, who has Preacher in custody, calls out from a car, "Hey, Bart! . . . We're savin' this bird up for *you!*" The hangman, standing at a doorway decorated with a Christmas wreath, calls back, "This time it'll be a privilege!" His smile is accompanied by a tip of his bowler.

Golden had the sense that at this point in the film, Laughton "was kind of floundering. . . . I had a feeling that he didn't know how to finish the thing." The lynch mob, for instance, seemed "out of place" to Golden, though he admitted that Laughton "went to a lot of trouble shooting that stuff."[18] The mob is an essential part of the novel, so Laughton naturally includes it in the film. In the book, however, the townsfolk swarm up the steps of the county jail. The hangman does not reappear in a comic reprise. Grubb leaves the impression that Harry Powell is about to be lynched. The suggestion of mob vengeance makes for a fittingly grue-some end to Preacher's violent life. In the first draft of the script, Agee includes the mob descending on the jailhouse, and he adds a line for Icey that signals Preacher's end: "*Harry Powell, prepare to meet yore God!*" ("NH," 278). The final screenplay gives us instead the scene in which Preacher is hustled out the rear door of the jailhouse and into a police car (*AF*, 350). Laughton made the change not, it would seem, because he was "floundering," but because he wanted to maintain the balance between horror and humor that we have already seen was important to him in other parts of the film. Here at the end, the story needs to shift from the lynch mob to the coda at Rachel's house. Thus, Laughton calls on Bryar to smile and make the transition to a bright finale for his film. "Christmas atmosphere," he tells Bryar and the actor playing the policeman. The shot of the jovial hangman is accompanied by a musical segue: Schumann's frenzied "mob" theme gives way to sleigh bells and pizzicato strings dancing playfully up and down the scale. By eliminating even a suggestion that Preacher is lynched, Laughton more or less strands his mob; the scenes of the marching townspeople go nowhere. No doubt that irresolution contributed to Golden's feeling that the lynch-mob sequence "didn't flow."[19] The scene is also our last view of Preacher in the film, and it is something of an anticlimax to see the devil incarnate seated passively in a car during a moment of lighthearted gallows humor. The outtakes silently reinforce the incon-sequential nature of Preacher's final appearance. An instant before the scene begins, Mitchum takes one last puff on a cigarette and tosses it out the window. Although the hangman's reappearance does have the effect of bringing the story full circle, the scene's blithe confidence that justice has prevailed is at odds with the dark visions of the film we have been watching. Bart's tipping of his hat, a stereotypical gesture better suited to the world of musical comedy, makes the moment all the more unreal-istic. By stylizing the scene, Laughton makes it difficult for the audience to connect this jaunty Bart with that other grim, reflective executioner from realistic scenes at the prison and at home. Bryar, however, main-tains a consistency within Laughton's inconsistent use of the hangman: his smile, the way he lifts his hat—all the details of his admittedly theat-rical presentation—remain understated.

Two women in the supporting cast are anything but understated. Evelyn Varden, as Icey Spoon, and the uncredited, still-unknown actress playing Miz Cunningham both relish the overbearing characters they embody.

In the novel and Agee's first-draft screenplay, Miz Cunningham greets John and Pearl by saying, "Ahhhh! If it ain't the poor little Harper lambs!" (*NH*, 33; "NH," 47). In the final script, the *ahhhh* is enlarged to *uh-hawwww!* which stands alone as an offscreen sound (*AF*, 274). In the first take of Miz Cunningham's scene, the actress forgets the exclamation and goes straight into her dialogue. Laughton, intent on hearing that all-important sound, has her begin again. The startling *awwww* (as it comes out on film) instantly establishes Miz Cunningham's domineering nature as she confronts the children with questions about their father's stolen money. With a minimum of gesture but with broad facial expressions and a theatrical screech, which lives up to the final screenplay's description of her voice as that of "a Tidewater Cockatoo" (*AF*, 274), the actress gives a memorable turn as a menacing old crone.

Varden, too, offers a broad, indelible portrait. In the matronly roles for which she is known, she is quite capable of restraint. As the stuffy but cordial school principal in *Cheaper by the Dozen* (1950), she reacts with mild amusement to the imperious Clifton Webb. In *The Bad Seed*, released the year after *The Night of the Hunter*, she plays Patty McCormack's doting aunt, another fatuous, gullible busybody, but tones the character down to everyday proportions. That performance— a suburban version of Icey Spoon—points up the way Varden pushes Grubb's country wife to the edge of caricature yet manages to create a fully dimensioned woman. "She put things into that characterization which she should have gotten *extra* for," Grubb told Preston Neal Jones. He admitted that Varden "is almost my favorite person in the whole film" (*HH*, 170). To capture Icey, Varden exaggerates the harshness of her high-pitched voice and, as specified in the shooting script, draws out her words: "It's for the pick-nick" (*AF*, 282) or "You-Hooooo! Mis-ter Paow-welll!" (*AF*, 309). She even has a knack for enhancing nonverbal sounds. Listening to Preacher explain that Willa ran off or hearing Walt read a postcard from Preacher, she utters sympathetic purrs, each one resonating with slightly different emotion. Late in the film, with Laughton's encouragement, Varden exaggerates her exaggerations. In a take for the trial scene, she yells, "Lynch him! Lynch him!" Laughton wants to do it again. "It's the word, the ugliness of the word," he tells her, and he draws the word out: "Lyyyynch!" He continues, "I want the staring eyes and the drunken face." In the take that follows, Laughton does not get the face he wants. "Now do it again with staring eyes," he says. Instead of calling "action," he says to Varden, "I'm the biggest so-and-so in the world! Come *on*!" In the take that appears in the film, Varden viciously rasps out, "*Lyyynch* him!" Vocally and physically, she matches one of Grubb's drawings, in which Icey's eyes are black, staring circles within circles, and her mouth is a gaping hole, half blackened in a way that gives her the appearance of a grotesque jack-o'-lantern. Walt, with black eyes and black, down-turned mouth, hovers over his wife's shoulder. His gaze is fixed on Icey, and his head is smaller than his wife's. Thus Grubb visualizes Walt's submission to Icey's potent force (see fig. 7.1). In the film, Beddoe conveys Walt's meekness by giving the man's anger the awkward quality of an emotion rarely used. In contrast, Icey easily channels her religious fervor into hatred. Even in scenes of rage, Beddoe and Varden maintain the contrast between a low-key and a flamboyant style of acting.

F. X. Feeney, in an article about the film's outtakes, comments on the acting of Mitchum and Shelley Winters in a way that helps to illuminate the work of Varden and Beddoe. Feeney compares the different acting techniques of Winters and Mitchum and says that "one can hear her Stanislavsky-ish self-immersion in her role clashing with Mitchum's more Zen 'Let's pretend' method—and one can overhear Laughton relishing the contrast, letting it inform their impossibility as a couple."[20] The opposing styles of Beddoe and Varden may not point to "their impossibility as a couple," but they reinforce an incompatibility that is evident in tensions when Walt expresses doubts about Preacher or in the sexual troubles made public by Icey at the picnic. In contrast to Beddoe's understated reaction to his sexual humiliation (a sudden look of chagrin, a lowering of the chicken leg he has been eating), Varden caps the scene with an exaggerated expression. Unable to drop the sexual theme, she says, "A woman's a *fool* to marry for that. That's somethin' for a *man*. The good Lord never meant for a decent woman to want *that*—not *really want* it! It's all just a *fake* and a *pipe*-dream." Varden, turning momentarily into a silent-screen actress, draws in her breath and registers a look of obvious yearning. Her lines, which are adapted from the novel (*NH*, 89), are not in Agee's first draft. Their reappearance in the final script (*AF*, 285), with emphases slightly different from those Varden uses in the film, suggests how much Laughton wants to stress

Figure 7.1
Icey and Walt Spoon at Preacher's trial.
Sketch for *The Night of the Hunter,* 1954, Davis Grubb.

Icey's sexual repression and her unhealthy interest in pushing Willa into Preacher's bed.

Acting styles also underline other relationships in the film. The extravagant performances of Varden and Mitchum yoke Icey and Preacher together. By fawning on "that man of God" and urging Willa to marry Preacher, Icey becomes Powell's unwitting partner in devilishness. When she realizes her mistake, she becomes, like Preacher, an avenger thirsting for blood. On the other hand, the naturalistic techniques of Gish and Chapin underscore the compatibility of Rachel and John.

It is fitting, then, for Willa Harper to be played in a style that oscillates between restraint and exaggeration. Such a divided technique is appropriate for a character torn between a mother's love for John and a wife's devotion to Preacher. It is equally fitting that Shelley Winters was cast in the role. From film to film, her performances move between small effects and broad strokes. In *A Double Life* (1947), she plays Pat Kroll, a waitress who thinks she might "try the modeling game." Serving Anthony John (Ronald Colman), Winters conveys sex appeal with a tilt of her head and the hint of a smile. She leans forward with a hope at once eager and shy when she suggests meeting him later: "We could, uh, tell each other our troubles, if you want to, huh?" Pat's quiet manner is a contrast to the later Dixie Evans in *The Big Knife* (1955). Squeezed into a black, off-the-shoulder dress with a plunging neckline, Dixie exudes a crass sexuality. "Hey, did you know that I'm perfectly proportioned?" she asks Charlie Castle (Jack Palance), and she stands up to show what she means. Dixie is an actress fighting for a break, and everything about her is bold: loud voice, large gestures, and big emotions that swivel from anger to despair to warm affection.

Gregory told Jones, "We wanted for the children's mother a voluptuous kind of actress, . . . someone that would be willing to let her hair blow, and be a little frowzy, but still have that pathetic quality" (*HH*, 87). Winters can be frowzy when necessary, as in *A Place in the Sun* (1951), where she plays Alice Tripp, a drab factory worker impregnated and abandoned by George Eastman (Montgomery Clift). Yet, as her performance in *The Big Knife* makes clear, she can certainly be a "voluptuous kind of actress." Scenes from Grubb's novel, which display Willa's sexual hunger with Ben, may not be in the film, but Winters manages to communicate the woman's sexual longing simply in the way she smiles or touches her hair as she readies herself for the honeymoon night with Preacher. Winters also reveals the vulnerability of her characters, and she is adept at shading each portrayal differently. Dixie from *The Big Knife*, for all her brassiness, has a plaintive quality that makes her seem at times like a confused and hurt child. "Oh, that lousy studio," she says during a tipsy, chattering monologue, in which we learn that the film studio has used her as a call girl and given her only a few small parts. "They louse you up, and then they call you a louse." Pat in *A Double Life* displays her own meekness in a less flamboyant manner. Standing by her bed in a nightgown, soon to be murdered by the insane Anthony, she says simply, "It's like I'm scared all the time I'm gonna get run over by a truck. Stuff like that." Like Pat, Willa Harper is lonely and desperate for companionship. Like Dixie, she is gullible, susceptible to the manipulations of men. Willa, however, channels her thwarted sexuality into religious passion. She has a fervor that, however misguided, gives her a spiritual resolve. Winters uses a gliding walk for Willa that expresses the woman's inner lightness. The walk is a striking contrast to the heavy, flat-footed step that Winters employs for the downtrodden Alice in *A Place in the Sun*. Although Laughton wanted only his former student for the role of Willa, Gregory felt that Betty Grable, "the ice-cream girl," with a "fresh" quality, would have been a more interesting choice.[21] Grubb recalled that Anne Baxter and Grace Kelly also wanted to play Willa.[22] Despite her unglamorous portrayal in *The Country Girl* (1954), Kelly is difficult to imagine in the role of the West Virginia widow. It is also hard to imagine Grable or even the versatile Baxter achieving the delicate combination of sensuality, plainness, meekness, and hysteria that Winters brings to the role.

Winters is at her most flamboyant in the revival meeting. While directing the scene, Laughton works to heighten the intensity of her performance. Softly, he asks her to get in the mood: "Do a prayer, quite high. Any kind of a prayer that you know." Then he shouts, "Now! Loud!" Her first prayer, bubbling instinctively from her Jewish upbringing, is in Hebrew: "Shmah Israel Adonai Eloheinu, Adonai Ehad!" In another take, she keeps to the realm of Willa's religion and recites her own version of the Twenty-third Psalm: "The shadow of the valley of death, I shall fear no evil, for thou art with me." In the film, tottering almost drunkenly on a stage lit by torches, Winters struggles for air as she speaks her lines: "You have all sinned! Which one of you can say [*gasp*] as I can say [*gasp*] that you drove a good man to murder [*gasp*] because I kept a-houndin' him for perfume and clothes and face paint?" Raising her arms to heaven, clasping her hands before her, Winters grows more and more agitated, keeping Willa at the very edge of hysteria. In outtakes for the scene, Winters plunges headlong over the edge. She screeches her lines, nearly choking on her words: "I drove a good man to *murder*," "Throw that money in the *river*, throw it in the *riverrrr*!" Although her manic performance is oddly compelling, one can understand why Laughton rejected these takes as too frenzied even for his purposes. The take he chose keeps the focus more on Willa's overwrought emotions and less on the histrionics of the actor.

For one of Willa's lines in the picnic sequence, Laughton made a different choice, with unfortunate results. After Preacher tells Willa the lie that Ben threw his stolen money into the river, Winters says beatifically, "I feel clean now. My whole body's just a-quivering with cleanness" (the word is *a-quiverin'* in the novel and the scripts). The words are taken directly from the book, where they read perfectly well (*NH*, 71). They do not, however, play well. Audiences invariably laugh at the speech. The "a-quivering with cleanness" line would be difficult for any actress to deliver. Nevertheless, Winters, in one take for the scene, speaks the line in a matter-of-fact way that makes it sound almost natural. Laughton, however, is not interested in even a semblance of naturalism at this point. He chooses the take in which Winters, turning from Preacher as though she were ready to float away, utters the line as a grand pronouncement.

In contrast, the murder scene shows Winters at her most restrained and controlled. The outtakes reveal Laughton striving for a minimalist performance. As Winters lies in bed under a tightly wrapped sheet, already resembling a corpse in its shroud, Laughton goes through several takes of the moment when Preacher slaps her face. "Cheerful and more calm," he tells Winters. "Smile a little softer this time." Later in the scene he tells her, "Keep your face still. . . . You're looking at His *dear* face." Her eyes, distant and serene, do indeed seem fixed on eternity. She remains utterly still, except when Preacher slaps her. Even then her face registers no emotion. Her head turns aside with the blow and mechanically returns to its original position. The uncanny stillness is matched by a soft, barely inflected voice. Directing Winters, Laughton speaks almost in a whisper, as though intoning a prayer. Caught up in his spell, Winters uses her liquid voice to achieve her own hypnotic effect: "He made you marry me so you could show me the way and the life and the salvation of my soul. Ain't that so, Harry?" Laughton's direction of Winters throughout the murder scene is tactful, even tender: "Now Shelley, sweetheart, just that darling smile of yours. . . . A little darling smile, like you smile at me. That's it. Smile, smile as if you'd like me—when you look at me when you trust me."

In the honeymoon sequence, however, Laughton's attitude after many takes is different. He says sharply, "Shelley, put your head up. . . .

Oh, Christ. . . . Keep your goddamn mouth closed." Eventually he says to her, "Well, if you want to scream, scream!" And she does. Whether the director was truly irritated with Winters, or whether, as Jones suggests, he was deliberately trying "to make her feel as belittled as Willa is supposed to feel" (*HH*, 181), Laughton never employs such a harsh manner with any other performer. When Gloria Castilo, playing Ruby, has difficulty keeping her chin down in the drugstore scene, Laughton tells her, "Don't get disgusted with yourself. You're disgusting anyway, but just try not to be." She understands the rough affection of his comment and laughs. Laughton's unique combination of restraint and aggression when directing Winters seems to arise from, and is perfectly suited to, the split in acting technique required for the creation of Willa.

Billy and Sally

The performances of Billy Chapin as John and Sally Jane Bruce as Pearl contain their own fluctuations of technique. In their cases, however, the oscillations stem from awkwardness on the part of the child actors and missteps by Laughton in his direction of them.

Accounts over the years have offered contradictory views of Laughton's relationship with Billy and Sally. Terry Sanders, for instance, recalled that Laughton was somewhat "insecure with the children," and Golden remembered that he was especially unhappy directing the little girl.[23] On the other hand, Beddoe, Gish, and Cortez all found that Laughton worked in a sensitive, fatherly way with the youngsters (*HH*, 279–81), and assistant cameraman Sy Hoffberg remembered that he was "very kind" to them.[24] Gregory said that Laughton had no problems with the children because "he was a child himself." During rehearsals at the director's house, "Laughton would get on the floor and play with the little girl."[25] Although Brown believed that Laughton was "marvelous" with the children, he said that because his son was the same age as John Harper, he had a clearer sense than Laughton "what little boys would do." For the scene in which Ben makes John swear to keep the secret of the money, Brown suggested a bit of business based on his own experience with his son. He thought Ben should say, "John, look me right in the eye, don't look around, look me right in the eye."[26] Here, then, is another example of Laughton's willingness to listen to his crew. The moment, not found in the novel or either draft of the script, is in the film. Ben says, "Now stand up straight and look me in the eye." According to Mitchum, he, too, helped Laughton. He either "very often" took over directing the children[27] or "in one case" took over because Laughton refused to direct them.[28] The outtakes reveal a few times when Mitchum offers brief direction to Sally. Alone with the children at the dinner table, Preacher flicks open his knife, and Mitchum tells the girl, "Soon as the blade comes out, start across." When he moves to the basement door with the children, he interrupts the take and says to Sally, "Once more. And remember not to look back at *me,* honey." Yet such moments seem to be the extent of Mitchum's direction.

At times Laughton, who cast Sally not because of her acting ability but because she had the "doll-like" quality he was looking for,[29] does have trouble getting her to do what he wants. In the first basement scene, Sally continually reacts too soon to Preacher's offscreen voice, holds her doll in the wrong position, and has trouble delivering the line "It's cold and spidery down here" in a natural way. Her awkwardness appears to have contributed to the eventual deletion of the scene. Through all such difficulties, however, Laughton remains unflappable and, indeed, fatherly. He speaks gently, calls Sally "darling" and "dear." In the same vein, he calls Billy "old man" or "old fellow" and is consistently patient and professional with him. Although one writer refers to Laughton's direction of Billy as "little short of vicious" when the director, trying to obtain an anguished look, "keeps hitting the boy in the stomach, lightly but earnestly, take after take,"[30] there is nothing cruel in Laughton's manner. Rather, his approach is that of a physical trainer working to improve his charge. Billy himself responds with complete professionalism, as he does in all of the outtakes, refining his reactions to give Laughton what he wants. "Billy adored Laughton," says an anonymous writer who interviewed Billy and his mother, "felt he was a marvelous director because he spent so much time with him and because he established such an immediate direct and warm working relationship."[31]

The outtakes show that Laughton generally tried to draw a naturalistic performance from each child. When Preacher threatens John with the switchblade, Laughton pretends to cry and tells Sally, "Cry, cry. He's trying to kill your brother, darling, you've got to make a noise about it. Look, look! Look at what's happening over here. Now cry out. Cry out real loud like that." Laughton utters a dramatic sob. "Like that!" Sally exhibits genuine anguish at the sight of her brother under the knife. To elicit the proper expression from Billy when the boy sees Rachel for the first time, Laughton tells him, "It's a sort of look of, uh, you don't believe, you wonder. . . . It's almost like somebody gave you an enormous big [knife?] like Mitch did the other day. It's that kind of a look. . . . No, it's more pleasant than that, Billy. It's almost crying. That's it." Billy achieves a subtle combination of wonder and contentment as he looks at Rachel. Under Laughton's careful tutelage, Billy creates a character with shadings very different from, say, the role of Gadge in *Tobor the Great* (1954). In that film, Billy's one-dimensional, wide-eyed manner ("I just gotta see Tobor! I just gotta!") conveys the idea of boyish enthusiasm. In *The Night of the Hunter,* Billy embodies a boy on the edge of adulthood. Sally many times gives an affecting, realistic performance of her own— peering in bewilderment through a basement window or turning back for a last, poignant look at a farm woman handing out food.

For all that, there are lapses in the children's portrayals. Sally often delivers her lines with unnatural emphases and rhythms: "It'll spoil our *sup*-per" or "You'll get awful *mad,* John, I did a sin. I didn't *tell* no one." At certain moments in the outtakes, Sally provides an amusing contrast to her affected screen manner. During a scene in the basement, she blurts out with natural honesty, "This is a hard way to make this movie." To Mitchum at the dinner table, she says, "Forgetting your lines again." Billy has his share of moments in which he is obviously pretending to feel an emotion: jumping up and exclaiming at the sight of his father's car or mustering an expression of outrage when he first sees Preacher with Pearl's doll.

Laughton occasionally contributes to the playacting quality of the children's performances. When Preacher corners John in the narrow hallway of the boy's house, he announces the impending marriage to Willa in Sistersville. "And when we get back," he says, "we're all going to be friends—and share our fortunes *together,* John." John's reply is to blurt out, "You think you can make me tell! But I won't! I won't! I won't!" In the first version of the scene, found among the outtakes, John claps the back of his hand to his forehead as he speaks. When he realizes what he has done, he covers his mouth with his hand. According to Helen Gould, who wrote a piece about Laughton's direction of Billy and Sally shortly after *The Night of the Hunter* finished shooting, Laughton had second thoughts about the scene. He sought the advice of Billy's mother and asked if a child would put a hand to his forehead in the way Laughton had directed the boy to do. " 'No, he wouldn't,' Mrs. Chapin answered. Viewing the rushes that night, Mr. Laughton voluntarily agreed: 'I was so wrong! We'll re-shoot it.' "[32] He did, and in the film Billy simply covers his mouth at the end of his line.

Billy's hand-to-forehead gesture looks like something out of what Roberta E. Pearson calls the "histrionic code" in stage and silent-screen acting—a set of stylized actions that refer "always to the theatrical event rather than to the outside world." Acting manuals that illustrated specific poses for specific emotions were common from the eighteenth century to the early twentieth century. Griffith's studio, Biograph, even had its own "gestural dictionary." A pose common to such guidebooks included a hand placed on the forehead to indicate "woe."[33] In the scene with Preacher and John, Laughton's version of that pose has no dramatic impact. It simply looks odd. To Laughton's credit, he recognized the problem and went to some trouble to improve the scene.

Yet the hand-over-mouth gesture that Laughton finally used is itself an exaggerated action rooted in the histrionic code. It is not the only such action in the film. Laughton's questioning of Billy's mother shows that he was not certain how children would act, and that uncertainty may help to explain why Laughton relied at times on a theatrical formula of acting for the children. As if determined to use John's rejected gesture somewhere, Laughton allows a sobbing Pearl to place her hand on her forehead after Preacher snaps at her for trying to touch his knife. At another point, John hears the distant whistle of a steamboat, and he puts a finger to his mouth, which is an iconic gesture indicating thought—in this case, the thought that he can escape to Uncle Birdie. In these examples, Laughton's use of silent-film technique does not result in effective stylized images. The histrionic gestures create, through awkward movements, artificial emotions.

From a critical standpoint, such artificiality does not seriously damage a film that often revels in artifice, whether it be visual stylization or the heightened reality of Mitchum's performance. But if viewers are unwilling to accept the very idea of such artifice, then the awkward qualities of the children and the mingling of acting styles among the adults can contribute only to a sense of an unbalanced, unsatisfying movie. That sense was precisely what most reviewers expressed when the film was released in 1955. Even a sympathetic reviewer like Dorothy

Manners of the *Los Angeles Examiner* disparaged "arty and off-beat" moments in Laughton's work. She, however, also predicted that "'word of mouth' publicity" would make the film a commercial success, especially because Mitchum, playing a "contemptible, fiendish, warped character" gives "his greatest and most polished performance on the screen."[34] United Artists had backed the film chiefly on the strength of Mitchum's name, and Mitchum had certainly given his all, but ultimately his name and his performance failed to bring in the customers.[35] The "'word of mouth' publicity" that Manners predicted never materialized. In another review of the work, François Truffaut was more prescient. He said, "Screenplays such as this are not the way to launch your career as a Hollywood director. The film runs counter to the rules of commercialism." Then he added a statement that was sadly prophetic: "it will probably be Laughton's single experience as a director."[36]

Eight

RECEPTION AND BEYOND

Promotion

The premiere, at least, was a success: searchlights; a red carpet; a motor-cade with celebrities like Marilyn Maxwell, Cesar Romero, and Agnes Moorehead acknowledging a crowd of thousands and then submitting to interviews with Don DeFore (who would later become well known as George Baxter on the NBC television series *Hazel*); even a nationwide broadcast of the revels on Steve Allen's *Tonight Show*. It was a night of the usual Hollywood hoopla. Except that it all took place in Des Moines, Iowa.[1]

According to Gregory, he had planned a sneak preview of the film in Des Moines, but the city asked if the screening could be turned into a public celebration (*HH*, 346). Thus, July 26, 1955, was designated "Paul Gregory Day," and the citizens of Des Moines turned out for *The Night of the Hunter*'s world premiere, filling all 1,700 seats at the Paramount Theater and paying $5 a plate for a banquet at Hotel Fort Des Moines to honor their Iowan son.[2] Proceeds from the night went to the building fund of the city's YMCA.[3] Although the Des Moines premiere did not originate with Gregory, it was in keeping with ideas that he and Laughton held about the reception of their film. In a piece for *Good Housekeeping* several months before the release of the movie, Laughton wrote: "Paul Gregory and I have made a movie called *The Night of the Hunter*, which is by a writer called Davis Grubb. We bought the story because we couldn't put it down, so we figured if we liked it that much, the chances were that Normal, Illinois, and Grand Forks, North Dakota, and Wilmington, North Carolina, would like it too."[4] Des Moines might have been the first stop in the sort of road-show marketing campaign that Gregory had hoped United Artists would let him pursue in his attempt to reach viewers in Normal and Grand Forks and Wilmington.

Instead, the Iowa premiere marked the only time audiences flocked to a theater to see *The Night of the Hunter*. "The week the picture opened in 1955," Pauline Kael remembers in *Kiss Kiss Bang Bang*, "I saw it in a theater with about two thousand seats, of which perhaps a dozen were occupied."[5] The film opened in New York on September 29, and by October 17 *Daily Variety* was reporting that *The Night of the Hunter* "lagged with $7,000 or less in four days of third Mayfair round." In Simon Callow's melancholy words, "The film slowly ground to a standstill around America." It ended up on a twin bill with a B Western.[6] Gregory blamed United Artists not only for its policy of mass booking the film but also for its calculated neglect. He believed that United Artists was less interested in *The Night of the Hunter* than it was in the more expensive Mitchum vehicle, *Not as a Stranger* (1955), and simply "sloughed it off."[7] "I had expectations of being able to sell [the film]," he said. In an unpublished article written before the film was released, Gregory explained his intention to generate advance interest in Laughton's work: "We have here an extremely subtle story on a theme as far removed from the run-of-the-mill film offering as a newsreel clip is from a musical comedy in Technicolor. We sensed from the beginning that our production would take special handling and very special treatment." He outlined a plan to take the film on a "'swing tour' of key cities before the picture opens" and to meet with reviewers as a "final step in pre-conditioning." Gregory also conceived a grassroots marketing strategy in which he would target specialized groups like photography buffs. United Artists never gave him the opportunity to put his ideas into effect.[8] But a failure to invest in marketing was only part of the problem. Just as significant was the quality of the ad campaign granted to *The Night of the Hunter*. Jack Moffitt, in a review of Laughton's movie for the *Hollywood Reporter*, felt that with "an especially intelligent selling job, such as was given 'Marty,' the film can probably be a financial success."[9] No such "selling job" materialized, partly because the marketing strategists seemed uncertain how to promote a film that did not fit easily into any genre.

Ads on the days leading up to the film's opening in Los Angeles featured individual pictures of Gish, Winters, and Mitchum. The marketers evidently hoped that personalities alone could draw in audiences, and there would be no need to define the film. Yet in oblique ways—unfortunately, not ways guaranteed to attract an audience—the copy in each ad refers to significant aspects of *The Night of the Hunter*. The picture of Gish is accompanied by words that evoke the silent era and point to Laughton's desire for the excitement he discovered in D. W. Griffith: "A great star brings the old greatness back to motion pictures . . . with a new warmth!"[10] The Mitchum and Winters ads touch on the unusual nature of the film, as though the marketers felt compelled for some sort of truth in advertising. I have italicized the pertinent words: "Robert Mitchum in a chilling performance unequalled in stature . . . *unconventional* in its sheer terror!"[11] "Shelley Winters dares to step into the *off-beat* role of a woman too hungry for love to see terror!"[12] An ad that features the ensemble of players does not attempt to define the film except in the most general terms: "Towering above all others . . . a motion picture that will not be easily matched or forgotten!" The pictures of the cast below the empty words reveal little about the nature of the characters or the drama. Winters is posed in the center of the ad, looking voluptuous in a low-cut dress with pearls around her neck.[13] This is the alluring actress whom Hollywood had been intent on creating at the start of Winters's career and now seemed reluctant to abandon for the sake of Laughton's film. (The "glamorous Shelley," as Winters wryly calls herself, is well documented in photographs from her autobiography, *Shelley: Also Known as Shirley*.)

Another ad more sensibly focuses on the film as a work of terror and suspense, even if the headline is a typical Madison Avenue gimmick: "The TERRORific Suspense Hit of the Year!" The centerpiece of the ad is a picture of Mitchum and Winters embracing against the backdrop of a full moon and dark clouds. Mitchum, looking at once romantic and fiendish, holds Winters with the hand labeled *love* while behind her back he clenches a knife with the fingers marked *hate*.[14] The mixture of lyricism and violence in the picture captures an important quality of the film. It would become a central image in the film's marketing, serving, for example, as the main picture on a five-foot, "full color standee" for theater lobbies.[15] Yet unless one has read the book, which, as a reminder to the audience, is granted a small image toward the bottom of the ad, one would have no idea that the plot turns on children being chased by the man with the knife. The idea of Mitchum threatening children might, one imagines, turn an audience away. But Mitchum threatening a submissive woman, especially if she is in a negligee, is a marketable idea. Therefore, another ad presents even more forcefully the film as a sexual conflict between a man and a woman. While Mitchum stands towering and stern in his vest and tie, Winters, wearing a nightgown, kneels at his side, tugging on his arm and gazing up at him with a pleading face. A quotation that is from neither the novel nor the film gives only a vague sense of what this supposedly marital drama is all about: "This morning we were married . . . and now you think I'm going to kiss you, hold you, call you my wife!" Words at the bottom of the ad do not clarify the situation: "The scenes . . . the story . . . the stars . . . but above all—the suspense!!!!"[16] The four exclamation points suggest the desperation of the marketers, who hope that punctuation will make an audience rush out to experience the suspense.

Tucked away in *The Night of the Hunter* study collection at the Library of Congress is an image by Saul Bass that points to a different sort of advertising campaign. Bass was an artist who had already created titles for Otto Preminger's *Carmen Jones* (1954) and who would become famous for imaginative title sequences on such films as *Vertigo* (1958), *North by Northwest* (1959), and *Walk on the Wild Side* (1962). To accompany a trade announcement that principal cinematography on *The Night of the Hunter* had been completed, Bass designed a picture of a black-sleeved arm jutting down into the frame. Fingers marked *hate* clench the neck of a rag doll, which dangles in midair, its smiling face tipped upside down. The stark image, a graphic depiction of innocence in the grip of evil, cuts to the essence of Grubb's novel and Laughton's film. Bass, however, apparently did no further work on *The Night of the Hunter,* and the film's advertising campaign followed a less imaginative path.

There were other promotions, many of them outlined in a packet of publicity ideas from the Arthur P. Jacobs public relations firm.[17] One can see that *The Night of the Hunter* received a more thorough promotional push than has generally been acknowledged. In April 1955, the *Los Angeles Herald and Express* serialized the film's screenplay.[18] Dell Publishing released a thirty-five-cent paperback edition of Grubb's novel, which became the center of a "promotional campaign valued at $210,000."[19] Van Heusen shirts joined the ballyhoo by running an ad featuring Mitchum in *Life* magazine and promoting the film with posters in stores that carried Van Heusen products.[20] Pieces about the film appeared in many periodicals, including *Collier's*, which published a fascinating comparative study of five Grubb drawings and five stills of the same scenes from the movie.[21] Paragraphs about Gloria Pall, the burlesque dancer in the film, even appeared in *Tops* magazine, the June cover of which trumpeted the lead article: "Jackie Gleason: TV's Sexmaster!" In a photo on page 27, Pall poses half dressed with Laughton, who is showing her a copy of the script (no doubt to show her exactly where to bump and where to grind).[22] On a more dignified plane, Laughton, introduced by Gregory, appeared on NBC radio just before the film's release, where he read excerpts from Grubb's novel to the accompaniment of Schumann's music.[23] (This sounds like a preview of the recording that was eventually released by RCA.) Other radio spots used a five-minute recorded interview with Laughton and Mitchum and "announcements stressing the suspense elements of the film."[24] Television promotions included plugs from Edward R. Murrow and, in what Gregory called a "unique and special kind of promotion," a live performance of scenes from the film by Mitchum, Gish, Winters, and Peter Graves on *The Ed Sullivan Show*.[25] Gregory also sent copies of the novel to film reviewers. In a page-long letter to Louella Parsons, he says, with perhaps a whiff of irony, "Knowing your very busy schedule, I thought that it might very easily be that, while you would intend to go and get [the book], it might slip your mind. So please know that it gives me great pleasure to herewith place in your hands the fabulous new novel, *The Night of the Hunter*, by Davis Grubb."[26] The effort in this case earned results. Her words stream above an ad that promotes the film as an adaptation of the best-selling novel: "Terrifying and brooding! 'Night of the Hunter' is the most completely different horror movie I have ever seen!" (quoted in *HH*, 347).

Louella Parsons, Ed Sullivan, Dell Publishing, and Van Heusen combined were unable to generate audiences for the film. Sterling reviews might have helped, but with few exceptions notices for *The Night of the Hunter* were not the kind that make people rush out to their local theaters.

Certainly the film had its champions. In *Photoplay*, Janet Graves hails it as "a suspense masterpiece," in which Laughton "uses the camera with the greatest imagination."[27] Charlotte B. Speicher of *Library Journal* admires the "remarkable, even loving, fidelity" to Grubb's novel and says that "in its sensitivity, its imaginative and often poetic photography, its haunting musical score, its skillful blending of hymns, and especially in its gripping, nerve-wracking narrative power, it proves an important and memorable achievement."[28]

At the other extreme were a few outright negative reviews. Although Dick Williams in the *Mirror-News* "found Davis Grubb's superb suspense story . . . one of last year's most absorbing novels," he believes that the film "got consciously arty and symbolic and it [presumably the artiness] lies like a heavy marsh fog over portions of this episodic picture."[29] In the same vein, Robert Kass in the *Catholic World* feels that Laughton "has so shrouded all of the suspense in symbolism and gracefully beautiful but meaningless camera shots that his film has all the clarity of a mud puddle by moonlight."[30] (At least the film inspired some reviewers to try their own hand at poetic flights of language.) Hazel Flynn of the *Daily NewsLife* is less concerned with the film's aesthetics. She notes the film's connection to Universal horror films and to *The Cabinet of Dr. Caligari* but therefore condemns the work for its "sustained terror" and possible ill effects on "the minds of children." In the same moralistic vein, she says, "Mitchum has long been under fire from church and other elements, and since he masquerades as a man of the cloth here— the role, despite the fact that he does a good acting job, is in bad taste."[31]

Nevertheless, most reviewers tried to balance praise and criticism, if not always in ways that offered a ringing endorsement of the film. Michael Winner, writing in *Films and Filming*, says, "Mr. Laughton has something of real worth to offer" in a film that "has some of the finest black-and-white photography I have ever seen." But then he adds, "Regrettably he seems so busy with new effects that he forgets these are only a means to an end."[32] Bosley Crowther in the *New York Times* admires the way Laughton catches "the ugliness and terror of certain ignorant, small-town types. . . . The scene of the wedding-night of Miss Winters and the preacher is one of the most devastating of its sort since Von Stroheim's 'Greed.'" Yet Crowther dislikes the stylization in the film, which "angles off into . . . strange, misty scenes composed of shadows and unrealistic silhouettes."[33] On the other hand, to William K. Zinsser at the *New York Herald-Tribune*, "silhouettes of houses and barns . . . look like a Thomas Hart Benton etching come to life. [Laughton] arranges patterns of night-time lights and shadows to create a dramatic effect." Even so, Zinsser feels that "sometimes Laughton gets too arty for his own good," though he concludes, "'The Night of the Hunter' has so much imagination that we can forgive these excesses."[34]

Robert Golden tells a story about a United Artists executive offering Laughton his opinion of the film: "It's too arty." To which Laughton replied, "What the hell do you know about art?"[35] One wonders whether Laughton responded in the same way, or worse, to the critics. Nearly every review, whether sympathetic or not, levels the charge of "artiness" at the film and thereby works against the picture's commercial success. A movie that is "too busy being arty to be scary" hardly sounds appealing.[36] Gregory, however, believed that despite tepid reviews, he "absolutely could have sold [the film]."[37] Impossible as it is to know how Gregory's efforts might have fared, one can say that he would have had a difficult time overcoming resistance to the film. The very nature of *The Night of the Hunter* militated against its acceptance by audiences in 1955.

Out of Sync

Jack Ravage paints the following picture of the era in which Laughton's film was released:

> The mid-fifties was a time in which the mass movie audi-
> ence was being inundated by CinemaScope productions,
> with highly saturated color and "spectacular" subject
> matter, such as *The Robe* (1953, Twentieth Century-Fox),
> *Oklahoma!* (1955, Magna Pictures), and *Around the World
> in Eighty Days* (1956, United Artists). Television was the
> new demon on the block and the studios were fighting for
> what they perceived to be their very existence. . . .
>
> It would seem a bad time for any studio to make a
> small-budget, black-and-white motion picture about sex,
> violence, religion, and child abuse.[38]

Yet sex, violence, and religion (minus the child abuse) were staples of many big-budget, color productions of the 1950s. The problem for

Laughton was not that he used those topics, but that he chose to be serious about them. *The Night of the Hunter* came out during a time of "'biblical blockbusters' and insipid trivialities . . . offered under the guise of 'religious films.'"[39] These biblical epics were nothing new in Hollywood history; they were part of a recurring cycle. At the very dawn of cinema, filmed versions of passion plays, occasionally fleshed out with slides, lectures, hymns, and organ music for presentations of ninety minutes or more, became popular spectacles.[40] Over the next fifteen years or so, when moving pictures were under attack from various moral quarters, producers of story films naturally turned to the Bible "to deal with the industry's most vociferous opponents, the clergy."[41] During the latter-day crisis of the fifties, in a contest with that "new demon," television, producers once more looked to the Bible not for spiritual comfort but for economic salvation. Where the earliest biblical films had stressed authenticity (Vitagraph even hired the Reverend Madison C. Peters as a consultant for its five-reel sensation *The Life of Moses* [1909–10]) and were careful not to "descend to the level of mere razzle-dazzle showmanship,"[42] the new films were in the mold of religious extravaganzas from the twenties. Indeed, *Quo Vadis* (1951), *Salome* (1953), *The Ten Commandments* (1956), and *Ben-Hur* (1959) were remakes of silent pictures. The full-color sagas of the fifties, like their silent counterparts, use biblical narrative as a means to secular ends. The story of Salome, for instance, undergoes a melodramatic rewrite: Salome (Rita Hayworth) experiences a sudden conversion, dances before King Herod to save John's life, and goes off to hear the Sermon on the Mount with Roman commander Stewart Granger. (Herod is played by Laughton, who was willing to act in the sort of film that ran counter to his directorial work on *The Night of the Hunter*.) As for spectacle, Cecil B. DeMille's VistaVision parting of the Red Sea nearly lives up to its billing as "the Single Most Spectacular Scene Ever Filmed."[43] In nearly every biblical film, scantily clad dancers add to the gleeful sexual quotient. One finds Virginia Mayo bathing naked in *The Silver Chalice* (1954), Victor Mature bare chested as Samson, and Hedy Lamarr as Delilah in assorted pinup poses (*Samson and Delilah* [1949]). All of this is balanced by sanctity. Over *Salome*'s concluding long shot of Christ on the Mount of Olives, the Roger Wagner Chorale chants a hymn while a title appears: "This Was the Beginning." (The religious message is only slightly undercut when Columbia's logo, the lady with her sparkling torch, fades in during the climax of the hymn to give the impression that the studio itself is the new Messiah.) *Quo Vadis* offers images from Christ's life to illustrate the history being recounted by Peter (Finlay Currie), including a re-creation of Leonardo da Vinci's *Last Supper*. The static scenes, each a single shot, are a throwback to the tableau style of the silent era. Unlike Laughton, who uses silent techniques as a way to simplify his storytelling, director Mervyn LeRoy inserts the shots as part of his overall spectacle. The scenes allow the audience to enjoy living pictures of memorable biblical incidents. For the studios, the biblical sagas could be highly profitable. *Quo Vadis* was MGM's biggest moneymaker since *Gone with the Wind* (1939). Paramount's *Ten Commandments* went on "to top $80 million world-wide."[44] Film audiences at the time reveled in a pious hedonism, which they certainly did not find in *The Night of the Hunter*.

Even more than in Grubb's novel, where Willa at least recalls her idyllic honeymoon night with Ben (*NH*, 126–27), sex in Laughton's film is presented in a negative light. The movie becomes a study in the effects of repression. Preacher perverts sex into something filthy that drives him to murder the objects of his lust. Willa forces her frustrated sexual needs into evangelism. Icey's self-denial leads to an emptiness in her married life and an unsavory interest in Willa's relations with men. Only Rachel exhibits a healthier view of sex, when she demonstrates a sensitive understanding of a young woman's sexual desire. In a line that James Agee wrote for her, Miz Cooper responds to Ruby's lustful adventures by saying, "Child! You were lookin' for love, Ruby, in the only foolish way you knew how." (The line in Agee's first draft reads, "you was lookin' for *love,* poor child, the only foolish way you knowed how" ["NH," 238].)

Religion in *The Night of the Hunter* is also a somber matter. When Andrew M. Greeley claims that "American filmmakers have produced movies about religion, movies which use religion, movies which exploit religion to titillate or terrify, but no religious movies," he overlooks *The Night of the Hunter*.[45] The film does terrify its audience, but part of that terror comes from its portrait of faith deformed. At the heart of the movie is a conflict between a religion driven by hatred and a religion rooted in love. Ending as it does on Christmas morning, when children have been delivered from evil, *The Night of the Hunter* comes down on the side of Christian belief, yet the progress toward that resolution forces the audience to look into the dark places of faith. In its depiction of religious hypocrisy, on both Preacher's grandiose scale and the everyday scale of the townsfolk, *The Night of the Hunter* takes the audience on an uncomfortable journey, not a pleasant tour of Sunday-school pictures come to life.

The censors, still hard at work in 1955, provide a glimpse of how some people at the time reacted to the film's portrayal of unwholesome religion. On May 19, 1955, the Legion of Decency gave the film a class B designation ("Morally Objectionable in Part for All") because of "suggestive sequences [that tend] to degrade the dignity of marriage." In October 1955, the Protestant Motion Picture Council deemed the film "objectionable" and said flatly, "This study in human terror will be offensive to most religious people."[46] When the movie opened in Memphis, Tennessee, the chairman of the city's censorship board, Lloyd T. Binford, banned the movie. In a letter to Tony Tedesco, the Memphis branch manager for United Artists, Binford called the film "the rawest I've ever seen."[47] The force of his eyewitness outrage is lessened somewhat by the fact that he never saw the film. He later admitted that only three female members of the board had attended a screening, and he explained that "he did not intend to imply by his letter that he had seen [the picture]."[48] According to Gregory, such opposition hurt the film commercially. Yet he had a plan to use that opposition to generate controversy and publicity. "I was going to instigate a major lawsuit. . . . I was being denied by the archdiocese the distribution of the film in Wyoming. And I was going to go after them. . . . I was all set to go with the thing, and then United Artists wouldn't let me have anything to do with it."[49]

The Night of the Hunter's spiritual battle between falsity and truth, though manifest in the plot and in the performances of Mitchum and Gish, finds its deepest expression within the visual scheme of the film. The picture's "unique style," as David Ashley King puts it, reveals a "spiritual presence" that carries the work "beyond the realm of the thriller genre to become a religious film."[50] Basing his argument on ideas in Paul Schrader's *Transcendental Style in Film*, King makes a convincing case that the minimalism of the film's design and the way Laughton "uses the devices unique to cinema to transform the ordinary" create a sense of mystery and transcendence.[51] To experience the holy through a film's style, however, requires a profound concentration on the part of the viewer. The fact that so many reviewers could look at Laughton's techniques and see chiefly a surface artiness points up how difficult it is to penetrate to the deeper meanings conveyed by those techniques.

Even an intelligent critic like John Beaufort of the *Christian Science Monitor,* who holds up "the distilled artistry of 'Forbidden Games'" as a contrast to Laughton's "theatricality," finds that "the technique of the telling seems constantly to impede the narrative."[52] He misses the point that the film's narrative moves forward on its style. The story of the children's journey on the river, with its otherworldly peace and its worldly dangers, is told in imagery that oscillates between the dreamlike and the realistic. The children's deliverance from evil is manifest in the way Miz Cooper and her pastoral world are depicted on screen. *The Night of the Hunter* illustrates an assertion by David Bordwell: "Style is not simply window-dressing draped over a script; it is the very flesh of the work."[53]

Out of step with the era's lavish, color spectaculars, *The Night of the Hunter* also stands apart stylistically from other small-scale, black-and-white films of its day. Even at that time of widescreen productions, after all, it was possible for a smaller film without color to reach a wide audience. *Marty,* for instance, released in the same year as *The Night of the Hunter,* was a popular success. The story of a lonely, plain-looking butcher who finds love with a plain-looking woman, the film even swept the Academy Awards for best screenplay (by Paddy Chayefsky, based on his television drama), best director (Delbert Mann), best actor (Ernest Borgnine), and best picture. *Marty* is a well-written, well-made film, but it is also a recognizable type of film: a slice-of-life, kitchen-sink drama. Even without its history as a television play, the movie would have been familiar to the 1955 audience.

In a newspaper article by Bob Thomas, syndicated shortly before *The Night of the Hunter*'s opening, Gregory was at once optimistic and defiant about the appeal of his less-than-familiar film:

> The picture is a departure from the usual methods of film making. Those who hate it are those film makers who insist on following the same patterns that have been established. . . .
>
> Some people say the picture will never sell. These are the same kind who predicted doom for "Don Juan in Hell," which grossed over three million dollars. They said the same about "John Brown's Body," which grossed $1,625,000 and could have gone three million if we had kept touring.[54]

Unfortunately, by grounding his expectations in the way theater audiences accepted the unconventional, Gregory miscalculated the extent to which a film audience would embrace "departure from the usual methods of film making." Critics at the time of the film's release had different ideas about the genre of the work in front of them. It was seen as a film of "helpless terror," a film "entirely in the horror vein," or, to have it both ways, a film of "horror, not unmixed with weird terror."[55] Other critics saw a modern fairy tale and "an authentic American fable" that "evokes some of the magic of *Huckleberry Finn*."[56] Although Grubb's novel can also be seen from many perspectives, each side of the book's eclectic nature fits comfortably into a well-known literary form. It satisfies reader expectations. The film thwarts expectations at nearly every turn.

If, as many ads suggest, *The Night of the Hunter* is a noirish suspense film, then its lyricism and its pastoral scenes are out of place. One would expect a film more like *The Window* (1949) or *Sudden Fear* (1952). *The Window*, set in New York City, is about a boy (Bobby Driscoll) prone to making up stories. He witnesses a murder but cannot make his parents believe him. The killers spend the film tracking the boy down. Both this movie and *The Night of the Hunter* portray violent worlds and a landscape of threatening shadows, but the urban setting makes *The Window* a more typical film noir. Also, the idea of a child alone and in danger is played out in a matter-of-fact manner, without lyrical commentary on the nature of innocence and evil. *Sudden Fear*, shot on location in San Francisco, is another urban noir of deep shadows and pools of light. It combines the romance and menace touted in the ads for *The Night of the Hunter*. Joan Crawford, who is better suited than Shelley Winters to the ad line "a woman too hungry for love to see terror,"[57] discovers that her beloved husband (Jack Palance) plans to murder her. She then creates a counterscheme to kill him. The plot and the structure—a leisurely love affair at the start, cat-and-mouse suspense in the middle, and a chase at the end—are predictable, but in that predictability lies the pleasure of the film. At one point, however, the film employs the techniques of German expressionism. A clock ticks off the seconds, while over a close-up of Crawford's eyes we see what she imagines: stalking her husband, murdering him, and framing his lover (Gloria Grahame) so that she is condemned to death. The sequence has a dreamlike quality, especially when Grahame, wearing a white dress in a black void, hears herself sentenced to die and screams hysterically. The expressionist technique here is used to show how cleverly the heroine's mind works and to give the audience essential information about the stages of the woman's murder scheme. The "arty" effects are made accessible by being knitted into the story. One can almost look past the stylistics of the sequence and concentrate on the plot.

If *The Night of the Hunter*, for all its suspense, lacks the form of a conventional thriller, it looks even less like a horror film of the fifties. The film does match in certain ways one of what Stuart Kaminsky identifies as "seven branches of the American horror film." Laughton's movie falls into category number 3, where the horror stems from "corrupt humans who worship evil." The villains, who sometimes wield knives, "are usually ordinary people whose normal appearance masks evil."[58] Villains in fifties horror films, however, are hardly ordinary, because they are rarely people. With *House of Dracula* in 1945, the long series of Universal horror movies came to an end, though a trio of monsters gathered again for a comic fling in *Abbott and Costello Meet Frankenstein* (1948). For several years there was a lull in the horror genre, and then in 1951 the Thing from another world emerged from the ice of the Arctic and ushered in a wave of science-fiction horrors. In this new cinematic age, a host of monsters came from the sky (*Invaders from Mars* [1953], *Earth Versus the Flying Saucers* [1956]), from the deep (*The Beast from 20,000 Fathoms* [1953], *Creature from the Black Lagoon* [1954], on which one of the art directors was Hilyard Brown), and from the earth when scientific experiments went wrong (the giant ants of *Them!* [1954], the giant spider in *Tarantula* [1955]. As outsized as Mitchum's Preacher is, the horror associated with him is less apocalyptic than that of aliens and sea beasts and gigantic bugs. And there is little psychological complexity in a rampaging behemoth or a hungry arthropod. Audiences at the time found the instinctive drives of such creatures more interesting than the complex psychology of a murderous religious fanatic.

Viewers who think *The Night of the Hunter* "makes a bid for the 'art' class of film" will find the work atypical even in that sphere.[59] In his book *Narration in the Fiction Film*, David Bordwell points out that "art-cinema narration" frequently calls attention to the film itself as "a construct," perhaps through "odd ('arty') camera angles" or through "stylized treatment of situations, settings, or props."[60] In these ways at least, *The Night of the Hunter* falls into the category of art cinema. But in other ways, it still fits the mold of classical cinema, which even at its best, as Lawrence W. Levine makes clear in *Highbrow/Lowbrow,* is often perceived as a "popular" cinema on the "lowbrow" end of a cultural hierarchy.[61] *The Night of the Hunter* maintains the "ongoing causal chain" of events common to classical cinema.[62] It is composed of segments that fit logically together in "smooth, careful linearity." Its protagonist, John Harper, is not the "drifting protagonist" whom Bordwell often finds in the art film, but rather a character who struggles to achieve specific goals—in this case, eluding Preacher and finding sanctuary.[63] Laughton, as an actor, a stage director, or a film director, had little use for distinctions between the "popular" and the "artistic." For him, it was perfectly natural to combine two modes of narration. For many viewers, it is a bewildering experience to watch a film that is a kind of narrational superimposition—say, an art-cinema horror movie. Even Terry Sanders once admitted, "I love the film, but it's very strange."[64]

Apart from its paradoxical form, *The Night of the Hunter* looks strange in comparison to other movies of its era because of its silent-film techniques. Leo Braudy, in his 1976 book *The World in a Frame,* makes a distinction between films of an "open style," in which "the world of the film is a momentary frame around an ongoing reality," and those of a "closed style," in which "the world of the film is the only thing that exists." To Braudy, "the closed style is potentially more static and pictorial and thus was the perfected product of the silent-film period." The color and sweep of many films in the fifties represented new explorations of the open style, where "the inner space of film could be expanded to farther and farther horizons." Thus, in the fifties "a truly enclosed film began to have a touch of the archaic about it." He identifies *The Night of the Hunter* as just such an "enclosed film." Although he speaks of "directors, writers, and cameramen" in the fifties as trying "to find a new synthesis, a new way of telling stories, that could eclectically mingle the best of the open and closed styles," he does not acknowledge that Laughton and his crew were using cinematic techniques from the past in a self-conscious manner as part of the director's own eclectic scheme.[65] Whatever the merits of Braudy's comments about the film, or about his open and closed classification, his view of *The Night of the Hunter* is a plausible representation of how filmgoers in the fifties saw Laughton's work. At a time when DeMille and others were dusting off silent films to refurbish them with a new gloss for a modern audience,

Laughton unveiled studied imitations of D. W. Griffith that looked "archaic" indeed.

The Night of the Hunter's unusual form separates it even from films of the fifties to which it is closer in theme and attitude. Emanuel Levy in *Small-Town America in Film* points out that "in the decade's most characteristic films, life in small towns was depicted as emotionally stifling, intellectually suffocating, and sexually repressive." In the typical narrative pattern of such films, an outsider arrives in town, disrupts an equilibrium, and precipitates conflicts of various kinds.[66] (The outsider narrative is not, of course, limited to films of the fifties. At a writing seminar, I once heard the novelist John Gardner say, with only a touch of facetiousness, that all literature boiled down to two plots: someone arrives in town; someone leaves town.) Levy's examples include *Picnic* (1955), *All That Heaven Allows* (1955), and *Peyton Place* (1957). *The Night of the Hunter* shares with these films a critical attitude toward small-town life. It even shares a similar ironic establishing shot with *All That Heaven Allows*. When first seen in Laughton's overhead shot, Cresap's Landing has the quaint charm of a peaceful river town. The view is not unlike Douglas Sirk's high-angle view of his deceptively idyllic Stonington, Connecticut. Each film is, in its own way, stylized, but otherwise Laughton's sui generis work is distinct from Sirk's romantic melodrama. The compression, even claustrophobia, of Laughton's film is still further removed from the entertaining, high-class soap opera contained in the multiple story lines of *Peyton Place* (four families, an exponential increase in personal and social traumas). And *Picnic,* for all the repressions and emotional voids within its story, has an expansive quality, a buoyancy, that allowed audiences at the time to enjoy it as a "romantically photographed episode in the national heartland."[67]

The Naked and the Dead

Although Laughton's film was at odds with cinematic trends of its era, Gregory was determined to keep Laughton up to date on the publishing front. He had bought the rights to yet another first novel, this one acclaimed as a significant literary event: *The Naked and the Dead* (1948), by Norman Mailer. Despite *The Night of the Hunter*'s disappointing reception, Laughton forged ahead on this new adaptation. It was a project that had long been in the works. In a letter to Agee dated April 16, 1954, Ilse Lahn passed along the news that Gregory wanted Agee to write the picture that would follow *The Night of the Hunter*. Gregory was secretive about the title, but Lahn surmised that it was *The Naked and the Dead*.[68] A few months before, Agee himself had included Mailer's novel in a list of jobs for film and television that were "embryonic, or hanging fire," though he mentioned no producer in connection with the project.[69] In Gregory's inquiry about Agee, just at the time screenwriting began on *The Night of the Hunter*, one can sense an eagerness to work with the versatile author. Yet there is no further record of interest in Agee for the Mailer film. By the following April, a month before Agee died of a heart attack in New York City, a newspaper article about *The Night of the Hunter*'s imminent release mentioned that Denis and Terry Sanders were "now associated with Paul Gregory on 'The Naked and the Dead.'"[70] Laughton's young protégés had indeed been hired to work on the screenplay. Given Laughton's eventual feelings about Agee's work, it is no surprise that Gregory did not employ Agee again. Other members of *The Night of the Hunter* crew, however, did reconvene with the Sanders brothers for the new film. Hilyard Brown returned as art director and "got a lot of work done" on the picture.[71] Milton Carter was back as assistant director. Stanley Cortez began planning the cinematography and was even sent to Hawaii with Carter to scout locations.[72] Laughton's preparations for the film sound like those for *The Night of the Hunter*. Once again, Laughton met with the novelist of the work he was adapting. Mailer recalled working with Laughton "for four or five days in his suite at the St. Moritz going through the book page and paragraph discussing every aspect of the movie." And once again Laughton asked his author to provide drawings of characters from the novel. When Mailer said, "'I don't know how to do it,' [Laughton] snorted and said, 'Nonsense, Mailer, anyone can draw. You go ahead and do it and that will give me some idea of what you have in your mind that you can't express.'"[73] Conferences about the script with the Sanders brothers were, as usual, interspersed with Laughton's readings from Dickens or Shakespeare, and gourmet lunches were once more provided by Heidel, the cook who so delighted *The Night of the Hunter* crew.[74]

Even apart from readings and lunches, however, the work proceeded slowly. After about six months, according to Terry, "it dawned on me that Charles didn't *want* to finish the script."[75] William Phipps, a close friend of Laughton's who acted out scenes from the screenplay as it was being written, noted that Laughton "was almost in despair" over his inability to adapt Mailer's novel. "I remember, he was very frustrated about that. . . . He couldn't get it to where he could say, 'This'll be a movie, I can shoot this'" (*HH,* 371). The Sanders brothers, eager to move on to other projects, grew impatient. "It was drawn out too long," said Terry, "so finally, very amicably, we resigned. . . . We had to. It would have gone on another six months."[76] Laughton eventually completed a screenplay on his own. In light of his outrage over Agee's long first draft for *The Night of the Hunter,* it is ironic that he himself delivered a long, dense draft of the Mailer adaptation. Gregory had found financial backing from a Philadelphia entrepreneur, William Goldman, but when Goldman was told that Laughton would need another year to revise the script, he refused to put up any more money. Laughton's work on the project came to an end.[77]

Separate Ways

The collapse of *The Naked and the Dead* also signaled the end of the professional relationship between Gregory and Laughton. Gish had once said to Laughton, "I hope nothing ever happens to you and Paul and your friendship." The intensity of his shocked response—"What, what could happen, what do you mean?"—surprised her. She said simply that "something could happen, time can change everything." Yet when things did finally change, she said, "I was shocked by their parting and have always wondered what came between them or what happened."[78] It is still not clear what happened exactly. Lanchester says that Laughton dissolved the partnership for personal reasons.[79] According to Gregory, Laughton's lawyer swayed his client to make the split for professional reasons (*HH,* 361). One can imagine that a collaboration between two such strong-willed men would have its share of strains, both personal and professional. What is clear from conversations with Gregory is that the relationship could be both deeply satisfying and difficult. In the end, whatever the precise reasons, the five-year partnership was ended swiftly, without ceremony, and each partner went his own way.[80]

Gregory's first task was to see *The Naked and the Dead* through to completion. Terry and Denis Sanders wrote an entirely new script, and the project ended up at Warner Bros., where Jack Warner offered one suggestion to Terry: "Don't have these guys slipping around in shit."[81] The Sanders draft, which Mailer admired, was eventually rewritten by other hands.[82] Directed by Raoul Walsh, the film that came out in 1958 was, as Terry put it, "a typical Warners World War II–type guts and glory movie. . . . It was basically a rape of the book."[83] Yet it was a commercial success. "*That* property just grossed millions and millions and millions," said Gregory, "and it was a lousy picture. Disheartening" (*HH,* 373). Gregory concentrated on such television work as *Crescendo,* a *DuPont Show of the Month* with Rex Harrison and an all-star musical cast (directed by Bill Colleran, CBS, September 29, 1957), and on theater. His interest in unusual stage presentations led him to produce Norman Corwin's dramatization of the Lincoln-Douglas debates, *The Rivalry,* which toured the country in 1957 with Raymond Massey, Martin Gabel, and Agnes Moorhead, and a *Hamlet* with Judith Anderson in 1970.[84] He also produced a more conventional work, *The Marriage-Go-Round,* a 1958 comedy with Charles Boyer, Claudette Colbert, and Julie Newmar, which ran on Broadway for more than a year.[85] It was, by Gregory's own admission, his "biggest success," even if it did not give him the "artistic satisfaction" of other projects (*HH,* 361). Trying to balance the artistic and the commercial became more and more disheartening, and when the entertainment business stopped entertaining him, he retired to Palm Springs, California.[86]

After the break with Gregory, Laughton went on to act in four more films: *Witness for the Prosecution* (1957), *Under Ten Flags* (1960), *Spartacus* (1960), and *Advise and Consent* (1962). Whatever disappointments he experienced as a film director did not lessen his intensity as an actor. The Laughton perfectionism, bane of such directors as William Dieterle and Josef von Sternberg, was a delight to Billy Wilder, cowriter (with Harry Kurnitz) and director of *Witness for the Prosecution:* "There were twenty versions of the way he could do a scene, and I would say, 'That's it! All right!' And then the next day, on the set, he comes and he says, 'I thought of something else.' And that was version number twenty-one. Better and better all the time."[87] Laughton also went back to the theater. He starred in and directed two plays: *Major Barbara* on Broadway (1956) and *The Party,* a new play by Jane Arden, in London

(1958). The following year, he went to Stratford-upon-Avon, where he played Bottom, in *A Midsummer Night's Dream,* and King Lear.[88]

When *The Night of the Hunter* came out, some reviewers saw it as the harbinger of a new, illustrious career for Laughton. To a critic in *Variety,* the film was "rich in promise of things to come." Another *Variety* critic agreed: "As a piece of film craftsmanship, 'Hunter' sometimes is brilliant, stamping Charles Laughton as a future important, creative director of pictures."[89] Two days after Bosley Crowther reviewed the film, he wrote a follow-up piece in the *New York Times* about first-time directors. Most of the article was devoted to Laughton. After carefully weighing the virtues and flaws of *The Night of the Hunter,* Crowther concluded, "One senses conglomeration and deliberate virtuosity in this film. Mr. Laughton was flexing his muscles. He'll hit harder next time, we feel sure."[90] But there was no next time. Although the theater still welcomed Laughton as a director, he never made another film. He died of bone cancer on December 15, 1962.

If one thinks of what Laughton achieved in *The Night of the Hunter,* it is tantalizing to imagine what else he might have accomplished on screen. Terry Sanders felt certain that if Laughton had directed *The Naked and the Dead,* "it would have been a great film." Gregory concurred: "*The Naked and the Dead* was not a war story; it was about men in war. And Laughton would have been superb."[91] Denis Sanders gave a sense of Laughton's continued interest in experimenting with the film medium: "Charles had a number of innovations in mind for [*The Naked and the Dead*]. He wished to show a sort of circular motion so that the person on the screen would be on the borders and his thoughts would be revealed in the center of the screen. It was an effect that he could never completely work out, but they were talking a great deal about doing their flashbacks in the actual order, going backwards rather than flashing back to a scene and then going forward chronologically. The idea was not used, but it was an intriguing one."[92] The "flashbacks in reverse" were Laughton's way of incorporating sections from the novel that Mailer titled "the time machine." These passages, reminiscent of the biographical sketches in the John Dos Passos trilogy *U.S.A.* (1937), periodically interrupt the narrative to give brief histories of the characters. Laughton's attempt to use the character sketches, while finding a distinctive way to film them, reveals him as a director once more looking to combine a faithful rendition of the novel with unconventional cinematic techniques. Whether Laughton's *Naked and the Dead* would have been "a great film" or not, his work on the project reinforces what we can surmise from *The Night of the Hunter:* had Laughton continued to make films, he would have been no commonplace director.

To Grubb, Laughton expressed his desire to make a movie of Thomas Wolfe's novel *You Can't Go Home Again* (1940), and on the last day he and Grubb ever saw each other, Laughton talked about making another film together. "We'll have a success next time," he said.[93] The close of Laughton's film-directing career has an almost tragic irony, in that his work abruptly ended just at the moment he discovered what might have been his ultimate vocation. *The Night of the Hunter* was the culmination of his life in film and of his many other interests. Callow makes the point eloquently: "Laughton had found, it would seem, his métier. Everything in his experience contributed to it: his love and knowledge of art, his gifts in shaping a script, his ability with actors, his deep immersion in all the process of movie-making. The man who loved words but could not write, the man who loved art but could not paint, the man who had authority but preferred to work with collaborators, had found his brush, his pen, his team."[94]

Cortez believed that *The Night of the Hunter*'s poor reception "broke Charles Laughton's heart," and Gregory felt that the film's box-office failure "devastated Charlie."[95] If so, it is especially poignant that Laughton did not live to see what Gregory, Cortez, and many others on the crew of *The Night of the Hunter* were able to witness: the film's critical reappraisal and its rebirth.

Nine

IT ENDURES

Reassessment

"I did at first think Laughton had ruined *The Night of the Hunter*," Davis Grubb told Preston Neal Jones. "His film was faithful to my book, but it wasn't faithful to the film I'd had in my head while I was writing it. . . . Since then, I've seen the film many times, and I've come to appreciate it for the fine work it is. . . . I think it's a wonderful picture, and I wouldn't want to change a single thing about it" (*HH*, 363). Grubb's shifting view of Laughton's adaptation mirrors historical changes in the response of audiences and critics. Rejected at the box office and sold off quickly by United Artists to television at a time when "Hollywood didn't allow movies that new to be shown on TV,"[1] *The Night of the Hunter* is now eagerly received on the repertory circuit and routinely billed as "an American classic."[2] New generations of critics praise aspects of the work once condemned as arty. Douglas Brode, writing in 1976, says, "The film juxtaposes the most obvious studio shots with vividly realistic images; but instead of clashing, they mesh into a strikingly original vision."[3] To Moylan C. Mills in 1988, the director's "stylistic daring . . . and his masterful manipulation of the mise-en-scène . . . enable Laughton to intensify the basic material. . . . *The Night of the Hunter* can be judged in retrospect as a work of cinematic brilliance."[4] In lauding the film, later critics implicitly support strong words by Stanley Cortez in defense of Laughton: "To me, the word 'arty' is a disgraceful, horrible, insulting word to use, it has connotations of being phony, or pretentious, of bad taste, of kitsch—all the things that Charles Laughton was not" (*HH*, 359).

For viewers schooled in films of the sixties and seventies, *The Night of the Hunter* appears less peculiar than it did on its first release. Alongside Jean-Luc Godard's *Weekend* (1967), a film both funny and grotesque that combines bourgeois drama, fantasy, and revolutionary rant, Laughton's eclecticism seems almost cautious. Laughton's mingling of classical narrative strategies with art-cinema techniques is less foreign to a viewer who has seen a Hollywood gangster story told in the elliptical, ambiguous manner of an art film (Godard's *Bande à part* [1964], François Truffaut's *Tirez sur le pianiste* [1960], or Jean-Pierre Melville's *Le doulos* [1962]). Laughton's self-conscious use of styles and genres from Hollywood's past align him with American filmmakers like Robert Altman, Roman Polanski, and Martin Scorsese, who refashion earlier forms for their own purposes (the Western in *McCabe and Mrs. Miller* [1971], the film noir in *Chinatown* [1974], and the musical in *New York, New York* [1977]). When *The Night of the Hunter* came out, it was easy to patronize the film as the first effort of a new director because, it was assumed, he would follow it with other, better movies. To a later generation, Laughton's only film becomes an object valued for its rarity. Even the work's flaws, often the slips of a brilliant novice, gain a certain charm.

In 1992, almost forty years after its release, *The Night of the Hunter* was selected by the Library of Congress for its National Film Registry, which was established in 1988 to preserve films "deemed 'culturally, historically, or aesthetically important.'"[5] By 2006, the Hollywood establishment also deemed the film important enough and classifiable enough to be included in a montage tribute to film noir at the Academy Awards.[6] While the film was being transformed from a failure to an established classic, Robert Gitt was overseeing the restoration of *The Night of the Hunter*'s outtakes. That work led to the restoration of the film itself. Image and sound were returned to their original clarity, and the impressive result, along with a sampling of outtakes, was unveiled at the New York Film Festival in 2001. Gitt has since toured internationally with a presentation called "Charles Laughton Directs *The Night of the Hunter*," in which he comments knowledgeably on a careful selection of outtakes.[7]

Cultural Artifact

Even before widespread acceptance of *The Night of the Hunter,* the film had entered the consciousness of popular culture. In his 1981 book *Cult Movies,* Danny Peary listed *The Night of the Hunter* among films that "are swiftly becoming cult favorites."[8] Six years before Peary's book, however, *Films and Filming* had already acknowledged the status of Laughton's film by including it as part of a series on "the cult movies."[9] An early piece by Ian Johnson, published in 1963, has the quality of a cultist's appreciation. The article, "And a Little Child Shall Lead Them," is largely a detailed synopsis of the film, as though Johnson, like an enthusiast who has just made a thrilling discovery, feels compelled to tell others about his find. Brief commentary on what he calls "a strange and wonderful film" is written in an awestruck, impressionistic vein: "We are children once more and the Devil may walk tonight. Shadows cast themselves in Gothic quadrangles, pools of darkness hold we know not What. A heavy chill envelops deep mystery, things unexplained. Beautiful, ugly, wonderful things. There is much to be discovered."[10] In the 1975 film *The Rocky Horror Picture Show,* bad-boy biker Eddie (Meatloaf) grips the handlebars of his cycle with fingers tattooed *love* and *hate. Rocky Horror* became the center of its own cult at midnight screenings, and the film's allusion to Preacher points up the cultish delight that cinephiles took in *The Night of the Hunter.*

Other allusions, however, carry Laughton's film beyond cult status. J. Hoberman, in an article about the film's 1992 revival at New York's Public Theater, points out more substantive references to the film: "Attuned as they are to *echt* Americana, the rock intelligentsia have recognized *The Night of the Hunter* as archetypal. *Rolling Stone* titled its classic 1970 report on Charles Manson 'Year of the Fork, Night of the Hunter'; Greil Marcus cites the movie in *Mystery Train* to contextualize the devils that haunted Robert Johnson."[11]

Preacher's tattooed fingers are of particular fascination for song-writers and filmmakers who look to contextualize their work. The frustration and fury within Preacher's hands epitomize the dark land-scape of "Death or Glory," a 1979 song by the punk-rock group the Clash:

Every cheap hood strikes a bargain with the world,
And ends up making payments on a sofa or a girl,
Love 'n' hate tattooed across the knuckles of his hands,
The hands that slap his kids around 'cause they don't
understand . . .
How death or glory becomes just another story.[12]

Bruce Springsteen adapts the image not for violence but for pathos in
his song from 1987, "Cautious Man," about Bill Horton, a "man of the
road" who settles down with a bride but lives suspended between two
worlds with an inner "coldness . . . that he couldn't name":

On his right hand Billy'd tattooed the word love and on his
left hand was the word fear
And in which hand he held his fate was never clear.

In the ambiguous conclusion of Springsteen's ballad, the murderous
image of Preacher standing over Willa's bed flickers behind this quiet,
poignant scene:

At their bedside he brushed the hair from his wife's face as
the moon shone on her skin so white
Filling their room in the beauty of God's fallen light.[13]

On film, Spike Lee uses the image of Preacher to add irony and
resonance to *Do the Right Thing* (1989), his story of racial tensions on a
sweltering summer day in Brooklyn. Lee's film counterpoints love and
hate. In keeping with the film's polarities, Radio Raheem (Bill Nunn)
wears gold brass knuckles that read *love* and *hate*. The outsized version
of Preacher's tattoos is fitting for a muscular character who towers over
everyone else and carries a giant boom box, which he plays at earsplit-
ting volume. "That boy's livin' *very* large," says one observer. Raheem
is by no means a villain, but like Preacher, he is an unsettling character
full of rage. At one point, he delivers Preacher's sermon "Right-Hand-
Left-Hand" directly to the camera in his own street lingo: "Hate! It was
with this hand that Cain iced his brother. . . . One hand is always fightin'
the other hand, and the left hand is kickin' much ass." Raheem's boxing
match between the hands is more violent than Preacher's arm wrestle;

the right hand of love becomes a battering fist. The pantomimed fight, in which love conquers hate, ironically prefigures the violent climax in which Raheem, having tried to kill Sal (Danny Aiello) for smashing his radio, is choked to death by a cop. At the instigation of Mookie (Spike Lee), a raging mob, unlike the mob in *The Night of the Hunter,* achieves its goal: Sal's pizza joint is burned to the ground. In Laughton's film, despite lingering anxieties, it is love that triumphs. In Lee's film, despite an uneasy rapprochement between Mookie and Sal, it is hate that triumphs. These reversals add texture to *Do the Right Thing,* which, like Laughton's work, stands outside the usual Hollywood fare in its subject matter, form, and mingling of tones.

A 1993 episode of *The Simpsons* contains a lighter homage that circles back to the early allusion in *The Rocky Horror Picture Show.* Sideshow Bob prepares to murder Bart Simpson, and as he lifts weights we see that his fingers bear tattoos similar to Preacher's. Sideshow Bob has only three fingers, however, so his tattoos read *luv* and *hāt*.[14] The casual nod to *The Night of the Hunter,* embedded in a show that is itself a parody of the Mitchum vehicle *Cape Fear,* illustrates the way Laughton's film has become a common point of reference. Nevertheless, a *Simpsons* Web site notes that many viewers saw Sideshow Bob's tattoos as a reference to *The Rocky Horror Picture Show.* One cult film occasionally trumps another.[15]

The Story Continues

Another version of Grubb's novel was made for television (ABC, 1991). Directed by David Greene, the film features Richard Chamberlain as Preacher and Burgess Meredith as Birdie, though now the old man has no bearing on the plot; he is merely John Harper's friend. In 1954, Laughton felt compelled to reproduce as many scenes as possible from a novel that had sold well and was fresh in the public's mind. The film-makers in 1992 were less concerned with fidelity to what was no longer a well-known book. Apart from a few scenes and the basic story of a false preacher terrorizing children to learn the secret of stolen money, very little from the novel ends up on the screen. Ben (Ray McKinnon) does not kill anyone, and he is not executed. Preacher inadvertently murders him in a prison hospital. It is John (Reid Binion) who hides the money in Pearl's doll. But it is Pearl (Amy Bebout) who flings the money at Preacher near the end. In swimming after the money in the river, Preacher is pulled over a waterfall to his death. The most significant change is the elimination of Miz Cooper. Without Rachel and her battle against Preacher, the film lacks the allegorical overtones of a spiritual war between good and evil. This production is interested only in the melodrama of a villain threatening a poor family. That melodrama could still make for a good, if less textured, movie. The changes to the novel do not in and of themselves hurt the film. Where the movie suffers chiefly is in its failure to develop its characters. When John and Pearl walk home together at the end of the film, John says, "The road's gonna be dark. But there's no monsters and no creepy-crawlies." Pearl replies, "That's okay, John. I ain't scared anymore." Unfortunately, the film has not provided any emotional connection to her fears, and it has not given a strong enough sense of John's determination to protect Pearl. Dialogue periodically hints at Preacher's life as an abused child, but the clues to his past do not give him the dimension that the screenwriter, Edmond Stevens, hoped for. And Mrs. Spoon (Mary Nell Santacroce) remains a distant character, even though the filmmakers work hard to make her sympathetic: in a wheelchair, she oversees a doll factory, which allows her the chance to give Pearl a gift of the all-important doll.

Comparison with Laughton's film is inevitable and, in this case, draws attention to all that Laughton achieved in his cinematic transformation of the story. The television movie updates the rural setting to contemporary times, and though the poverty of the region is stressed, one misses the Depression atmosphere and the sense of an entire society threatened from within that are an integral part of the original film. The movie is in color, but apart from the murder of Willa (Diana Scarwid) in the headlights of a car, color is not used to create mood or emotion. One waits in vain for color effects comparable to the arresting visuals created in black and white by Cortez. A mood of terror is generally lacking in the remake. It is typical of this version that the children escape from Preacher in broad daylight. They spend only a few minutes on the river—no lyrical journey here—before Preacher, chasing them in a car, catches up to their boat. The actors, especially Richard Chamberlain in a mustache and slicked-back hair, also dim by comparison. Chamberlain delivers the sermon "Right-Hand-Left-Hand" from the pulpit of a church, but even in his dominant position at the altar he is a feeble preacher. His version of the struggling hands is barely a finger wrestle, with none of Mitchum's thundering force. A *Night of the Hunter* without a charismatic Preacher is no *Night of the Hunter*.

In 1996, *The Night of the Hunter* turned up onstage. Lonny Price directed a reading of a work in progress, a musical based on Grubb's novel, with music by Claibe Richardson and book and lyrics by Stephen Cole. The score was subsequently recorded and released on CD.[16]

Cole makes a significant change for his book: he eliminates Uncle Birdie. One misses hearing Birdie say, in reference to his wife's photograph, "Dead and gone these twenty-five years and never takes her eyes off me," or seeing him rock drunkenly while he prays, "Sweet heaven, save poor old Uncle Birdie," yet leaving him out helps to streamline the story for the musical stage. Otherwise, the libretto follows the book closely. It includes bits left out of Laughton's movie, such as the children's references to the "blue men" and a scene in which Icey, Walt, and Willa consult a Ouija board to learn the name of Willa's next husband. Like Agee and Laughton, Cole takes dialogue nearly verbatim from the novel, even using it in his lyrics. In "Wedding Night," for example, Preacher sings to Willa, "You thought that the minute you walked through the door, I would paw you and feel you in the miserable way that men are supposed to. You thought! Ain't that right?" At the end of the show, Rachel sings words from her monologue in the novel, "The wind blows and the rain is cold," though Cole adds his own effective words to her refrain: "And the river runs wild and wide."

Richardson, too, stays close to the spirit of Grubb's novel by incorporating music that evokes America of the thirties: harmonies and rhythms in a Gershwin vein, specifically echoes of *Porgy and Bess* during Preacher's "Right-Hand-Left-Hand" sermon; ragtime for Preacher's account of the widows he has killed (rhythms that suggest he takes perverse pleasure in his murders); and the sound of a burlesque-hall orchestra in "Ruby at the Drug Store." The music, melodic and varied, stands on its own (Ben's fading call to John, "Remember, boy, remember," is especially effective), but it cannot dispel the echoes of Schumann's score. During the river journey onstage, Preacher's continued threat to the children is conveyed by a clash of the lyrical and the atonal. The idea is good, but after one has heard Mitchum's disembodied voice sing, "Leaning . . . leaning," anything else is a disappointment. Even allowing for the different medium, and granted excellent performances by Martin Vidnovic (Preacher), Carolee Carmello (Willa), and Mary Catherine

Wright (Rachel), one misses Mitchum, Winters, and Gish. Laughton's cast has put their stamp too indelibly on the roles for other voices and other personalities to suffice.

Overall, the musical's very fidelity to Grubb's novel works against it because the show calls to mind the same scenes and dialogue in Laughton's film. Also, the musical frames the story as the film does: Rachel opens the show delivering a Bible lesson to a group of children, and she closes it by singing, "They endure and abide." Admittedly, that framing structure, which gives the show a satisfying sense of closure, is irresistible, but its similarity to Laughton's work only invites further comparison. In short, although the musical shapes the novel intelligently and is affecting on the stage, it simply cannot escape the shadow of Laughton's adaptation.

Davis Grubb himself is shadowed by Laughton. In Pedro Almodóvar's film *Talk to Her* (2002), the camera, panning over objects beside the hospital bed of Alicia (Leonor Watling), comes upon a novel with a bookmark in it. The novel that Alicia has yet to finish is a Spanish edition of *The Night of the Hunter*—*La noche del cazador*. On the cover is the familiar image of Mitchum standing at Miz Cooper's back steps. Rare for *Night of the Hunter* allusions, this is a homage to both the novel and the film (Almodóvar adjusts the focus to make certain that we can read the title), yet the image from the film is what registers first and identifies the book. A British edition put out by Prion Books for its Film Ink Series in 1999 also uses a picture of Mitchum on the cover, this time the image of Preacher scowling from his seat in the burlesque house. Where the film had at times been sold with references to the best-selling novel, now the novel is promoted as the source for the well-known film.

It is a film, as Truffaut says, that "makes us fall in love again with an experimental cinema that truly *experiments,* and a cinema of discovery that, in fact, *discovers.*"[17] And it is a film that continues to be a source of discovery. Just as I saw it for the first time on television, my daughter caught her first glimpse of *The Night of the Hunter* on Turner Classic Movies. John and Pearl were in the skiff on the river, and the studio stars were twinkling in the night sky. I was about to begin a Disney sing-along video, but my daughter called out, "No! This!" And she watched, in rapt attention, the entire river journey, the appearance of Miz Cooper, and the bathing of John. She was two years old. The film's evocation of childhood clearly has the power to captivate a child. On the other hand, college students who also had never seen the film expressed their own fascination after a screening at the University of Tennessee in April 2005. *Modern, bizarre,* and *wonderful* were terms they used to describe the work. The cinematography, Mitchum's performance, and the music were singled out for praise. Implicitly, the students were commenting on Laughton's collaborative method. As Barrie Hayne, in program notes for a *Night of the Hunter* screening at the Toronto Film Society, puts it, "Yet though the personal, even eccentric, quality of the vision makes this film distinctly Laughton's, it is also, to varying degrees, Davis Grubb's, James Agee's, Stanley Cortez's, Lillian Gish's, and Robert Mitchum's."[18] One should add at least the names of Billy Chapin, Hilyard Brown, Robert Golden, and Paul Gregory, the motivating force behind the entire adaptation. Gregory once said that Laughton was "basically a teacher."[19] If so, he chose to teach through stories, whether from the stage or from the screen. "So Paul Gregory and I have made a picture called *The Night of the Hunter,* and we hope you like it," Laughton says in an article written several months before the release of his film, when expectations for its success were still high. He concludes: "I know I hope you [like it], as I live to tell you stories as actor or reader or director. And I hope you will want to listen to me until I am too gone to care, which I don't think will happen till I am dead."[20]

Dead and gone these forty years, and the storyteller continues to speak to us.

NOTES

Preface

1. *New York Times*, "Best Seller List," March 14, 1954–July 4, 1954.

2. Higham, *Charles Laughton*, 195–96.

3. Xan Brooks, "The Best Family Films of All Time," *Guardian*, December 10, 2005, http://film.guardian.co.uk/features/featurepages/0,,1663635,00.html.

4. Jones, *Heaven and Hell*, 399 (hereafter cited in notes and parenthetically in text as *HH*).

5. Couchman, "Night," 5.

6. Bluestone, *Novels into Film*, 67.

7. Chatman, *Coming to Terms*, 163.

8. Wagner, *Novel and the Cinema*, 222, 223, 226. For other categories and discussions of fidelity in adaptation, see Beja, *Film and Literature*, 82; Klein and Parker, *English Novel and the Movies*, 9–10; Andrew, *Concepts in Film Theory*, 98–101.

9. Stam, "Beyond Fidelity," 54.

10. Sarris, "Notes on the *Auteur* Theory," 133–34.

11. Paul Gregory, personal interview with the author, Desert Hot Springs, Calif., August 10, 2000.

12. Robert Golden, interview with Nigel Algar (producer-director with Barraclough Carey Productions), Newport Beach, Calif., 1994, for *Night of the Hunter* segment, *Moving Pictures*, BBC2, February 19, 1995. Transcript courtesy of Nigel Algar.

13. Hammond, "Melmoth," 109.

14. Wood, "*Night of the Hunter*," 68.

15. Higham, *Charles Laughton*, 185–86.

16. Neale Lanigan to "Dear Librarian," September 24, 1986, *The Night of the Hunter* clipping file, Billy Rose Theatre Division, New York Public Library for the Performing Arts.

17. Anderson, "Screenwriters Get Their Due."

18. Wood, "*Night of the Hunter*," 70.

19. Robert Gitt, "The Hidden *Hunter*," *Guardian*, June 6, 2003, http://film.guardian.co.uk/features/featurepages/0,4120,971008,00.html.

20. Couchman, "Labor of Love," 92–94.

21. F. X. Feeney, "Night Vision: Charles Laughton Directs," *LA Weekly,* August 9–15, 2002, http://www.laweekly.com/ink/02/38/film-feeney.php.

Introduction

1. Grubb, "Valley of the Ohio," 56.

2. Welch, *Davis Grubb,* 3–4.

3. Grubb, "Valley of the Ohio," 56.

4. Grubb, *Night of the Hunter,* 26 (hereafter cited parenthetically in text as *NH*).

5. Wood, "New Creative Writers," 373.

6. Welch, *Davis Grubb,* 17.

7. Grubb, "Valley of the Ohio," 135.

8. Welch, *Davis Grubb,* 11–12.

9. Grubb to Don Congdon, October 17, 1953, quoted in Welch, *Davis Grubb,* 22.

10. Douglass, foreword to *Fools' Parade,* by Davis Grubb, xx–xxi.

11. Welch, *Davis Grubb,* 30, 49, 51.

12. Don Congdon, "Davis Grubb" (chapter from Congdon's manuscript presently titled "An Agent's Story," n.d.), 57. Reprinted with permission of Don Congdon. All rights reserved.

13. Douglass, foreword to *Fools' Parade,* by Davis Grubb, viii–ix.

14. Grubb, *Fools' Parade,* 115.

15. Grubb, *Barefoot Man,* 143.

16. Ibid., 53.

17. Welch, *Davis Grubb,* 72.

18. Grubb, *Dream of Kings,* 355–56.

19. Grubb, *Fools' Parade,* 249.

20. Ibid., 122.

21. Norman Lloyd, personal interview with the author, New York, N.Y., November 28, 2007; *HH,* 392.

22. Welch, *Davis Grubb,* 56; Davis Grubb, "The Morning After *The Night of the Hunter*" (typescript of unpublished essay, [1974?]), 4. Permission from Estate of Davis Grubb.

23. Callow, *Charles Laughton,* 49.

24. J. Danvers Williams, "Five Years After," *Film Weekly,* February 19, 1938, quoted in Callow, *Charles Laughton,* following page 142.

25. Callow, *Charles Laughton,* 43.

26. Lanchester, *Elsa Lanchester Herself,* 164.

27. "The Epic That Never Was," directed by Bill Duncalf, BBC, December 24, 1965, bonus feature on *I, Claudius,* DVD, directed by Herbert Wise (1976; Chatsworth, Calif.: Image Entertainment, 2000).

28. Callow, *Charles Laughton,* 58.

29. Lanchester, *Elsa Lanchester Herself*, 155.

30. Laughton, *Tell Me a Story*, 1.

31. Viertel, *Kindness of Strangers*, 316.

32. Higham, *Charles Laughton*, 134.

33. Brecht, *Brecht on Theatre*, 165.

34. Brecht, *Life of Galileo*.

35. Brecht, *Brecht on Theatre*, 167–68.

36. Lanchester, *Charles Laughton and I*, 96. The Internet Broadway Database still lists Laughton as director and Jed Harris as producer: *The Fatal Alibi*, by Michael Morton, based on *The Murder of Roger Ackroyd*, by Agatha Christie, Booth Theatre, New York, February 8, 1932–March 1, 1932, http://www.ibdb.com/production.asp?ID=7904.

37. Callow, *Charles Laughton*, 197; Higham, *Charles Laughton*, 146–48, 163.

38. Callow, *Charles Laughton*, 204–6.

39. Gregory, interview with author.

40. Ibid.

41. Johnson, "Art of Paul Gregory," 15–16.

42. "Feature Story Manual," typescript, 1955, p. 50, *The Night of the Hunter* study collection, Motion Picture, Broadcasting and Recorded Sound Division, Library of Congress (hereafter cited as *The Night of the Hunter* study collection).

43. Johnson, "Art of Paul Gregory," 16.

44. Charles Laughton, "How Mr. Laughton Became the Devil," *New York Times Magazine*, March 23, 1952, 21.

45. Johnson, "Art of Paul Gregory," 17.

46. Bob Thomas, "Inside Hollywood: Paul Gregory, Due to Be Honored by Iowa, Has More Unusual Productions Planned," *Newark Evening News*, July 15, 1955.

47. Callow, *Charles Laughton*, 137.

48. "Feature Story Manual," 50–51; *HH*, 34.

49. Johnson, "Art of Paul Gregory," 19–20; Thomas, "Inside Hollywood."

50. Johnson, "Art of Paul Gregory," 20–21.

51. Gregory, interview with author.

Chapter 1

1. Johnson, "Art of Paul Gregory," 21; Gregory, interview with author. Gregory recalled that the Chambord was on Second Avenue. Restaurant listings of the time place the restaurant on Third Avenue near Fiftieth Street ("Restaurants in New York City [Originally Published 1940]," http://www.oldandsold.com/articles06/new-york-city-51.shtml). In a 1950 review of the Chambord, Jane Nickerson says that the restaurant opened in 1936 ("Veal Is Really Good, but How to Cook It? Owner and Chef of Famed Cafe Explain," News of Food, *New York Times*, May 30, 1950).

2. Higham, *Charles Laughton,* 155.

3. *Time,* "The Happy Ham," March 31, 1952, http://www.time.com/time/magazine/article/0,9171,935604,00.html. An episode guide for *Toast of the Town,* the original name of *The Ed Sullivan Show,* on TV.com shows that Laughton was on the CBS broadcast of March 6, 1949 (http://www.tv.com/toast-of-the-town/show/5696/episode_guide.html?season=2&tag=season). A clip from that appearance is included in *The Ed Sullivan Show: 10th Anniversary,* CBS, June 23, 1958 (available for on-site viewing at the Paley Center for Media, New York). There are few "balletlike turnings," because Laughton is seated in an armchair in front of imposing bookshelves, peering through glasses at the Bible he holds in his lap. For a finale he removes his glasses and intones the concluding lines of his tale to the audience. The performance is intimate, restrained, and compelling. A complete rendition of the "fiery furnace" story can be heard on an audio recording that is similar in tone to Laughton's *Toast of the Town* recitation (*Charles Laughton: Readings from the Bible,* Decca 33 rpm DL-8031, [1958?]). Laughton presented another, more theatrical reading of the "fiery furnace" scene on *The Ed Sullivan Show,* February 14, 1960 (http://www.tv.com/the-ed-sullivan-show/show/1156/episode_guide.html?season=13&tag=season_dropdown;dropdown;12). The performance is a bonus feature on the DVD *Inspirational Treasures from "The Ed Sullivan Show"* (New York: Good Times Entertainment, 2003). For his reprise of the 1949 appearance ("Ed asked me to read the first thing I read on his show," he tells us), Laughton stands on a darkened stage beside a lectern, never looks at the Bible, and this time does employ "turnings" and gestures to accompany his more flamboyant presentation. A clip of that second reading is in *The Ed Sullivan Show: 15th Anniversary,* June 23, 1963 (available for on-site viewing at the Paley Center for Media). Sullivan, in his inimitable way, mistakenly introduces the clip as "the late Charles Laughton in his TV debut."

4. Johnson, "Art of Paul Gregory," 22.

5. Gregory, interview with author; Harris, *Always on Sunday,* 74. According to the Internet Broadway Database, the Maxine Elliott Theater was named CBS Studio 51 in 1949 (http://www.ibdb.com/venue.aspx?id=1267).

6. Peter Graves, telephone interview with the author, January 29, 1996; "The Ed Sullivan Show," TV.com, http://www.tv.com/the-ed-sullivan-show/robert-mitchum---lillian-gish---rocky-marciano/episode/116884/summary.html?tag=ep_list;ep_title;0. Electronic and print sources give conflicting dates for the Sullivan show's change of title, citing either September 18, 1955, or September 25, 1955. Contemporary television listings, however, prove that the title was *Toast of the Town* on September 18 and *The Ed Sullivan Show* on September 25. See, for instance, *Independent Press-Telegram* (Long Beach, Calif.), September 18, 1955, and September 25, 1955, http://www.newspaperarchive.com/.

7. Gregory, interview with author.

8. Lanchester, *Elsa Lanchester Herself,* 201–2.

9. Laughton, "How Mr. Laughton Became the Devil," 21; *Time,* "Happy Ham."

10. Callow, *Charles Laughton*, 208.

11. Johnson, "Art of Paul Gregory," 35–37.

12. Laughton, *Tell Me a Story*, 1–2; "Mr. Pickwick's Christmas," read by Charles Laughton, music by Hanns Eisler, 1944, side 2 of *Charles Dickens Classics: "A Christmas Carol" and "Mr. Pickwick's Christmas*," MCA, audiocassette MCAC-15010, 1983.

13. Lanchester, *Elsa Lanchester Herself*, 194.

14. Johnson, "Art of Paul Gregory," 63–64.

15. George Bernard Shaw, *Don Juan in Hell*, directed by Charles Laughton, Columbia Masterworks, 33 rpm SL-166, 1952.

16. Benét, *John Brown's Body*, xvi.

17. Stephen Vincent Benét, *John Brown's Body*, adapted and directed by Charles Laughton, Columbia Masterworks, 33 rpm SL-181, 1953.

18. Lanchester, *Elsa Lanchester Herself*, 167.

19. Norman Corwin, e-mail to author, July 15, 2005; Stephen Vincent Benét, *John Brown's Body*, directed by Norman Corwin, *Columbia Workshop*, CBS, July 20, 1939, The Vintage Radio Place, compact disc 51676, http://www.OTRSite.com.

20. Higham, *Charles Laughton*, 181.

21. Seymour Peck, "Play from the Log of the *Caine*," *New York Times*, January 17, 1954. The play opened to generally excellent notices that often praised the restraint of Laughton's direction (see Johnson, "Art of Paul Gregory," 158, and Callow, *Charles Laughton*, 227). Brooks Atkinson, for instance, writes, "Having had some very basic experience with concert-style drama, Mr. Laughton is not loading the play down with non-essentials" (At the Theatre, *New York Times*, January 21, 1954). *Caine Mutiny* ran from January 20, 1954, to January 22, 1955 (http://www.ibdb.com/production.asp?ID=2435).

22. Laughton, *Fabulous Country*, 49.

23. Hilyard Brown, personal interview with the author, Los Angeles, August 9, 1995.

24. Edwin Schallert, "Hollywood's Still No. 1 to Gregory," *Los Angeles Times*, January 23, 1955.

25. Hardwicke, *Victorian in Orbit*, 270.

26. Johnson, "Art of Paul Gregory," 95.

27. Massey, *Hundred Different Lives*, 355–56.

28. Johnson, "Art of Paul Gregory," 131, 157.

29. Schallert, "Hollywood's Still No. 1."

30. James Agee, *Night of the Hunter*, in *Agee on Film*, vol. 2, 292 (hereafter cited parenthetically in text as *AF*). Copyright © 2009 by The James Agee Trust, reprinted with permission of The Wylie Agency.

31. Benét, *John Brown's Body*, Columbia Masterworks SL-181.

32. Johnson, "Art of Paul Gregory," 97.

33. Schumann, "*Night of the Hunter*," 13, 15.

34. Johnson, "Art of Paul Gregory," 44.

35. Jacques Barzun, Notes, *Don Juan in Hell,* by George Bernard Shaw, Columbia Masterworks SL-166.

36. Singer, *Laughton Story,* 259.

37. Massey, *Hundred Different Lives,* 356.

38. Johnson, "Art of Paul Gregory," 98.

39. James Agee, "The Night of the Hunter," typescript of final screenplay, 1954, Script Collection, Margaret Herrick Library, Academy of Motion Picture Arts and Sciences, Beverly Hills, Calif. (hereafter cited as "Margaret Herrick Library"). Copyright © 2009 by The James Agee Trust, reprinted with permission of The Wylie Agency.

40. Benét, *John Brown's Body,* Columbia Masterworks SL-181.

41. Lillian Gish, summary of conversation with unknown interviewer, New York, N.Y., December 18, 1967, p. 5, Elsa Lanchester papers, Margaret Herrick Library.

42. Gregory, interview with author.

43. Paul Gregory, interview with Nigel Algar (producer-director with Barraclough Carey Productions), Los Angeles, Calif., 1994, for *Night of the Hunter* segment, *Moving Pictures,* BBC2, February 19, 1995. Transcript courtesy of Nigel Algar.

44. Ibid.

45. Ibid.

46. Johnson, "Art of Paul Gregory," 27.

47. Higham, *Charles Laughton,* 157.

48. Johnson, "Art of Paul Gregory," 28.

49. Gregory, interview with author.

50. Preliminary Inventory, Paul Gregory Collection, American Heritage Center, University of Wyoming (Laramie).

51. Lanchester, *Elsa Lanchester Herself,* 203.

52. *This Is Charles Laughton,* produced by Paul Gregory, 1953, rereleased by Quality Productions, 1977, Motion Picture, Broadcasting and Recorded Sound Division, Library of Congress; *Charles Laughton: Readings from the Bible,* Decca, 33 rpm DL-8031, [1958?]; *The Story-Teller: A Session with Charles Laughton,* Capitol, 33 rpm (2 discs) STBO 1650, [1961?].

53. Johnson, "Art of Paul Gregory," 70–73, 109–10; *Don Juan in Hell,* Carnegie Hall, October 22, 1951; New Century Theatre, November 29, 1951–December 31, 1951; Plymouth Theatre, New York, April 6, 1952–May 24, 1952, http://www.ibdb.com/production.asp?ID=12833; *John Brown's Body,* New Century Theatre, February 14, 1953–April 11, 1953, http://www.ibdb.com/production.asp?ID=2217.

54. Houseman, "Drama Quartette"; *Time,* "Happy Ham."

55. Higham, *Charles Laughton,* 157.

56. *The Night of the Hunter,* by Davis Grubb, produced by Paul Gregory, narrated by Charles Laughton, music by Walter Schumann, orchestration by Arthur Morton, recorded August 26, 1955, compact disc, RCA, 74321720532, 1999.

57. Gregory, interview with author.

58. Laughton, *Tell Me a Story*, 169.

59. Lanchester, *Elsa Lanchester Herself*, 204.

60. Callow, *Charles Laughton*, 239.

61. Lanchester, *Elsa Lanchester Herself*, 235–36.

62. Gregory, interview with author.

63. *HH*, 50; Davis Grubb, summary of conversation with unknown interviewer, [1968?], p. 1, Elsa Lanchester papers, Margaret Herrick Library.

64. Gregory, interview with author.

65. Grubb, summary of conversation with unknown interviewer, 1.

66. Gregory, interview with author.

67. Grubb, summary of conversation with unknown interviewer, 1.

Chapter 2

1. Douglass, foreword to *Fools' Parade*, by Davis Grubb, xiii; *HH*, 51.

2. Laughton, *Tell Me a Story*, 20, 192.

3. Grubb, summary of conversation with unknown interviewer, 1.

4. Allen, "New Novels," 51; Jackson, "A Study in Human Terror"; Hughes, "Novels Reviewed," 72; Prescott, Books of the *Times*.

5. *Time*, "Killer in Cresap's Landing," 92; Anthony West, "Arcadia Run to Seed," 121.

6. Palmer, *Thrillers*, 132.

7. Carroll, *Philosophy of Horror*, 99.

8. *The Handbook to Gothic Literature*, ed. Marie Mulvey-Roberts (New York: New York University Press, 1998), s.v. "Terror" (by David Punter), 235.

9. Wilt, *Ghosts of the Gothic*, 5.

10. Punter, *Literature of Terror*, 1: 40–44.

11. Palmer, *Thrillers*, 122.

12. MacAndrew, *Gothic Tradition in Fiction*, 7.

13. Walpole, *Castle of Otranto*, 25.

14. Lewis, *Monk*, 383.

15. Punter, *Literature of Terror*, 1:62; Radcliffe, *Italian*, 23, 43.

16. Lewis, *Monk*, 387.

17. Messadié, *History of the Devil*, 275.

18. Lewis, *Monk*, 156.

19. Maturin, *Melmoth the Wanderer*, 230–34.

20. Ibid., 323.

21. Sage, introduction to *Melmoth*, by Charles Robert Maturin, xxv.

22. Welch, *Davis Grubb*, 59.

23. Carroll, *Philosophy of Horror*, 4.

24. Ibid., 16.

25. Christopher Morley, "*The Night of the Hunter* by Davis Grubb," *Book-of-the-Month Club News*, February 1954, 6.

26. *Handbook to Gothic Literature,* s.v. "American Gothic" (by Allan Lloyd Smith), 2, 3. The first nine chapters of *Arthur Mervyn* were published in *Weekly Magazine* during 1798. Hence Smith's date in the text. The entire first part of *Arthur Mervyn*—twenty-three chapters—was published as a book in 1799. The second part of the novel came out in 1800. Hence the dates in my list of works cited. (Brown, *Three Gothic Novels,* 903–4.)

27. Ringe, *American Gothic,* 13.

28. Brown, *Wieland,* 159.

29. Brown, *Edgar Huntly,* 641.

30. Ringe, *American Gothic,* 50.

31. MacAndrew, *Gothic Tradition in Fiction,* 244.

32. *Handbook to Gothic Literature,* s.v. "Southern Gothic" (by A. Robert Lee), 217–20.

33. Warren, *World Enough and Time,* 27.

34. O'Connor, *Wise Blood,* 59–60, 110–11, 116–22.

35. Ibid., 8, 126.

36. Ron Havern, "Havern's Grubbiana," typescript, variously dated summaries of conversations between Havern and Grubb, January 16–18, 1981, p. 6, Davis Grubb Collection, Clarksburg-Harrison Public Library, Clarksburg, W.Va.

37. O'Connor, *Mystery and Manners,* 44.

38. Melville, *Moby Dick,* 308.

39. O'Connor, *Wise Blood,* 110–11.

40. Faulkner, *As I Lay Dying,* 356.

41. Wolfe, *Look Homeward, Angel,* 1.

42. Wolfe, *Of Time and the River,* 345.

43. Grubb to Congdon, February 2, 1953, quoted in Welch, *Davis Grubb,* 57.

44. Twain, *Life on the Mississippi,* 29.

45. Twain, *Adventures of Huckleberry Finn,* 97.

46. Margaret Atwood, "Why I Love *Night of the Hunter,*" *Guardian,* March 19, 1999.

47. Welch, *Davis Grubb,* 39.

48. Strong, "New Novels," 70.

49. Arnow, "Youth and Terror," 19.

50. Allen, "New Novels," 51.

51. Caldwell, *Tobacco Road,* 119.

52. Jacobs, "Humor of *Tobacco Road,*" 285.

53. Fiedler, *Love and Death,* 134.

54. Havern, "Havern's Grubbiana," July 19, 1980, p. 3.

55. Douglass, foreword to *Fools' Parade,* by Davis Grubb, xiv.

56. Atwood, "Why I Love *Night of the Hunter.*"

57. King, "*Christ-Haunted,*" 43.

58. Alpert, "Terror on the River," 21.

59. Terry Sanders, production notebook for second-unit locations on *The Night of the Hunter,* personal collection of Sanders.

60. Bettelheim, *Uses of Enchantment,* 11.

61. Ibid., 8–13.

62. Davis Grubb, "Rough Script for RCA Victor Recording of *The Night of the Hunter,*" spring 1955, p. 1, *The Night of the Hunter* study collection. Permission from Estate of Davis Grubb.

63. Welch, *Davis Grubb,* 160.

64. Rohmer, *Insidious Dr. Fu-Manchu,* vi, 2.

65. Welch, *Davis Grubb,* 14–15.

66. Douglass, foreword to *Fools' Parade,* by Davis Grubb, xix.

67. Pyle, *Merry Adventures of Robin Hood,* 1–4.

68. Pyle, *Otto of the Silver Hand,* 4.

69. Grubb, *Twelve Tales of Suspense and the Supernatural.*

70. Grubb, note "To Whom It May Concern," preface to "Gentleman Friend," May 8, 1974, A&M 2797, West Virginia and Regional History Collection, Charles C. Wise Library, Morgantown. Permission from Estate of Davis Grubb.

71. Welch, *Davis Grubb,* 27–28.

72. Havern, "Havern's Grubbiana," February 6, 1981, p. 1; July 19, 1980, p. 4.

73. Grubb, "Gentleman Friend," typescript of unpublished story, August 10, 1950, p. 12, A&M 2797, West Virginia and Regional History Collection, Charles C. Wise Library, Morgantown (hereafter cited parenthetically in text as "GF"). Permission from Estate of Davis Grubb.

74. James Agee, "The Night of the Hunter," typescript of first-draft screenplay, 1954, p. 112, box 4, folder 29, James Agee and James Agee Trust Collection, Special Collections, University of Tennessee (hereafter cited parenthetically in text as "NH"). Copyright © 2009 by The James Agee Trust, reprinted with permission of The Wylie Agency.

75. Welch, *Davis Grubb,* 27.

76. Douglass, foreword to *Fools' Parade,* by Davis Grubb, xiii.

77. Callow, *Night of the Hunter,* 12, 18.

78. Allen, "New Novels," 51–52.

79. Anthony West, "Arcadia Run to Seed," 122.

80. Holzhauer, "Children of Night," 123.

81. Ibid.

82. Anthony West, "Arcadia Run to Seed," 122.

83. Don Congdon, "Davis Grubb," 58 (see introduction, n. 12).

84. Herbert F. West, "A Heritage Full of Dread," 4–5; Baro, "A Terrifying and Impassioned Narrative," 5; Cavendish, "Magic of Fine Writing," 5.

85. Arnow, "Youth and Terror," 19.

86. Herbert F. West, "A Heritage Full of Dread," 4, 5.

87. Hughes, "Novels Reviewed," 72.

88. Baro, "Terrifying and Impassioned Narrative," 5.

89. Jackson, "Study in Human Terror."

90. *New York Times Book Review,* "Best Seller List," March 14, 1954–July 4, 1954.

91. *Book-of-the-Month Club News,* February 1954, 5.

92. *Reader's Digest Condensed Books.* Other works in the volume are *God and My Country,* by MacKinlay Kantor, *Not as a Stranger,* by Morton Thompson, *The Best Cartoons from France,* edited by Edna Bennett, and *The Young Elizabeth,* by Jennette and Francis Letton.

93. Terry Sanders, personal interview with the author, Santa Monica, Calif., August 7 and 11, 2000.

94. Ibid.

95. Gregory, interview with author.

Chapter 3

1. Welch, *Davis Grubb,* 50, 78.

2. Grubb, "Morning After," 5 (see introduction, n. 22).

3. Harvey, "*Night of the Hunter,*" 48.

4. Douglass, foreword to *Fools' Parade,* by Davis Grubb, xvi.

5. Harvey, "*Night of the Hunter,*" 48.

6. Laughton to Grubb, n.d., ca. April 1954, quoted in Jones, "Heaven and Hell to Play With," 88–89.

7. Grubb to Laughton, April 19, 1954, *The Night of the Hunter* study collection. Permission from Estate of Davis Grubb.

8. Johnson, "Art of Paul Gregory," 228.

9. Gregory, interview with author.

10. Allan, "Widows and Orphans, Beware!" 72.

11. Davis Grubb, letter "To Whom It May Concern," preface to drawings for Charles Laughton, August 10, 1973, *The Night of the Hunter* sketches, Margaret Herrick Library. Permission from Estate of Davis Grubb.

12. Davis Grubb, "The Bottom Lands," research maps for *The Night of the Hunter,* April 30, [1954], Elsa Lanchester papers, Margaret Herrick Library. Grubb inadvertently dated the maps 1953 instead of 1954. Permission from Estate of Davis Grubb.

13. Hilyard Brown, personal interview with the author, Los Angeles, August 9, 1995; Stanley Cortez, personal interview with the author, Los Angeles, August 11, 1995; Robert Golden, personal interview with the author, Newport Beach, Calif., August 8, 1995; Gregory, interview with author; Seymour (Sy) Hoffberg, personal interview with the author, Woodland Hills, Calif., August 12, 1995.

14. Gregory, interview with Algar.

15. Denis Sanders, summary of conversation with unknown interviewer, May 29, 1968, p. 2, Elsa Lanchester papers, Margaret Herrick Library; Brown, interview with author.

16. Fultz, "Poetry and Danger of Childhood," 97.

17. Ibid. The words that Fultz quotes are from *NH,* 72.

18. Eisner, *Haunted Screen*, 17.

19. *The Penguin Dictionary of Literary Terms and Literary Theory*, 4th ed., ed. J. A. Cuddon (rev. C. E. Preston) (New York: Penguin, 1998), s.v. "Expressionism."

20. Cortez, interview with author; Terry Sanders, interview with author.

21. Higham, *Charles Laughton*, 187.

22. Gloria Pall, "Gloria Pall Page," http://www.gloriapall.com/gpall.htm.

23. Brown, interview with author.

24. Turner, "Creating *The Night of the Hunter*," 1337.

25. Grubb, "To Whom It May Concern," *The Night of the Hunter* sketches.

26. Grubb to Laughton, April 19, 1954, p. 5, *The Night of the Hunter* study collection.

27. Grubb, "To Whom It May Concern."

Chapter 4

This chapter incorporates my article "Credit Where Credits Are Due: The Agee-Laughton Collaboration on *The Night of the Hunter*," from *Agee Agonistes: Essays on the Life, Legend, and Works of James Agee*, ed. Michael A. Lofaro (Knoxville: University of Tennessee Press, 2007).

1. Welch, *Davis Grubb*, 50; *HH*, 40–41.

2. Gregory, interview with Algar.

3. Gregory, interview with author.

4. Grubb, summary of conversation with unknown interviewer, 2 (see chap. 1, n. 63).

5. Ibid., 1.

6. Ibid., 3.

7. Gregory, interview with author.

8. Bergreen, *James Agee*, 364, 389–90.

9. Folks, "James Agee's Filmscript," 153.

10. Wolfe, "Thomas Wolfe to F. Scott Fitzgerald," 643.

11. Server, *Robert Mitchum*, 267.

12. Gregory, interview with Algar.

13. John Collier, *The African Queen*, typescript, April 11, 1947, John Huston papers, Margaret Herrick Library; Grobel, *Hustons*, 366; Huston, *Open Book*, 213–15.

14. Agreement to write *The Night of the Hunter* screenplay for Gregory Associates, signed by James Agee, May 31, 1954, *The Night of the Hunter* study collection.

15. Terry Sanders, interview with author; Gregory, interview with author.

16. Terry Sanders, interview with author; Gregory, interview with author; Robert Mitchum, interview with Nigel Algar (producer-director with Barraclough

Carey Productions), Santa Barbara, Calif., 1994, for *Night of the Hunter* segment, *Moving Pictures,* BBC2, February 19, 1995. Transcript courtesy of Nigel Algar.

17. Johnson, "Art of Paul Gregory," 217.

18. Higham, *Charles Laughton,* 188.

19. Bergreen, *James Agee,* 392.

20. Paul Sprecher, e-mail to author, August 11, 2003.

21. Ibid.

22. Kashner and MacNair, *Bad and the Beautiful,* 185.

23. Seib, *James Agee,* 106.

24. Taylor, review of *Agee on Film,* 47.

25. Barson, *A Way of Seeing,* 169.

26. Higham, *Charles Laughton,* 188.

27. Lanchester, *Elsa Lanchester Herself,* 236.

28. Grubb, "Morning After," 5 (see introduction, n. 22).

29. Agee and Evans, *Let Us Now Praise,* 365.

30. Laughton to Agee, April 12, 1954, box 1, folder 21, James Agee and James Agee Trust Collection, Special Collections, University of Tennessee. I am grateful to John Wranovics, author of *Chaplin and Agee: The Untold Story of the Tramp, the Writer, and the Lost Screenplay* (New York: Palgrave, 2005), for discovering the letter and bringing it to my attention.

31. Grubb to Laughton, April 19, 1954, 1–2, *The Night of the Hunter* study collection.

32. Bergreen, *James Agee,* 392.

33. Agee to Paul Gregory, January 14, 1955, *The Night of the Hunter* study collection.

34. Gregory to Reva Frederick, July 2, 1954, *The Night of the Hunter* study collection.

35. Gregory to Winters, July 29, 1954, *The Night of the Hunter* study collection.

36. Lanchester, *Elsa Lanchester Herself,* 236.

37. Terry Sanders, interview with author.

38. Agee to Gregory, January 14, 1955, *The Night of the Hunter* study collection.

39. Laughton to Agee, April 12, 1954, James Agee and James Agee Trust Collection.

40. Lanchester, *Elsa Lanchester Herself,* 236.

41. Agee to Laughton, April 1954, *The Night of the Hunter* study collection.

42. Server, *Robert Mitchum,* 268.

43. Agee to Laughton, April 1954, *The Night of the Hunter* study collection.

44. James Agee, "Interiors and Exteriors for *The Night of the Hunter,*" typescript, n.d., ca. June 1954, 2–3, Elsa Lanchester papers, Margaret Herrick Library.

45. Gish, summary of conversation with unknown interviewer, 3–4 (see chap. 1, n. 41).

46. Robert Mitchum, telephone interview with the author, August 22, 1995.

47. Gow, "Cult Movies," 48.

48. Burch, *Life to those Shadows,* 214–16.

49. Grubb to Laughton, April 19, 1954, 2–3, *The Night of the Hunter* study collection.

50. Stanley Cortez, interview with Nigel Algar (producer-director with Barraclough Carey Productions), Los Angeles, 1994, for *Night of the Hunter* segment, *Moving Pictures,* BBC2, February 19, 1995. Transcript courtesy of Nigel Algar.

51. Ibid.

52. Kramer, *James Agee,* 64.

53. Agee, "Notes for a Moving Picture," 48, 55, 53.

54. Agee, *Noa Noa,* 6.

55. Grubb, summary of conversation with unknown interviewer, 3–4.

56. Callow, *Night of the Hunter,* 22–24.

57. Callow, *Charles Laughton,* 230.

58. Callow, *Night of the Hunter,* 79.

59. Gregory to Kohner, July 3, 1954; July 9, 1954; July 15, 1954; July 22, 1954; July 29, 1954; August 5, 1954, Paul Kohner papers, Archiv der Stiftung Deutsche Kinemathek, Berlin, Germany. I am indebted to the indefatigable John Wranovics for providing me with copies of the Kohner correspondence.

60. Lahn to Agee, August 23, 1954, Paul Kohner papers.

61. Laughton to Agee, memo, July 16, 1954, *The Night of the Hunter* study collection. Laughton had good reason to be concerned about the Breen Office, the moral watchdog of the American film industry. Formally known as the Production Code Administration (PCA), the office was headed for twenty autocratic years (1934–54) by a former journalist and public relations executive named Joseph I. Breen. The PCA read every script from every studio in Hollywood to evaluate, among a long list of moral concerns, language, sexual propriety, and respect for religion. No film could be profitably released without the Production Code Seal. For a lively history, see Leff and Simmons, *Dame in the Kimono.* The Production Code and various amendments are printed in Steinberg, *Reel Facts,* 459–75.

62. Laughton to Mrs. James Agee, cable, May 19, 1955, *The Night of the Hunter* study collection.

63. Agee to Gregory, January 14, 1955, *The Night of the Hunter* study collection.

64. Fitzgerald, "Memoir," 85.

65. Gregory, interview with author; *HH,* 102.

66. Gregory to Agee, February 10, 1955, *The Night of the Hunter* study collection.

67. Macdonald, "Jim Agee, a Memoir," 176.

68. Folks, "James Agee's Filmscript," 152.

69. Feeney, "Let Us Now Praise James Agee," *Written By* (forthcoming). Manuscript courtesy of F. X. Feeney.

Chapter 5

1. Hilyard Brown, interview with Nigel Algar (producer-director with Barraclough Carey Productions), Los Angeles, 1994, for *Night of the Hunter* segment, *Moving Pictures*, BBC2, February 19, 1995. Transcript courtesy of Nigel Algar.

2. Golden, interview with author.

3. Brown, interview with author.

4. Turner, "Creating *The Night of the Hunter*," 1274.

5. Golden, interview with author.

6. Brown, interview with Algar.

7. Cortez, interview with Algar.

8. Brown, interview with author.

9. Brown, interview with Algar.

10. Brown, interview with author.

11. Gregory, interview with Algar.

12. Gregory, interview with Algar; Brown, interview with author.

13. Brown, interview with author.

14. Brown, interview with Algar.

15. Terry Sanders, interview with author.

16. Terry Sanders, interview with Algar. Lanchester gives a vivid picture of Heidel as an essential member of the Laughton household, *Elsa Lanchester Herself*, 189–90.

17. Denis Sanders, summary of conversation with unknown interviewer, 1–2 (see chap. 3, n. 15).

18. Cortez, interview with author.

19. Lahn to Agee, August 23, 1954, Paul Kohner papers.

20. Mitchum, telephone interview with author.

21. Robert Mitchum, summary of conversation with unknown interviewer, June 20, 1968, p. 6, Elsa Lanchester papers, Margaret Herrick Library.

22. Mitchum, telephone interview with author.

23. Gish, summary of conversation with unknown interviewer, 4 (see chap. 1., n. 41).

24. Gregory, interview with author.

25. Gish, summary of conversation with unknown interviewer, 4.

26. Brown, interview with author.

27. Cortez, interview with Algar.

28. Gregory, interview with Algar.

29. Gregory, interview with author.

30. Gregory, interview with Algar; Gregory, interview with author.

31. Gregory, interview with Algar.

32. Cortez, interview with author.

33. Golden, interview with author.

34. Ibid.

35. Ibid.

36. Ibid.

37. Hilyard Brown, "From the Cast and Crew of *The Night of the Hunter*," drawing, autumn 1954, *The Night of the Hunter* study collection.

38. Golden, interview with author.

39. Brown, interview with author.

40. Ibid.

41. Ibid.

42. Bauer, "Oedipus Again," 624.

43. Lanchester, *Elsa Lanchester Herself,* 189.

44. Golden, interview with Algar; Mitchum, interview with Algar.

45. Roizman, "ASC Close-up," 104.

46. Higham, *Hollywood Cameramen,* 167; Cortez, interview with Algar; Cortez, interview with author.

47. Higham, *Hollywood Cameramen,* 100.

48. Cortez, interview with Algar.

49. Higham, *Hollywood Cameramen,* 101–3.

50. Brady, *Citizen Welles,* 326.

51. Higham, *Hollywood Cameramen,* 110–11.

52. Cortez, interview with author.

53. Turner, "Creating *The Night of the Hunter*," 1274.

54. Callow, *Charles Laughton,* 202.

55. Turner, "Creating *The Night of the Hunter*," 1274; Cortez, interview with author; *HH,* 82.

56. Higham, *Hollywood Cameramen,* 111.

57. Cortez, interview with Algar.

58. Higham, *Hollywood Cameramen,* 99.

59. Brady, *Citizen Welles,* 319.

60. Cortez, interview with author.

61. Lanchester, *Elsa Lanchester Herself,* 240.

62. Terry Sanders, interview with author.

63. Terry Sanders, production notebook. Jones reproduces the notebook page (*HH,* 267).

64. Brown, interview with author.

65. Brown, interview with Algar.

66. Terry Sanders, production notebook. Jones reproduces a Sanders sketch (*HH,* 266).

67. Cortez, interview with author.

68. Brady, *Citizen Welles,* 320.

69. Carringer, *Making of "Citizen Kane,"* 128, 129.

70. Mitchum, telephone interview with author.

71. Higham, *Hollywood Cameramen,* 115.

72. Grubb, summary of conversation with unknown interviewer, 4 (see chap. 1, n. 63).

73. Higham, *Hollywood Cameramen,* 111.

74. Cortez, interview with author.

75. Cortez, interview with Algar.

76. Brown, interview with Algar.

77. *Encyclopedia of Painting,* 4th rev. ed., ed. Bernard S. Myers (New York: Crown, 1979), s.v. "Expressionism."

78. Internet Movie Database, "*A Midsummer Night's Dream* (1935), Full Cast and Crew," http://www.imdb.com/title/tt0026714/fullcredits. Cortez is listed as "camera operator (uncredited)."

79. Maltin, *Behind the Camera,* 125.

80. Kracauer, *From Caligari to Hitler,* ix; see illustration no. 6 at the back of the book.

81. Brown, interview with author.

82. Hammond, "Melmoth," 109.

83. Eisner, *Haunted Screen,* 123–26.

84. Schatz, *Genius of the System,* 88.

85. Gregory, interview with author.

86. Brown, interview with author; Cortez, interview with author.

87. Cortez, interview with author.

88. Damico, "Film Noir," 95–105.

89. Borde and Chaumeton, "Towards a Definition," 18.

90. Ibid., 20.

91. Durgnat, "Paint It Black," 47–50.

92. Ibid., 49.

93. Ibid., 47.

94. Borde and Chaumeton, "Towards a Definition," 24.

95. Bordwell, Staiger, and Thompson, *Classical Hollywood Cinema,* 76.

96. Borde and Chaumeton, "Towards a Definition," 25.

97. Porfirio, "No Way Out," 92.

98. Truffaut, "Charles Laughton," 120.

99. Johnson, "And a Little Child," 18.

100. Robinson, *History of World Cinema,* 80, 81; Thompson and Bordwell, *Film History,* 63–69.

101. Thompson and Bordwell, *Film History,* 68.

102. Robinson, *History of World Cinema,* 82.

103. *Dallas Times Herald,* "*Night of the Hunter:* Laughton's New Command Post Is From the Director's Chair," August 23, 1955.

104. St. Johns, *Love, Laughter and Tears,* 78–79.

105. Gish, summary of conversation with unknown interviewer, 1–2.

106. Cortez, interview with author.

107. Terry Sanders, interview with Algar.

108. Terry Sanders, interview with author.

109. Bitzer, *Billy Bitzer,* 69.

110. Terry Sanders, interview with Algar.

111. Terry Sanders, interview with author.

112. Henderson, *D. W. Griffith*, 78.

113. Bitzer, *Billy Bitzer*, 69.

114. Agee, "David Wark Griffith," 316.

115. Schickel, *D. W. Griffith*, 182.

116. Henry King, interview with David Shepard, *Tol'able David*, DVD, directed by Henry King (1921; Los Angeles: Image Entertainment, 1999).

117. Agee, "Interiors and Exteriors," 2 (see chap. 4, n. 44).

118. Affron, *Star Acting*, 19.

119. Denis Sanders, summary of conversation with unknown interviewer, 2 (see chap. 3, n. 15).

120. Callow, *Charles Laughton*, 230.

121. Agee to Gregory, January 14, 1955.

122. Cortez, interview with author.

123. Jesionowski, *Thinking in Pictures*, 39.

124. Terry Sanders, interview with Algar.

125. Jesionowski, *Thinking in Pictures*, 89.

126. Graves, telephone interview with author.

127. Ibid.

128. Pechter, "On Agee on Film," 152.

Chapter 6

1. Mills, "Charles Laughton's Adaptation," 55.

2. Brown, interview with author.

3. Alpert, "Terror on the River," 21.

4. Couchman, "A Labor of Love," 90.

5. Cortez, "Tri-X in Feature Film Production," 44.

6. Turner, "Creating *The Night of the Hunter*," 1337.

7. Ravage, "*Night of the Hunter* (On Videotape)," 46.

8. Turner, "Creating *The Night of the Hunter*," 1338.

9. Golden, interview with author.

10. Grubb, summary of conversation with unknown interviewer, 2 (see chap. 1, n. 63).

11. Hammond, "Melmoth," 107.

12. Hammond, "Melmoth,"107; Bauer, "Oedipus Again," 628.

13. Hammond, "Melmoth," 107.

14. Leff and Simmons, *Dame in the Kimono*, 213.

15. Laughton to Shurlock, August 4, 1954, *The Night of the Hunter*, Motion Picture Association of America (MPAA), Production Code Administration Records, Margaret Herrick Library (hereafter cited as *The Night of the Hunter*, MPAA).

16. Terry Sanders, interview with author.

17. Gregory, interview with author.

18. Golden, interview with author.

19. Schumann, "*Night of the Hunter,*" *Film Music,* 13 (hereafter cited parenthetically in text as *FM*).

20. Brown, interview with Algar.

21. Golden, interview with author.

22. Unless otherwise indicated, the musical examples in this chapter, notated by Greg Pliska, follow those that Schumann created for his *Film Music* article.

23. Gorbman, *Unheard Melodies,* 3.

24. Turner, "Creating *The Night of the Hunter,*" 1337.

25. Walter Schumann, "Uncle Birdie," bars 1–8, *The Night of the Hunter* score, 1955, Music Division, Library of Congress. The score titles the Rachel Cooper theme "Rachel and the Kids."

26. Schumann, "The Muddy Place," bars 50–54, *Night of the Hunter* score.

27. A copy of Grubb's handwritten lyrics for "Pretty Fly" is in *The Night of the Hunter* study collection. Permission from Estate of Davis Grubb. Jones reproduces the page of lyrics (*HH,* 253).

28. Grubb to Laughton, April 19, 1954, p. 6, *The Night of the Hunter* study collection.

29. Davis Grubb, "Lullaby," from *The Night of the Hunter,* music by Walter Schumann, words by Davis Grubb. Copyright © 1955 by Bourne Co. Copyright renewed. All rights reserved. International copyright secured. ASCAP.

30. Cortez, interview with author.

31. Higham, *Hollywood Cameramen,* 113–14.

32. Cortez, interview with author.

33. Schumann, "Willa's Waltz," bars 47–58; "There Goes Willa," bars 82–89, *Night of the Hunter* score.

34. Arthur P. Jacobs, "*The Night of the Hunter:* Publicity and Exploitation Campaign," December 1, 1954, Marty Weiser Papers, Margaret Herrick Library.

35. Paul Francis Webster, "Willa's Waltz (the Theme from *The Night of the Hunter*)," (New York: Bourne, 1955), music by Walter Schumann, words by Paul Francis Webster. Copyright © 1955 by Bourne Co. Copyright renewed. All rights reserved. International copyright secured. ASCAP.

36. Hammond, "Melmoth," 109.

37. Brown, *Overtones and Undertones,* 16. Brown defines "mickey-mousing" as "the split-second synchronizing of musical and visual action, so called because of its prevalent use in animated cartoons."

38. Breen to Cohn, January 18, 1954, *The Night of the Hunter,* MPAA.

39. Jacobs, "*Night of the Hunter:* Publicity and Exploitation Campaign."

40. George A. Heimrich to Breen, August 23, 1954, *The Night of the Hunter,* MPAA.

41. Heimrich to Gregory, August 23, 1954, *The Night of the Hunter,* MPAA.

42. Geoffrey Shurlock, memo, August 30, 1954, *The Night of the Hunter,* MPAA.

43. King, "*Christ-Haunted,*" 13.

Chapter 7

1. Mitchum, telephone interview with author.

2. Gregory, interview with author; "The Day Lincoln Was Shot," *Ford Star Jubilee,* produced by Paul Gregory, directed by Delbert Mann, teleplay by Denis Sanders, Terry Sanders, and Jean Holloway, based on the book by Jim Bishop, narrated by Charles Laughton, with Jack Lemmon, Raymond Massey, Lillian Gish, Billy Chapin, and Paul Bryar, CBS, February 11, 1956 (available for on-site viewing at the Paley Center for Media, New York). As the foregoing cast list shows, the production was something of a *Night of the Hunter* reunion. At times Laughton delivers his perfectly modulated narration on camera in a familiar pose: seated before a music stand, dressed in a tuxedo. Gish as Mary Todd Lincoln is surprisingly awkward at first, but she gives a wrenching performance in scenes of hysteria at Lincoln's deathbed. Bryar is a memorable Andrew Johnson; one feels the helpless woe of a weak-willed man. It is remarkable that Gregory saw dramatic potential in Lemmon at a time when the actor was known for comic roles. Lemmon had just won an Academy Award for his hilarious turn as Ensign Pulver in *Mister Roberts* (1955). His breakthrough dramatic performance in feature films was yet to come: in *Days of Wine and Roses* (1962). Gregory's instincts were sound. Lemmon creates a chilling portrait of the obsessed, vainglorious John Wilkes Booth.

3. Agee, reviews of twenty-five films, *Agee on Film,* 301.

4. Mitchum, telephone interview with author.

5. Callow, *Charles Laughton,* 167–68.

6. Mitchum, telephone interview with author.

7. Gregory, interview with author.

8. Callow, *Night of the Hunter,* 65.

9. Esslin, *Brecht,* 130.

10. Wagenknecht, *Lillian Gish,* 241.

11. Barthes, *Mythologies,* 56.

12. Dyer, "White Star," 24.

13. Gregory to Gish, February 13, 1956, *The Night of the Hunter* study collection.

14. Laughton to Grubb, n.d., ca. April 1954, quoted in Jones, "Heaven and Hell to Play With," 89; Laughton to Agee, April 12, 1954, James Agee and James Agee Trust Collection. To Grubb, Laughton says that Barrymore "is rather Hudson than Ohio River Valley." To Agee, he writes, "Barrymore's grandeur is rather of the Hudson than the Ohio River Valley."

15. Dyer, "White Star," 22.

16. Server, *Robert Mitchum,* 80.

17. Davis Grubb, *The Night of the Hunter* sketches. Jones reproduces the drawing (*HH,* 160).

18. Golden, interview with author.

19. Ibid.

20. Feeney, "Night Vision."

21. Gregory, interview with author.

22. Grubb, summary of conversation with unknown interviewer, 3 (see chap. 1, n. 63).

23. Terry Sanders, interview with author; Golden, interview with author.

24. Hoffberg, interview with author.

25. Gregory, interview with author.

26. Brown, interview with author.

27. Mitchum, telephone interview with author.

28. Mitchum, summary of conversation with unknown interviewer, 3 (see chap. 5, n. 21).

29. Gregory, interview with author.

30. Nigel Andrews, "The Making of a Mighty Pantomime," *Financial Times,* July 1, 2005.

31. Summary of telephone conversation by unknown interviewer with Billy Chapin and his mother, [1968?], p. 1, Elsa Lanchester papers, Margaret Herrick Library.

32. Helen Gould, "C. Laughton: Tot Tutor," *New York Times,* October 31, 1954.

33. Pearson, *Eloquent Gestures,* 21–24.

34. Manners, "New Laughton Screen Play Hair Raiser."

35. Gregory, interview with author.

36. Truffaut, "Charles Laughton," 120.

Chapter 8

1. Robert Barewald, "Grand Avenue Jammed in Gala Climax to Gregory Day," *Des Moines Register,* June 27, 1955; *The Tonight Show,* with live hookup to Des Moines, Iowa, NBC, July 26, 1955 (available for on-site viewing at UCLA Film and Television Archive's Research and Study Center).

2. Barewald, "Grand Avenue."

3. *Motion Picture Daily,* "*Hunter* Premiere Funds to YMCA," July 15, 1955.

4. Laughton, "What I Live For," 118.

5. Kael, *Kiss Kiss Bang Bang,* 317.

6. Crowther, "Bogeyman Plus"; *Daily Variety,* "*Trial* 95G, *Okla* 36G On 1st 4 B'way Days; B. O. Rises From Storm Cellar," October 17, 1955; Callow, *Night of the Hunter,* 55; Brode, *Films of the Fifties,* 145.

7. Lanchester, *Elsa Lanchester Herself,* 240.

8. Gregory, interview with author; Paul Gregory, "Reviewing the Bidding," typescript, n.d., ca. June 1954, pp. 3, 4, *The Night of the Hunter* study collection. A note at the top of the manuscript reads, "For *Films in Review.*" The piece never went to print.

9. Moffitt, Review of *The Night of the Hunter.*

10. *Los Angeles Examiner,* advertisement for *The Night of the Hunter,* directed by Charles Laughton, August 22, 1955.

11. *Los Angeles Examiner,* advertisement for *The Night of the Hunter,* directed by Charles Laughton, August 24, 1955.

12. *Mirror-News,* advertisement for *The Night of the Hunter,* directed by Charles Laughton, August 23, 1955.

13. *Los Angeles Examiner,* advertisement for *The Night of the Hunter,* directed by Charles Laughton, August 23, 1955.

14. *Citizen-News,* advertisement for *The Night of the Hunter,* directed by Charles Laughton, September 27, 1955.

15. Press book for *The Night of the Hunter,* directed by Charles Laughton, personal collection of Preston Neal Jones.

16. *Mirror-News,* advertisement for *The Night of the Hunter,* directed by Charles Laughton, August 25, 1955.

17. Jacobs, "*Night of the Hunter:* Publicity and Exploitation Campaign" (see chap. 6, n. 34).

18. *Los Angeles Herald and Express,* "*Night of the Hunter* Starts in *Herald-Express* Monday," April 20, 1955.

19. *Film Daily,* "Campaign Backs *Hunter,*" August 4, 1955.

20. *Showmen's Trade Review,* "Book Promotion Sparks National *Hunter* Drive," August 13, 1955.

21. Harvey, "*Night of the Hunter,*" 48–49.

22. *Tops in Human Highlights,* June 1955, 27, clipping in *The Night of the Hunter* study collection.

23. *New York Times,* "Change of Scene for *Miss Brooks,*" August 16, 1955.

24. *Showmen's Trade Review,* "Book Promotion," August 13, 1955.

25. Jacobs, "*Night of the Hunter:* Publicity and Exploitation Campaign"; Gregory to Gish, telegram, August 25, 1955, Elsa Lanchester papers, Margaret Herrick Library; *The Ed Sullivan Show,* CBS, September 25, 1955, http://www .tv.com/the-ed-sullivan-show/robert-mitchum---lillian-gish---rocky-marciano/ episode/116884/summary.html?tag=ep_list;ep_title;0. The *Sullivan* promotion, including a scene from Grubb's novel that was not in the film, was originally scheduled for September 4 ("*Night of Hunter* on Sullivan Show," *New York Times,* August 27, 1955) but was postponed until September 25 after Winters became ill (Gregory to Gish, telegram, August 31, 1955; http://www.tv.com/ toast-of-the-town/show/5696/episode_guide.html?season=8&tag=season_ dropdown;dropdown;7). An excerpt from the presentation appears in *The Ed Sullivan Show: 15th Anniversary,* June 23, 1963 (available for on-site viewing at the Paley Center for Media, New York). On television, Mitchum and Winters stand in a replica of the set for Spoon's ice-cream parlor. She never says a word; she merely listens intently while Mitchum performs "the little story of Right-Hand-Left-Hand." His dialogue differs slightly from both the film and the novel. Perhaps the changes, along with the fact that he and Winters were petrified in front of the live audience (Winters, *Shelley II,* 115), caused Mitchum to stumble over his first

line: "Just yesterday, Ma'am, I resi—resigned from the state penitentiary." Winters recalls that Mitchum held up the wrong hand when he referred to his tattooed fingers (*Shelley II*, 115–16), but he does, in fact, hold up the proper hand at the proper moment. He even emphasizes the wickedness of the left hand by slapping it repeatedly with his right index finger—a gesture invented for the telecast.

26. Gregory, "Reviewing the Bidding," 3; Gregory to Parsons, June 19, 1954, *The Night of the Hunter* study collection.

27. Graves, Let's Go to the Movies, 13.

28. Speicher, "New Films from Books," 2231.

29. Williams, "*Night of the Hunter* Consciously Arty."

30. Kass, Film and TV, 465.

31. Flynn, "Mitchum as Minister."

32. Winner, review of *The Night of the Hunter*, 22–23.

33. Crowther, "Bogeyman Plus."

34. Zinsser, Screen.

35. Golden, interview with author.

36. *Life*, "Diabolic Preacher," 49.

37. Gregory, interview with author.

38. Ravage, "*Night of the Hunter* (On Videotape)," 43.

39. May and Bird, *Religion in Film*, 13.

40. Musser, *Emergence of Cinema*, 209–10.

41. Uricchio and Pearson, *Reframing Culture*, 165.

42. Ibid., 167, 184.

43. Morella, Epstein, and Clark, *Those Great Movie Ads*, 32.

44. Eames, *MGM Story*, 244; Eames, *Paramount Story*, 218.

45. Andrew M. Greeley, "Why Hollywood Never Asks the God Question," *New York Times*, Arts and Leisure section, January 18, 1976.

46. "Scorecard," *The Night of the Hunter*, MPAA. The Legion of Decency classifications can be found in Steinberg, *Reel Facts*, 494.

47. Binford to Tedesco, ca. July 1955, quoted in *Variety*, "Memphis Censor Bans *Night of Hunter* As 'Rawest (N)ever Seen,'" July 19, 1955.

48. *Motion Picture Daily*, "Memphis Bans *Hunter;* Refuses to Re-Review 3 Other Pictures," July 19, 1955.

49. Gregory, interview with author.

50. King, "*Christ-Haunted*," 22.

51. Ibid., 25. King's interesting discussion covers pages 23–79.

52. Beaufort, review of *The Night of the Hunter*.

53. Bordwell, *On the History of Film Style*, 8.

54. Thomas, "Inside Hollywood" (see introduction, n. 46).

55. Manners, "New Laughton Screen Play"; Flynn, "Mitchum as Minister"; Schallert, "*Night of Hunter* Eerie, Powerful."

56. Milt., "Film Review"; *Life*, "Diabolic Preacher," 49.

57. Advertisement for *The Night of the Hunter*, directed by Charles Laughton, *Mirror-News*, August 23, 1955.

58. Kaminsky, *American Film Genres,* 152–53.

59. Bongard, "*Night of the Hunter* Has Strange, Eerie Complexion."

60. Bordwell, *Narration in the Fiction Film,* 210–11.

61. Levine, *Highbrow/Lowbrow,* 1–2.

62. Bordwell, *Narration in the Fiction Film,* 207.

63. Ibid., 158, 207.

64. Terry Sanders, interview with author.

65. Braudy, *World in a Frame,* 46, 94–95.

66. Levy, *Small-Town America,* 115–16.

67. Wood, *America in the Movies,* 162.

68. Lahn to Agee, April 16, 1954, Paul Kohner papers.

69. Agee, "James Agee to Father Flye," 213.

70. Philip K. Scheuer, "Laughton Strikes a Strange and Symbolic Note in *Hunter,*" *Los Angeles Times,* April 17, 1955.

71. Brown, interview with author.

72. Higham, *Charles Laughton,* 199; *HH,* 366.

73. Higham, *Charles Laughton,* 197–98.

74. Terry Sanders, interview with author.

75. Callow, *Charles Laughton,* 237.

76. Terry Sanders, interview with author.

77. Higham, *Charles Laughton,* 199–200.

78. Gish, summary of conversation with unknown interviewer, 5 (see chap. 1, n. 41).

79. Lanchester, *Elsa Lanchester Herself,* 246.

80. Ibid.

81. Terry Sanders, interview with author.

82. Denis Sanders, summary of conversation with unknown interviewer, 8 (see chap. 3, n. 15).

83. Terry Sanders, interview with author.

84. Gregory, interview with author; Johnson, "Art of Paul Gregory," 184–93; *Hamlet,* directed by William Ball, toured America in 1970 and played Carnegie Hall, January 14–15, 1971 (see "Dame Judith Anderson," National Library of Australia, http://www.nla.gov.au/collect/prompt/andersn.html).

85. *The Marriage Go-Round,* by Leslie Stevens, directed by Joseph Anthony, Plymouth Theatre, New York, October 29, 1958–February 13, 1960, http://www .ibdb.com/production.asp?ID=2708.

86. Gregory, interview with author.

87. Crowe, *Conversations with Billy Wilder,* 30.

88. Callow, *Charles Laughton,* 305. Callow provides a detailed list of Laughton's plays, films, and recordings, 300–313.

89. Gene., review of *The Night of the Hunter;* Milt., "Film Review."

90. Bosley Crowther, "Directorial Ambition: Charles Laughton Joins Megaphoners with *The Night of the Hunter,*" *New York Times,* October 2, 1955.

91. Terry Sanders, interview with author; Gregory, interview with author.

92. Denis Sanders, summary of conversation with unknown interviewer, 8–9.

93. Grubb, summary of conversation with unknown interviewer, 6 (see chap. 1, n. 63).

94. Callow, *Charles Laughton,* 236.

95. Cortez, interview with author; Gregory, interview with Algar.

Chapter 9

1. Robert Gitt, telephone interview with the author, September 24, 2001.

2. *Film Forum 2 Spring–Summer 2003 Repertory Preview* (New York: Film Forum, 2003).

3. Brode, *Films of the Fifties,* 145.

4. Mills, "Charles Laughton's Adaptation," 55, 57.

5. FCRC of Illinois, "U. S. National Film Registry—Titles," efilmcenter, http://www.film-center.com/registry.html.

6. "78th Annual Academy Awards," directed by Louis J. Horvitz, film noir sequence by Chuck Workman, ABC, March 5, 2006.

7. Couchman, "Labor of Love"; Gitt, "Hidden *Hunter."*

8. Peary, *Cult Movies,* 394.

9. Gow, "Cult Movies," 48–53.

10. Johnson, "And a Little Child," 16, 18.

11. J. Hoberman, "Down by the River," *Village Voice,* July 28, 1992. The works cited in Hoberman's quotation are David Felton and David Dalton, "Book One: Year of the Fork, Night of the Hunter," *Rolling Stone,* June 25, 1970, 24–26; and Greil Marcus, *Mystery Train: Images of America in Rock 'n' Roll Music,* 5th rev. ed. (New York: Plume, 2008).

12. Joe Strummer, Mick Jones, Paul Simonon, and Topper Headon, "Death or Glory," *London Calling,* compact disc, Epic, EK 63885, 1999. © 1979 Nineden Ltd. (PRS). All rights in the U.S. and Canada administered by Universal-PolyGram Intl. Publ. Inc. (ASCAP). Used by permission. All rights reserved.

13. Bruce Springsteen, "Cautious Man," *Tunnel of Love,* compact disc, Columbia, CK 40999, 1987. "Cautious Man" by Bruce Springsteen. Copyright © 1987 Bruce Springsteen (ASCAP). Reprinted by permission. International copyright secured. All rights reserved.

14. *The Simpsons,* "Cape Feare," directed by Rich Moore, teleplay by Jon Vitti, Fox, October 7, 1993.

15. Don Del Grande, ed., "Cape Feare," *The Simpsons Archive,* http://www.snpp.com/episodes/9F22.html.

16. Claibe Richardson and Stephen Cole, *The Night of the Hunter,* based on the novel by Davis Grubb (concert reading, directed by Lonny Price, Vineyard Theatre, New York, N.Y., June 1996); Claibe Richardson and Stephen Cole, *The Night of the Hunter,* based on the novel by Davis Grubb, compact disc, Varèse Sarabande, VSD-5876, 1998.

17. Truffaut, "Charles Laughton," 120.

18. Barrie Hayne, program notes for *The Night of the Hunter,* directed by Charles Laughton (Toronto: Toronto Film Society, April 30, 1984), *The Night of the Hunter* clipping file, Margaret Herrick Library.

19. Gregory, interview with Algar.

20. Laughton, "What I Live For," 118.

WORKS CITED

Literature

Affron, Charles. *Star Acting: Gish, Garbo, Davis.* New York: Dutton, 1977.

Agee, James. *The African Queen.* In Agee, *Agee on Film,* vol. 2, 149–259.

———. *Agee on Film.* Vol. 1, *Reviews and Comments by James Agee.* 1958. Reprint, Boston: Beacon, 1964.

———. *Agee on Film.* Vol. 2, *Five Film Scripts by James Agee.* New York: McDowell, 1960.

———. *The Blue Hotel.* In Agee, *Agee on Film,* vol. 2, 391–488.

———. *The Bride Comes to Yellow Sky.* In Agee, *Agee on Film,* vol. 2, 355–90.

———. "David Wark Griffith." In Agee, *Agee on Film,* vol. 1, 313–18. Reprinted from *The Nation,* September 4, 1948, 264–66.

———. *A Death in the Family.* New York: McDowell, 1957.

———. *James Agee: Film Writing and Selected Journalism.* Edited by Michael Sragow. New York: Library of America, 2005.

———. James Agee to Father Flye, January 5, 1954. In *Letters of James Agee to Father Flye,* edited by James Harold Flye, 213–14. New York: Braziller, 1962.

———. *The Morning Watch.* 1950. Reprint, New York: Ballantine, 1966.

———. *The Night of the Hunter.* In Agee, *Agee on Film,* vol. 2, 261–354.

———. *Noa Noa.* In Agee, *Agee on Film,* vol. 2, 1–147.

———. "Notes for a Moving Picture: the House." In *New Letters in America,* edited by Horace Gregory, 37–55. New York: Norton, 1937. Reprinted in *The Collected Short Prose of James Agee,* edited by Robert Fitzgerald, 149–73. Boston: Houghton, 1968.

———. "Reviews of Twenty-Five Films." In Agee, *Agee on Film,* vol. 1, 300–302. Reprinted from *The Nation,* April 24, 1948, 449–50.

Agee, James, and Walker Evans. *Let Us Now Praise Famous Men.* 1941. Reprint, New York: Ballantine, 1966.

Allan, Rupert. "Widows and Orphans, Beware!" *Look,* September 6, 1955, 72.

Allen, Walter. "New Novels." Review of *The Night of the Hunter,* by Davis Grubb. *New Statesman and Nation,* July 10, 1954, 51–52.

Alpert, Hollis. "Terror on the River." Review of *The Night of the Hunter*, directed by Charles Laughton. *SR* Goes to the Movies. *Saturday Review*, August 13, 1955, 21.

Anderson, John. "Screenwriters Get Their Due." Review of *The Schreiber Theory: A Radical Rewrite of American Film History*, by David Kipen. *Newsday*, February 19, 2006, http://pqasb.pqarchiver.com/newsday/advancedsearch.html.

Andrew, J. Dudley. *Concepts in Film Theory.* New York: Oxford University Press, 1984.

Arnow, Harriette. *The Dollmaker.* 1954. Reprint, New York: Harper, Avon, 1972.

———. *Hunter's Horn.* New York: Macmillan, 1949.

———. "Youth and Terror." Review of *The Night of the Hunter*, by Davis Grubb. *Saturday Review*, February 20, 1954, 19.

Baro, Gene. "A Terrifying and Impassioned Narrative." Review of *The Night of the Hunter*, by Davis Grubb. *New York Herald Tribune Book Review*, February 21, 1954, 5.

Barson, Alfred. *A Way of Seeing: A Critical Study of James Agee.* Amherst: University of Massachusetts Press, 1972.

Barthes, Roland. *Mythologies.* Translated by Annette Lavers. New York: Hill, 1972.

Bauer, Stephen F. "Oedipus Again: A Critical Study of Charles Laughton's *The Night of the Hunter.*" *Psychoanalytic Quarterly* 68, no. 4 (1999): 611–36.

Beaufort, John [as J. B.]. Review of *The Night of the Hunter*, directed by Charles Laughton. *Christian Science Monitor*, October 11, 1955.

Beja, Morris. *Film and Literature: An Introduction.* New York: Longman, 1979.

Benét, Stephen Vincent. Foreword, in *John Brown's Body*, edited by Jack L. Capps and C. Robert Kemble, xv–xvii. New York: Holt, 1968.

———. *John Brown's Body.* Edited by Jack L. Capps and C. Robert Kemble. New York: Holt, 1968.

Bergreen, Laurence. *James Agee: A Life.* New York: Dutton, 1984.

Bettelheim, Bruno. *The Uses of Enchantment: The Meaning and Importance of Fairy Tales.* 1975. Reprint, New York: Random, Vintage, 1989.

Bitzer, Billy. *Billy Bitzer: His Story.* New York: Farrar, 1973.

Blake, William. "The Tyger." In *Blake: Complete Writings*, edited by Geoffrey Keynes, 214. London: Oxford University Press, 1972.

Bluestone, George. *Novels into Film.* 1957. Reprint, Berkeley: University of California Press, 1973.

Bongard, David. "*Night of the Hunter* Has Strange, Eerie Complexion." Review of *The Night of the Hunter*, directed by Charles Laughton. *Los Angeles Herald and Express*, August 27, 1955.

Borde, Raymond, and Étienne Chaumeton. "Towards a Definition of Film Noir." In Silver and Ursini, *Film Noir Reader*, 17–25.

Bordwell, David. *Narration in the Fiction Film.* Madison: University of Wisconsin Press, 1985.

————. *On the History of Film Style.* Cambridge, Mass.: Harvard University Press, 1997.

Bordwell, David, Janet Staiger, and Kristin Thompson. *The Classical Hollywood Cinema: Film Style and Mode of Production to 1960.* New York: Columbia University Press, 1985.

Brady, Frank. *Citizen Welles: A Biography of Orson Welles.* 1989. Reprint, New York: Doubleday, Anchor, 1990.

Braudy, Leo. *The World in a Frame: What We See in Films.* Garden City, N.Y.: Doubleday, Anchor, 1976.

Brecht, Bertolt. *Brecht on Theatre.* Edited and translated by John Willet. New York: Hill, 1964.

————. *Galileo.* English version by Charles Laughton. 1940. Reprint, edited by Eric Bentley, New York: Grove, 1966.

————. *Life of Galileo.* Translated by John Willett. Edited by John Willett and Ralph Manheim. 1980. Reprint, New York: Arcade, 1994.

Brode, Douglas. *The Films of the Fifties: "Sunset Boulevard" to "On the Beach."* Secaucus, N.J.: Citadel, 1976.

Brown, Charles Brockden. *Arthur Mervyn; or, Memoirs of the Year 1793.* 1799–1800. Reprinted in Brown, *Three Gothic Novels,* 229–637.

————. *Edgar Huntly; or, Memoirs of a Sleep-Walker.* 1799. Reprinted in Brown, *Three Gothic Novels,* 639–898.

————. *Three Gothic Novels.* Edited by Sydney J. Krause. New York: Library of America, 1998.

————. *Wieland; or, The Transformation: An American Tale.* 1798. Reprinted in Brown, *Three Gothic Novels,* 1–227.

Brown, Royal S. *Overtones and Undertones: Reading Film Music.* Berkeley: University of California Press, 1994.

Burch, Noël. *Life to those Shadows.* Translated and edited by Ben Brewster. Berkeley: University of California Press, 1990.

Caldwell, Erskine. *Tobacco Road.* 1932. Reprinted in *The Caldwell Caravan: Novels and Stories by Erskine Caldwell,* 13–132. Cleveland, Ohio: World, 1946.

Callow, Simon. *Charles Laughton: A Difficult Actor.* London: Methuen, 1987.

————. *The Night of the Hunter.* BFI Film Classics. London: BFI, 2000.

Carringer, Robert L. *The Making of "Citizen Kane."* 1985. Reprint, Berkeley: University of California Press, 1996.

Carroll, Noël. *The Philosophy of Horror; or, Paradoxes of the Heart.* New York: Routledge, 1990.

Cavendish, Henry. "Magic of Fine Writing." Review of *The Night of the Hunter,* by Davis Grubb. *Chicago Tribune Magazine of Books,* February 21, 1954, 5.

Chatman, Seymour. *Coming to Terms: The Rhetoric of Narrative in Fiction and Film.* Ithaca, N.Y.: Cornell University Press, 1990.

Cortez, Stanley. "Tri-X in Feature Film Production." *American Cinematographer* 36, no. 1 (1955): 33, 44–47.

Couchman, Jeffrey. "A Labor of Love (Sans Hate)." *American Cinematographer* 83, no. 1 (2002): 86–100.

———. "The Night of *The Night of the Hunter*." *Journal of Film Preservation* 64 (April 2002): 4–8.

Crowe, Cameron. *Conversations with Billy Wilder*. New York: Knopf, 1999.

Crowther, Bosley. "Bogeyman Plus." Review of *The Night of the Hunter*, directed by Charles Laughton. *New York Times*, September 30, 1955.

Damico, James. "Film Noir: A Modest Proposal." In Silver and Ursini, *Film Noir Reader*, 95–105.

Dickens, Charles. *David Copperfield*. 1850. Edited by Jerome H. Buckley. Norton Critical Editions. New York: Norton, 1990.

———. *Martin Chuzzlewit*. 1844. Reprint, London: Dent, Everyman, 1963.

———. *Oliver Twist*. 1846. Edited by Fred Kaplan. Norton Critical Editions. New York: Norton, 1993.

Dos Passos, John. *U.S.A.* New York: Random, Modern, 1937.

Douglass, Thomas E. Foreword, in Grubb, *Fools' Parade*, vii–xxv.

Durgnat, Raymond. "Paint It Black: The Family Tree of the *Film Noir*." In Silver and Ursini, *Film Noir Reader*, 37–51.

Dyer, Richard. "A White Star." *Sight and Sound* 3, no. 8 (1993): 22–24.

Eames, John Douglas. *The MGM Story: The Complete History of Fifty Roaring Years*. New York: Crown, 1975.

———. *The Paramount Story*. New York: Crown, 1985.

Eisner, Lotte H. *The Haunted Screen: Expressionism in the German Cinema and the Influence of Max Reinhardt*. Translated by Roger Greaves. 1969. Reprint, Berkeley: University of California Press, 1973.

Esslin, Martin. *Brecht: The Man and His Work*. Garden City, N.Y.: Doubleday, Anchor, 1961.

Faulkner, William. *As I Lay Dying*. 1930. Reprinted in *The Sound and the Fury and As I Lay Dying*. New York: Random, Modern, 1946.

———. *Sanctuary*. 1931. Reprint, New York: Random, Modern, 1932.

Fiedler, Leslie A. *Love and Death in the American Novel*. 1960. Reprint, Normal, Ill.: Dalkey Archive Press, 1997.

Fitzgerald, Robert. "A Memoir." In *Remembering James Agee*, 2nd ed., edited by David Madden and Jeffrey J. Folks, 37–88. Athens: University of Georgia Press, 1997.

Flynn, Hazel. "Mitchum as Minister Makes *Hunter* a Nightmare Movie." Review of *The Night of the Hunter*, directed by Charles Laughton. *Daily NewsLife*, August 29, 1955.

Folks, Jeffrey J. "James Agee's Filmscript for *The Night of the Hunter*." *Southern Quarterly* 33, no. 2–3 (1995): 151–60.

Fultz, James R. "The Poetry and Danger of Childhood: James Agee's Film Adaptation of *The Night of the Hunter*." *Western Humanities Review* 34, no. 1 (1980): 90–98.

Gene. Review of *The Night of the Hunter*, directed by Charles Laughton. *Variety*, July 20, 1955.

Gorbman, Claudia. *Unheard Melodies: Narrative Film Music*. Bloomington: Indiana University Press, 1987.

Gow, Gordon. "The Cult Movies: 4 *The Night of the Hunter*." *Films and Filming* 21, no. 5 (1975): 48–53.

Graves, Janet. Let's Go to the Movies with Janet Graves. Review of *The Night of the Hunter*, directed by Charles Laughton. *Photoplay*, October 1955, 13.

Grobel, Lawrence. *The Hustons*. New York: Scribner, 1989.

Grubb, Davis. *Ancient Lights*. New York: Viking, 1982.

———. *The Barefoot Man*. New York: Simon, 1971.

———. "Checker-Playing Fool." In Grubb, *You Never Believe Me*, 189–96. Originally published [under Dave Grubb] in *Collier's*, June 23, 1945, 26.

———. *A Dream of Kings*. New York: Scribner, 1955.

———. *Fools' Parade*. 1969. Reprint, Knoxville: University of Tennessee Press, 2001.

———. *The Golden Sickle*. New York: World, 1968.

———. "The Horsehair Trunk." In Grubb, *Twelve Tales*, 88–99, and in Grubb, *You Never Believe Me*, 197–206. Originally published [under Dave Grubb] in *Collier's*, May 25, 1946, 46, 81–84.

———. *The Night of the Hunter*. New York: Harper, 1953.

———. *Shadow of My Brother*. New York: Holt, 1966.

———. "The Siege of 318." In Grubb, *Siege*, 1–12. Originally published as "Cry Havoc" in *Ellery Queen's Mystery Magazine*, August 1976, 69–78.

———. *The Siege of 318: Thirteen Mystical Stories*. Webster Springs, W.Va.: Back Fork Books, 1978.

———. *A Tree Full of Stars*. New York: Scribner, 1965.

———. *Twelve Tales of Suspense and the Supernatural*. 1964. Reprint, Greenwich, Conn.: Fawcett, 1964.

———. "The Valley of the Ohio: A Journey in Place and Time." *Holiday*, July 1960, 56–57, 129–37.

———. *The Voices of Glory*. New York: Scribner, 1962.

———. *You Never Believe Me and Other Stories*. New York: St. Martin's, 1989.

Hammett, Dashiell. *The Maltese Falcon*. New York: Knopf, 1929.

Hammond, Paul. "Melmoth in Norman Rockwell Land . . . on *The Night of the Hunter*." *Sight and Sound* 48, no. 2 (1979): 105–9.

Hardwicke, Sir Cedric. *A Victorian in Orbit: The Irreverent Memoirs of Sir Cedric Hardwicke*. Garden City, N.Y.: Doubleday, 1961.

Harmetz, Aljean. *The Making of "The Wizard of Oz."* 1977. Reprint, New York: Hyperion, 1998.

Harris, Michael David. *Always on Sunday: Ed Sullivan; An Inside View*. New York: Meredith, 1968.

Harvey, Evelyn. "*The Night of the Hunter*." *Colliers*, June 10, 1955, 48–49.

Henderson, Robert M. *D. W. Griffith: The Years at Biograph.* New York: Farrar, 1970.

Higham, Charles. *Charles Laughton: An Intimate Biography.* Garden City, N.Y.: Doubleday, 1976.

———. *Hollywood Cameramen: Sources of Light.* Bloomington: Indiana University Press, 1970.

Holzhauer, Jean. "Children of Night." Review of *The Night of the Hunter,* by Davis Grubb. *Commonweal* 60, no. 5 (1954): 123–24.

Houseman, John. "Drama Quartette." *Theatre Arts,* August 1951, 14–15, 96–97.

Hughes, Riley. "Novels Reviewed." Review of *The Night of the Hunter,* by Davis Grubb. Books. *Catholic World* 180, no. 1,075 (1954): 71–72.

Huston, John. *An Open Book.* 1980. Reprint, New York: Ballantine, 1981.

Jackson, Joseph Henry. "A Study in Human Terror." Review of *The Night of the Hunter,* by Davis Grubb. Bookman's Notebook. *San Francisco Chronicle,* February 23, 1954.

Jacobs, Robert D. "The Humor of *Tobacco Road.*" In *The Comic Imagination in American Literature,* edited by Louis D. Rubin Jr., 285–94. New Brunswick, N.J.: Rutgers University Press, 1973.

Jesionowski, Joyce E. *Thinking in Pictures: Dramatic Structure in D. W. Griffith's Biograph Films.* Berkeley: University of California Press, 1987.

Johnson, Ian. "And a Little Child Shall Lead Them." *Motion* no. 6 (Autumn 1963): 16–18.

Johnson, James Lester. "The Art of Paul Gregory: An Examination of Gregory's Historic, Aesthetic and Pedagogic Contributions to Interpretation and Theatre." Ph.D. diss., University of Southern California, 1981.

Jones, Preston Neal. *Heaven and Hell to Play With: The Filming of "The Night of the Hunter."* New York: Limelight, 2002.

———. "Heaven and Hell to Play With: The Filming of *The Night of the Hunter.*" In *Performing Arts: Motion Pictures,* edited by Iris Newsom, 52–99. Washington, D.C.: Library of Congress, 1998.

Kael, Pauline. *Kiss Kiss Bang Bang.* Boston: Little, Atlantic, 1968.

Kaminsky, Stuart M. *American Film Genres: Approaches to a Critical Theory of Popular Film.* 1974. Reprint, New York: Dell, Laurel, 1977.

Kashner, Sam, and Jennifer MacNair. *The Bad and the Beautiful: Hollywood in the Fifties.* New York: Norton, 2002.

Kass, Robert. Film and TV. Review of *The Night of the Hunter,* directed by Charles Laughton. *Catholic World* 181, no. 1,086 (1955): 465.

King, David Ashley. *"Christ-Haunted": Religion and the South in Four American Films.* Ann Arbor, Mich.: University Microfilms, 2002.

Klein, Michael, and Gillian Parker, eds. *The English Novel and the Movies.* New York: Ungar, 1981.

Kracauer, Siegfried. *From Caligari to Hitler: A Psychological History of the German Film.* 1947. Reprint, Princeton, N.J.: Princeton University Press, 1970.

Kramer, Victor. *James Agee.* Boston: Twayne, 1975.

Lanchester, Elsa. *Charles Laughton and I.* London: Faber, 1938.

———. *Elsa Lanchester Herself.* New York: St. Martin's, 1983.

Laughton, Charles, ed. *The Fabulous Country: An Anthology.* New York: McGraw, 1962.

———. "How Mr. Laughton Became the Devil," *New York Times Magazine,* March 23, 1952, 21.

———, ed. *Tell Me a Story: An Anthology.* New York: McGraw, 1957.

———. "What I Live For." *Good Housekeeping,* February 1955, 16, 118.

Leff, Leonard J., and Jerold L. Simmons. *The Dame in the Kimono: Hollywood, Censorship, and the Production Code from the 1920s to the 1960s.* 1990. Reprint, New York: Doubleday, Anchor, 1990.

Levine, Lawrence W. *Highbrow/Lowbrow: The Emergence of Cultural Hierarchy in America.* 1988. Reprint, Cambridge, Mass.: Harvard University Press, 1990.

Levy, Emanuel. *Small-Town America in Film: The Decline and Fall of Community.* New York: Continuum, 1991.

Lewis, Matthew. *The Monk.* 1796. Edited by Howard Anderson. Reprint, Oxford: Oxford University Press, 1998.

Life. "A Diabolic Preacher Runs Amok." Review of *The Night of the Hunter,* directed by Charles Laughton. August 1, 1955, 49–51.

MacAndrew, Elizabeth. *The Gothic Tradition in Fiction.* New York: Columbia University Press, 1979.

Macdonald, Dwight. "Jim Agee, a Memoir." In *Remembering James Agee,* edited by David Madden and Jeffrey J. Folks, 163–85. 2nd ed. Athens: University of Georgia Press, 1997.

Mailer, Norman. *The Naked and the Dead.* New York: Holt, 1948.

Maltin, Leonard. *Behind the Camera: The Cinematographer's Art.* New York: New American, Signet, 1971.

Manners, Dorothy. "New Laughton Screen Play Hair Raiser." Review of *The Night of the Hunter,* directed by Charles Laughton. *Los Angeles Examiner,* August 27, 1955.

Massey, Raymond. *A Hundred Different Lives: An Autobiography by Raymond Massey.* Boston: Little, 1979.

Maturin, Charles Robert. *Melmoth the Wanderer.* 1820. Edited by Victor Sage. Reprint, London: Penguin, 2000.

May, John R., and Michael Bird, eds. *Religion in Film.* Knoxville: University of Tennessee Press, 1982.

Melville, Herman. *Moby Dick.* 1851. Edited by Harrison Hayford and Hershel Parker. Reprint, New York: Norton, 1976.

Messadié, Gerald. *A History of the Devil.* Translated by Marc Romano. New York: Kodansha, 1996.

Mills, Moylan C. "Charles Laughton's Adaptation of *The Night of the Hunter.*" *Literature/Film Quarterly* 16, no. 1 (1988): 49–57.

Milt. "Film Review: *The Night of the Hunter* (*Melodrama*)." Review of *The Night of the Hunter,* directed by Charles Laughton. *Daily Variety,* July 20, 1955.

Moffitt, Jack. Review of *The Night of the Hunter,* directed by Charles Laughton. *Hollywood Reporter,* July 20, 1955.

Morella, Joe, Edward Z. Epstein, and Eleanor Clark. *Those Great Movie Ads.* New York: Galahad Books, 1972.

Musser, Charles. *The Emergence of Cinema: The American Screen to 1907.* History of the American Cinema, 1. 1990. Reprint, Berkeley: University of California Press, 1994.

O'Connor, Flannery. *Mystery and Manners: Occasional Prose.* Edited by Sally and Robert Fitzgerald. New York: Farrar, 1969.

———. *Wise Blood.* 1952. Reprinted in *Three by Flannery O'Connor,* 7–126. New York: New American, Signet, 1964.

Palmer, Jerry. *Thrillers: Genesis and Structure of a Popular Genre.* New York: St. Martin's, 1979.

Pearson, Roberta E. *Eloquent Gestures: The Transformation of Performance Style in the Griffith Biograph Films.* Berkeley: University of California Press, 1992.

Peary, Danny. *Cult Movies: The Classics, the Sleepers, the Weird, and the Wonderful.* New York: Delta, Dell, 1981.

Pechter, William S. "On Agee on Film." *Sight and Sound* 33, no. 3 (1964): 148–53.

Porfirio, Robert G. "No Way Out: Existential Motifs in the *Film Noir.*" In Silver and Ursini, *Film Noir Reader,* 77–93.

Prescott, Orville. Books of the Times. Review of *The Night of the Hunter,* by Davis Grubb. *New York Times,* September 26, 1955.

Punter, David. *The Literature of Terror: A History of Gothic Fictions from 1765 to the Present Day.* 2 vols. 1980. Reprint, London: Longman, 1996.

Pyle, Howard. *The Merry Adventures of Robin Hood of Great Renown, in Nottinghamshire.* 1883. Reprint, New York: Dover, 1968.

———. *Otto of the Silver Hand.* 1888. Reprint, New York: Dover, 1967.

Radcliffe, Ann. *The Italian; or, The Confessional of the Black Penitents: A Romance.* 1796. Edited by Robert Miles. Reprint, London: Penguin, 2000.

Ravage, Jack. "*The Night of the Hunter* (On Videotape)." *Film Quarterly* 42, no. 1 (1988): 43–46.

Reader's Digest Condensed Books. Vol. 17, *Spring 1954 Selections.* Pleasantville, N.Y.: Reader's Digest, 1954.

Ringe, Donald A. *American Gothic: Imagination and Reason in Nineteenth-Century Fiction.* Lexington: University Press of Kentucky, 1982.

Robinson, David. *The History of World Cinema.* 1973. Reprint, New York: Stein and Day, 1974.

Rohmer, Sax. *The Insidious Dr. Fu-Manchu: Being a Somewhat Detailed Account of the Amazing Adventures of Nayland Smith in His Trailing of the Sinister Chinaman.* 1913. Reprint, Mineola, N.Y.: Dover, 1997.

Roizman, Owen. "ASC Close-up." *American Cinematographer* 85, no. 8 (2004): 104.

Sage, Victor. Introduction. In Maturin, *Melmoth the Wanderer,* vii–xxix.

Sarris, Andrew. "Notes on the *Auteur* Theory in 1962." In *Film Culture Reader,* edited by P. Adams Sitney, 121–35. New York: Praeger, 1970.

Schallert, Edwin. "*Night of Hunter* Eerie, Powerful." Review of *The Night of the Hunter,* directed by Charles Laughton. *Los Angeles Times,* August 27, 1955.

Schatz, Thomas. *The Genius of the System: Hollywood Filmmaking in the Studio Era.* 1988. Reprint, New York: Holt, Metro, 1996.

Schickel, Richard. *D. W. Griffith: An American Life.* 1984. Reprint, New York: Limelight, 1996.

Schrader, Paul. *Transcendental Style in Film: Ozu, Bresson, Dreyer.* Berkeley: University of California Press, 1972.

Schumann, Walter. "*The Night of the Hunter.*" *Film Music* 15, no. 1 (1955): 13–17.

Seib, Kenneth. *James Agee: Promise and Fulfillment.* Pittsburgh: University of Pittsburgh Press, 1968.

Server, Lee. *Robert Mitchum: "Baby, I Don't Care."* New York: St. Martin's, 2001.

Shaw, George Bernard. *Man and Superman.* In *Plays by George Bernard Shaw,* 236–405. New York: New American, Signet, 1960.

Shelley, Mary. *Frankenstein; or, The Modern Prometheus.* 1818. Edited by Maurice Hindle. Reprint, London: Penguin, 1992.

Silver, Alain, and James Ursini, eds. *Film Noir Reader.* New York: Limelight, 1996.

Singer, Kurt. *The Laughton Story: An Intimate Story of Charles Laughton.* Philadelphia: Winston, 1954.

Smollett, Tobias. *The Adventures of Ferdinand Count Fathom.* 1753. Edited by Paul-Gabriel Bouce. Reprint, London: Penguin, 1990.

Speicher, Charlotte B. "New Films from Books." Review of *The Night of the Hunter,* directed by Charles Laughton. *Library Journal* 80, no. 18 (1955): 2231.

Stam, Robert. "Beyond Fidelity: The Dialogics of Adaptation." In *Film Adaptation,* edited by James Naremore, 54–76. New Brunswick, N.J.: Rutgers University Press, 2000.

Steinberg, Cobbett. *Reel Facts: The Movie Book of Records.* New York: Random, Vintage, 1978.

St. Johns, Adela Rogers. *Love, Laughter and Tears: My Hollywood Story.* Garden City, N.Y.: Doubleday, 1978.

Stoker, Bram. *Dracula.* 1897. Reprint, New York: Dell, Laurel, 1965.

Strong, L. A. G. "New Novels." Review of *The Night of the Hunter,* by Davis Grubb. *Spectator,* July 9, 1954, 70.

Stuart, Jesse. "Split Cherry Tree." In *The Best-Loved Short Stories of Jesse Stuart,* edited by H. Edward Richardson, 135–47. New York: McGraw, 1982. Originally published in *Esquire,* January 1939, 52–53, 99–100.

Taylor, John Russell. Review of *Agee on Film: Five Film Scripts by James Agee. Sight and Sound* 30, no. 1 (1960–61): 46–47.

Thompson, Kristin, and David Bordwell. *Film History: An Introduction*. New York: McGraw-Hill, 1994.

Thomson, David. "A Child's Demon." *Sight and Sound* 9, no. 4 (1999): 20–22.

Time. "Killer in Cresap's Landing." Review of *The Night of the Hunter*, by Davis Grubb. Books. March 1, 1954, 92.

Truffaut, François. "Charles Laughton: *The Night of the Hunter*." In *The Films in My Life*, translated by Leonard Mayhew, 119–20. 1978. Reprint, New York: Da Capo, 1994.

Turner, George E. "Creating *The Night of the Hunter*." *American Cinematographer* 64, no. 12 (1982), 1272–76, 1335–41.

Twain, Mark [Samuel Langhorne Clemens]. *Adventures of Huckleberry Finn*. 1885. Edited by Sculley Bradley, Richmond Croom Beatty, E. Hudson Long, and Thomas Cooley. 2nd ed. Norton Critical Editions. New York: Norton, 1977.

———. *Life on the Mississippi*. 1883. Edited by John Seelye. Reprint, Oxford: Oxford University Press, 1990.

Uricchio, William, and Roberta E. Pearson. *Reframing Culture: The Case of the Vitagraph Quality Films*. Princeton, N.J.: Princeton University Press, 1993.

Viertel, Salka. *The Kindness of Strangers*. New York: Holt, 1969.

Wagenknecht, Edward. *Lillian Gish: An Interpretation*. In *Movies in the Age of Innocence*, by Edward Wagenknecht, 237–48. 1962. Reprint, New York: Ballantine, 1971. Originally published as University of Washington Chapbooks 7. Seattle: University of Washington Bookstore, 1927.

Wagner, Geoffrey. *The Novel and the Cinema*. Rutherford, N.J.: Fairleigh Dickinson University Press, 1975.

Walpole, Horace. *The Castle of Otranto: A Gothic Story*. 1764. Edited by W. S. Lewis. Reprint, London: Oxford University Press, 1969.

Warren, Robert Penn. *World Enough and Time: A Romantic Novel*. New York: Random, 1950.

Welch, Jack. *Davis Grubb: A Vision of Appalachia*. Ann Arbor, Mich.: University Microfilms, 1980.

West, Anthony. "Arcadia Run to Seed." Review of *The Night of the Hunter*, by Davis Grubb. *New Yorker*, March 20, 1954, 120–22.

West, Herbert F. "A Heritage Full of Dread." Review of *The Night of the Hunter*, by Davis Grubb. *New York Times Book Review*, February 21, 1954, 4–5.

Williams, Dick. "*Night of the Hunter* Consciously Arty." Review of *The Night of the Hunter*, directed by Charles Laughton. *Mirror-News*, August 27, 1955.

Wilt, Judith. *Ghosts of the Gothic: Austen, Eliot, and Lawrence*. Princeton, N.J.: Princeton University Press, 1980.

Winner, Michael. "The Night of the Hunter." Review of *The Night of the Hunter*, directed by Charles Laughton. *Films and Filming*, January 1956, 22–23.

Winters, Shelley. *Shelley: Also Known as Shirley*. 1980. Reprint, New York: Ballantine, 1981.

————. *Shelley II: The Middle of My Century.* 1989. Reprint, New York: Simon, Pocket Books, 1990.

Wolfe, Thomas. *Look Homeward, Angel: A Story of the Buried Life.* 1929. Reprint, New York: Scribner, 1957.

————. *Of Time and the River: A Legend of Man's Hunger in His Youth.* 1935. Reprint, New York: Scribner, 1999.

————. Thomas Wolfe to F. Scott Fitzgerald, July 26, 1937. In *The Letters of Thomas Wolfe,* edited by Elizabeth Nowell, 641–45. New York: Scribner, 1956.

————. *You Can't Go Home Again.* New York: Harper, 1940.

Wood, Ann, ed. "New Creative Writers: 48 Novelists Whose First Work Appears This Season." *Library Journal* 79, no. 4 (1954): 370–77.

Wood, Michael. *America in the Movies; or, "Santa Maria, It Had Slipped My Mind."* New York: Basic Books, 1975.

Wood, Robin. "*Night of the Hunter*/Novel into Film." Test market edition, *On Film* 1, no. zero (December 1970): 68–71. Reprinted as "Charles Laughton on Grubb Street" in *The Modern American Novel and the Movies,* edited by Gerald Peary and Roger Shatzkin, 204–14. New York: Ungar, 1978.

Wouk, Herman. *The Caine Mutiny Court-Martial: A Drama in Two Acts.* Garden City, N.Y.: Doubleday, 1954.

Zinsser, William K. Screen. Review of *The Night of the Hunter,* directed by Charles Laughton. *New York Herald-Tribune,* September 30, 1955.

Films

Abbott and Costello Meet Captain Kidd. Directed by Charles Lamont. Cinematography by Stanley Cortez. With Charles Laughton. Warner Bros., 1952.

Abbott and Costello Meet Frankenstein. Directed by Charles T. Barton. Art direction by Hilyard Brown and Bernard Herzbrun. Universal, 1948.

The Adventures of Dollie. Directed by D. W. Griffith. Biograph, 1908.

Advise and Consent. Directed by Otto Preminger. With Charles Laughton. Columbia, 1962.

The African Queen. Directed by John Huston. Screenplay by James Agee and John Huston. Based on the novel by C. S. Forester. United Artists, 1951.

All That Heaven Allows. Directed by Douglas Sirk. Universal, 1955.

Around the World in Eighty Days. Directed by Michael Anderson. United Artists, 1956.

Arsenic and Old Lace. Directed by Frank Capra. With James Gleason. Warner Bros., 1944.

Badlands of Dakota. Directed by Alfred E. Green. Cinematography by Stanley Cortez. Universal, 1941.

The Bad Seed. Directed by Mervyn LeRoy. With Evelyn Varden. Warner Bros., 1956.

Bande à part. Directed by Jean-Luc Godard. Columbia, 1964.

The Barretts of Wimpole Street. Directed by Sidney Franklin. With Charles Laughton. MGM, 1934.

The Beast from 20,000 Fathoms. Directed by Eugene Lourie. Warner Bros., 1953.

Ben-Hur. Directed by William Wyler. MGM, 1959.

The Best Years of Our Lives. Directed by William Wyler. With Don Beddoe. RKO, 1946.

The Big Knife. Directed by Robert Aldrich. With Shelley Winters. United Artists, 1955.

The Big Steal. Directed by Don Siegel. With Robert Mitchum. RKO, 1949.

The Birth of a Nation. Directed by D. W. Griffith. Epoch, 1915.

The Black Cat. Directed by Albert S. Rogell. Cinematography by Stanley Cortez. Universal, 1941.

The Black Cat. Directed by Edgar G. Ulmer. Universal, 1934.

Black Tuesday. Directed by Hugo Fregonese. Cinematography by Stanley Cortez. Art direction by Hilyard Brown. Edited by Robert Golden. With Peter Graves. United Artists, 1954.

Broken Blossoms. Directed by D. W. Griffith. With Lillian Gish. United Artists, 1919.

The Cabinet of Dr. Caligari. Directed by Robert Wiene. Decla, 1920.

Cape Fear. Directed by J. Lee Thompson. With Robert Mitchum. Universal, 1962.

Captain Blood. Directed by Michael Curtiz. Warner Bros., 1935.

Carmen Jones. Directed by Otto Preminger. Title sequence by Saul Bass. Twentieth Century-Fox, 1954.

Cheaper by the Dozen. Directed by Walter Lang. With Evelyn Varden. Twentieth Century-Fox, 1950.

Chinatown. Directed by Roman Polanski. Paramount, 1974.

Citizen Kane. Directed by Orson Welles. Assistant art direction by Hilyard Brown [uncredited]. RKO, 1941.

The Clock. Directed by Vincente Minnelli. With James Gleason. MGM, 1945.

The Cobweb. Directed by Vincente Minnelli. With Lillian Gish. MGM, 1955.

The Country Girl. Directed by George Seaton. Paramount, 1954.

Creature from the Black Lagoon. Directed by Jack Arnold. Art direction by Hilyard Brown and Bernard Herzbrun. Universal, 1954.

Days of Wine and Roses. Directed by Blake Edwards. Warner Bros., 1962.

Dead Man's Gulch. Directed by John English. With Emmett "Pappy" Lynn. Republic, 1943.

Devil and the Deep. Directed by Marion Gering. With Charles Laughton. Paramount, 1932.

Do the Right Thing. Directed by Spike Lee. Universal, 1989.

Double Indemnity. Directed by Billy Wilder. Paramount, 1944.

A Double Life. Directed by George Cukor. With Shelley Winters. Universal, 1947.

Dracula. Directed by Tod Browning. Universal, 1931.

Dr. Mabuse: The Gambler. Directed by Fritz Lang. UFA, 1922.

Duel in the Sun. Directed by King Vidor. With Lillian Gish. Selznick, 1946.

Earth versus the Flying Saucers. Directed by Fred F. Sears. Columbia, 1956.

False Colors. Directed by George Archainbaud. With Bob Mitchum. United Artists, 1943.

Faust. Directed by F. W. Murnau. UFA, 1926.

Flesh and Fantasy. Directed by Julien Duvivier. Cinematography by Stanley Cortez and Paul Ivano. Universal, 1943.

Fools' Parade. Directed by Andrew V. McLaglen. Based on the novel by Davis Grubb. Columbia, 1971.

Forbidden Games. Directed by René Clément. Films Corona, 1952.

The Forgotten Woman. Directed by Harold Young. Cinematography by Stanley Cortez. Universal, 1939.

The Four Horsemen of the Apocalypse. Directed by Rex Ingram. Metro, 1921.

Frankenstein. Directed by James Whale. Universal, 1931.

Frankenstein Meets the Wolf Man. Directed by Roy William Neill. Universal, 1943.

The Golem: How He Came into the World. Directed by Paul Wegener and Carl Boese. UFA, 1920.

Gone with the Wind. Directed by Victor Fleming. MGM, 1939.

Grandma's Boy. Directed by Fred Newmeyer. Pathé, 1922.

The Grapes of Wrath. Directed by John Ford. Twentieth Century-Fox, 1940.

Greed. Directed by Erich von Stroheim. MGM, 1924.

Here Comes Mr. Jordan. Directed by Alexander Hall. With James Gleason. Columbia, 1941.

Hobson's Choice. Directed by David Lean. With Charles Laughton. British Lion, 1954.

House of Dracula. Directed by Erle C. Kenton. Universal, 1945.

The Hunchback of Notre Dame. Directed by William Dieterle. With Charles Laughton. RKO, 1939.

Intolerance. Directed by D. W. Griffith. With Lillian Gish. Wark, 1916.

Invaders from Mars. Directed by William Cameron Menzies. Twentieth Century-Fox, 1953.

I Want to Live! Directed by Robert Wise. MGM, 1958.

The Killers. Directed by Robert Siodmak. Universal, 1946.

Le doulos. Directed by Jean-Pierre Melville. Pathé, 1962.

Les misérables. Directed by Richard Boleslawski. With Charles Laughton. United Artists, 1935.

The Life of Moses. Directed by J. Stuart Blackton. Vitagraph, 1909–10.

M. Directed by Fritz Lang. Vereinigte, 1931.

The Magnificent Ambersons. Directed by Orson Welles. Cinematography by Stanley Cortez. RKO, 1942.

The Maltese Falcon. Directed by John Huston. Screenplay by John Huston. Based on the novel by Dashiell Hammett. Warner Bros., 1941.

The Man on the Eiffel Tower. Directed by Burgess Meredith [Irving Allen and Charles Laughton uncredited]. Cinematography by Stanley Cortez. With Charles Laughton. RKO, 1949.

Marty. Directed by Delbert Mann. Screenplay by Paddy Chayefsky. Based on his television play (*Goodyear Television Playhouse*, NBC, May 24, 1953), United Artists, 1955.

McCabe and Mrs. Miller. Directed by Robert Altman. Warner Bros., 1971.

A Midsummer Night's Dream. Directed by Max Reinhardt and William Dieterle. Warner Bros., 1935.

Mister Roberts. Directed by John Ford and Mervyn LeRoy. Warner Bros., 1955.

Mother Goose Goes Hollywood. Directed by Wilfred Jackson. RKO, 1938.

The Mummy. Directed by Karl Freund. Universal, 1932.

Mutiny on the Bounty. Directed by Frank Lloyd. With Charles Laughton. MGM, 1935.

The Naked and the Dead. Produced by Paul Gregory. Directed by Raoul Walsh. Screenplay by Denis Sanders and Terry Sanders. RKO, 1958.

Napoléon. Directed by Abel Gance. MGM, 1927.

New York, New York. Directed by Martin Scorsese. United Artists, 1977.

The Night of the Hunter. Directed by Charles Laughton. Based on the novel by Davis Grubb. Screenplay by James Agee [Charles Laughton uncredited]. Cinematography by Stanley Cortez. Art direction by Hilyard Brown. Edited by Robert Golden. Music by Walter Schumann. With Robert Mitchum, Shelley Winters, Lillian Gish, James Gleason, Evelyn Varden, Peter Graves, Don Beddoe, Billy Chapin, and Sally Jane Bruce. United Artists, 1955.

North by Northwest. Directed by Alfred Hitchcock. Title sequence by Saul Bass. MGM, 1959.

Nosferatu. Directed by F. W. Murnau. Prana-Film, 1922.

Not as a Stranger. Directed by Stanley Kramer. With Robert Mitchum. United Artists, 1955.

Oklahoma! Directed by Fred Zinneman. Magna, 1955.

The Old Dark House. Directed by James Whale. With Charles Laughton. Universal, 1932.

On Dangerous Ground. Directed by Nicholas Ray. RKO, 1952.

Orphans of the Storm. Directed by D. W. Griffith. With Lillian Gish. United Artists, 1921.

The Outlaw and His Wife. Directed by Victor Sjöström. Svenska, 1918.

Out of the Past. Directed by Jacques Tourneur. With Robert Mitchum. RKO, 1947.

The Patsy. Directed by King Vidor. MGM, 1928.

Peyton Place. Directed by Mark Robson. Twentieth Century-Fox, 1957.

Picnic. Directed by Joshua Logan. Columbia, 1955.

A Place in the Sun. Directed by George Stevens. With Shelley Winters. Paramount, 1951.

Portrait of Jennie. Directed by William Dieterle. With Lillian Gish. Selznick, 1948.

The Private Life of Henry VIII. Directed by Alexander Korda. With Charles Laughton and Elsa Lanchester. United Artists, 1933.

Quo Vadis. Directed by Mervyn LeRoy. MGM, 1951.

Rachel and the Stranger. Directed by Norman Foster. With Robert Mitchum. RKO, 1948.

Rebecca of Sunnybrook Farm. Directed by Marshall Neilan. Paramount, 1917.

Rembrandt. Directed by Alexander Korda. With Charles Laughton and Elsa Lanchester. United Artists, 1936.

The Robe. Directed by Henry Koster. Twentieth Century-Fox, 1953.

The Rocky Horror Picture Show. Directed by Jim Sharman. Twentieth Century-Fox, 1975.

Ruggles of Red Gap. Directed by Leo McCarey. With Charles Laughton. Paramount, 1935.

Salome. Directed by William Dieterle. With Charles Laughton. Columbia, 1953.

Samson and Delilah. Directed by Cecil B. DeMille. Paramount, 1949.

The Scarlet Letter. Directed by Victor Seastrom. With Lillian Gish. MGM, 1926.

The Sea Hawk. Directed by Michael Curtiz. Warner Bros., 1940.

Secret Beyond the Door. Directed by Fritz Lang. Cinematography by Stanley Cortez. Republic, 1948.

Shadow of a Doubt. Directed by Alfred Hitchcock. Universal, 1943.

Shock Corridor. Directed by Samuel Fuller. Cinematography by Stanley Cortez. Allied Artists, 1963.

The Sign of the Cross. Directed by Cecil B. DeMille. With Charles Laughton. Paramount, 1932.

The Silver Chalice. Directed by Victor Saville. Warner Bros., 1954.

Since You Went Away. Directed by John Cromwell. Cinematography by Stanley Cortez and Lee Garmes. United Artists, 1944.

Singin' in the Rain. Directed by Gene Kelly and Stanley Donen. MGM, 1952.

The Sorrows of Satan. Directed by D. W. Griffith. Paramount, 1926.

Spartacus. Directed by Stanley Kubrick. With Charles Laughton. Universal, 1960.

Stalag 17. Directed by Billy Wilder. With Peter Graves. Paramount, 1953.

Steamboat Bill, Jr. Directed by Charles F. Reisner. United Artists, 1928.

Sudden Fear. Directed by David Miller. RKO, 1952.

Sunrise: A Song of Two Humans. Directed by F. W. Murnau. Fox, 1927.

Talk to Her. Directed by Pedro Almodóvar. Sony, 2002.

Tarantula. Directed by Jack Arnold. Universal, 1955.

The Ten Commandments. Directed by Cecil B. DeMille. Paramount, 1956.

Terje Vigen. Directed by Victor Sjöström. Svenska, 1917.

Them! Directed by Gordon Douglas. Warner Bros., 1954.

The Thing from Another World. Directed by Christian Nyby. RKO, 1951.

The Three Faces of Eve. Directed by Nunnally Johnson. Cinematography by Stanley Cortez. Twentieth Century-Fox, 1957.

A Time out of War. Directed by Denis Sanders. Cinematography by Terry Sanders. Screenplay by Denis Sanders. Based on the story "The Pickets" by Robert W. Chambers. Carnival Productions, 1954.

Tirez sur le pianiste. Directed by François Truffaut. Cocinor, 1960.

Tobor the Great. Directed by Lee Sholem. With Billy Chapin. Republic, 1954.

Tol'able David. Directed by Henry King. First National, 1921.

Touch of Evil. Directed by Orson Welles. Universal, 1958.

Under Ten Flags. Directed by Duilio Coletti. With Charles Laughton. Paramount, 1960.

Vertigo. Directed by Alfred Hitchcock. Title sequence by Saul Bass. Paramount, 1958.

Wagon Train. Directed by Edward Killy. With Emmett Lynn. RKO, 1940.

Walk on the Wild Side. Directed by Edward Dmytryk. Title sequence by Saul Bass. Columbia, 1962.

Way Down East. Directed by D. W. Griffith. With Lillian Gish. United Artists, 1920.

Weekend. Directed by Jean-Luc Godard. Athos, 1967.

The White Sister. Directed by Henry King. With Lillian Gish. Metro, 1923.

The Wind. Directed by Victor Seastrom. With Lillian Gish. MGM, 1928.

The Window. Directed by Ted Tetzlaff. RKO, 1949.

Witness for the Prosecution. Directed by Billy Wilder. With Charles Laughton and Elsa Lanchester. United Artists, 1957.

The Wolf Man. Directed by George Waggner. Universal, 1941.

Wyoming Renegades. Directed by Fred F. Sears. With Don Beddoe. Columbia, 1954.

CREDITS

Art

Figures 3.1, 3.3, 3.4, 3.6, 3.7, 3.8, 3.9, 3.10, 3.11, and 7.1 are reprinted courtesy of the Margaret Herrick Library, Academy of Motion Picture Arts and Sciences and with permission from the Estate of Davis Grubb.

Figure 3.2 is reprinted from *Blake's Illustrations for the Book of Job* (New York: Dover, 1995), 21.

Figure 3.5 is reprinted from *George Grosz: Die Gezeichneten* (Berlin: Malik-Verlag, 1930), 121. Art © 1929 Estate of George Grosz/Licensed by VAGA, New York, New York.

Figures 5.1, 5.2, 5.3, 5.4, 5.5, and 5.6 are reprinted courtesy of Terry Sanders.

Music

Unless otherwise indicated, the musical examples in chapter 6, notated by Greg Pliska, follow those that Schumann created for his *Film Music* article.

Example 6.1 is from "Main Title" from *The Night of the Hunter*, by Walter Schumann. Copyright © 1955 by Bourne Co. Copyright renewed. All rights reserved. International copyright secured. ASCAP.

Examples 6.2 and 6.7 are from "The Muddy Place" from *The Night of the Hunter*, by Walter Schumann. Copyright © 1955 by Bourne Co. Copyright renewed. All rights reserved. International copyright secured. ASCAP.

Example 6.3 is from "Main Title" from *The Night of the Hunter*, music by Walter Schumann, words by Davis Grubb. Copyright © 1955 by Bourne Co. Copyright renewed. All rights reserved. International copyright secured. ASCAP.

Example 6.4 is from "Uncle Birdie" from *The Night of the Hunter*, by Walter Schumann. Copyright © 1955 by Bourne Co. Copyright renewed. All rights reserved. International copyright secured. ASCAP.

Example 6.5 is from "Rachel and the Kids" from *The Night of the Hunter*, by Walter Schumann. Copyright © 1955 by Bourne Co. Copyright renewed. All rights reserved. International copyright secured. ASCAP.

Example 6.6 is from "Pretty Fly (Part One)" from *The Night of the Hunter,* music by Walter Schumann, words by Davis Grubb. Copyright © 1955 by Bourne Co. Copyright renewed. All rights reserved. International copyright secured. ASCAP.

Examples 6.8 and 6.10 are from "Willa's Waltz" from *The Night of the Hunter,* by Walter Schumann. Copyright © 1955 by Bourne Co. Copyright renewed. All rights reserved. International copyright secured. ASCAP.

Examples 6.9 and 6.11 are from "There Goes Willa" from *The Night of the Hunter,* by Walter Schumann. Copyright © 1955 by Bourne Co. Copyright renewed. All rights reserved. International copyright secured. ASCAP.

Example 6.12 is from "Willa's Waltz," music by Walter Schumann, words by Paul Francis Webster. Copyright © 1955 by Bourne Co. Copyright renewed. All rights reserved. International copyright secured. ASCAP.

Example 6.13 is reprinted from *Hymns of the Christian Life: A Book of Worship in Song Emphasizing Evangelism, Missions, and the Deeper Life* (Harrisburg, Pa.: Christian, 1936), 310.

Credits for textual material appear in the notes upon first citation of each source for which permission to reprint has been obtained.

INDEX

Callow, Simon, 11, 14, 48, 214; on Brechtian acting, 176–77; on Laughton–Agee partnership, 87; on Laughton as director, 106; on reception of *Night of the Hunter,* 196; on start of Laughton–Gregory partnership, 17
Cape Fear (film, 1962), 122, 175, 219
Captain Blood (film, 1935), 154
Carmello, Carolee, 221
Carmen Jones (film, 1954), 198
Carringer, Robert L., xxiv
Carroll, Noël, 34
Carter, Milton, 98, 99, 123
Castilo, Gloria, 134, 140, 167, 190. *See also* Ruby (character)
Castle of Otranto (Walpole), 31, 32
"Cautious Man" (Springsteen song), 218
Cavalier magazine, 45
Chamberlain, Richard, 219, 220
Chandler, Raymond, 121
Chapin, Billy, 133, 140, 180, 187, 223, 243n2; double (stand-in) for, 108; Laughton's direction and, 144, 146; performance as John, 190–93. *See also* Harper, John (character)
"Charles Laughton Directs *The Night of the Hunter*" (Gitt), 216
Chatman, Seymour, xxi
Chaumeton, Étienne, 120
Chautauqua movement, 7, 25
Chayefsky, Paddy, 205
Cheaper by the Dozen (film, 1950), 184
"Checker-Playing Fool" (Grubb), 45
Chekhov, Anton, 11
Cherry Orchard, The (Chekhov play), 13
children: fairy-tale heroes and, 43; Grubb's view of, 9; "Hing, hang, hung" song and, 86; point of view of, 103; viewing of *Night of the Hunter* and, xx, 222
Chinatown (film, 1974), 216
Christianity/religion, 77, 201, 203–4; biblical epics of 1950s and, 202–3; hypocrisy in the church and, 48; Pietà imagery and, 107; revival meeting scene and, 188–89; Southern gothic and, 36–38
CinemaScope, xxvii, 201

cinematography, xx, 104, 106–7, 223; balanced shots, 21; "close pull shot," 102; cut back to master shot, 124–25, 130; day-for-night, 108; dolly shots, 102; helicopter shots, 55, 83, 94, 126, 152; iris, 84–85, 86; light and shadow, 107, 108–9, 117–18, 120–21, 128, 136–37; silent-film techniques, 129–34; union regulations and, 125
Cinerama, xxvii
Citizen Kane (film, 1941), 110
Clary (character), 132, 140, 173
Clash (punk-rock group), 217–18
Clemons, Mary Ellen, 140
Clift, Montgomery, 187
Clock, The (film, 1945), 181
Clyde, Andy, 175
Cobweb, The (film, 1955), 179
Coco, Anne, xxiv
Cohn, Harry, 166
Colbert, Claudette, 212
Cole, Stephen, 221
Colgate Comedy Hour, The (TV show), 4
Colleran, Bill, 212
Collier, John, 74
Collier's magazine, 45
Collins, Ray, 105
Colman, Ronald, 187
Columbia Pictures, 202–3
Columbia Workshop, The (radio show), 20
Coming to Terms (Chatman), xxi
Congdon, Don, 39, 49
Congreve, William, 11
Cooper, Lovey (character), 77, 92
Cooper, Rachel (character), 31, 39, 115; absence from television adaptation, 220; in Agee's screenplay, 77, 81; based on friend of Grubb's, 9; biblical stories/quotations told by, 141, 146, 172; casting for, 54–55, 69, 179; Christian teachings and, 37–38, 42; gift of watch to John, 145–46; Gish's performance as, 174, 177, 179–80; gothic tradition and, 32, 34–35; in Grubb's sketches, 69; harmony with nature, 123; as ideal of goodness, 34, 42, 121; John

carried in Pietà image, 107; John's conflict with, 78; as keeper of narrative, 146–48; literary kin of, 40–41, 48, 49; musical score and, 152, 154, 167–68; night vigil of, 94; orphans and, 132; plot synopsis of novel and, 6; Preacher defeated by, 143–45, 171; on Ruby's sexual desires, 203; in stage musical version, 221–22; visual scheme of film and, 137. *See also* Gish, Lillian

Cortez, Ricardo, 104

Cortez, Stanley, xxv, 21, 62, 134, 190, 223; *Black Tuesday* and, 99; career of, 104–5; cinematography of, 104, 220; enthusiasm for working with Laughton, 98; Grubb's sketches and, 65; on iris shot of children in basement, 86; Laughton defended by, 215–16; on Laughton's lack of technical knowledge, 101; Laughton's working relationship with, 105–13; *Magnificent Ambersons* and, xx, 105, 107, 109; musical score and, 162; Tri-X film stock used by, 136–37; unified synthesis of film and, 135

Corwin, Norman, 20, 212

Costello, Dolores, 105

Costello, Lou, 3–4

Cotten, Joseph, 174

Country Girl, The (film, 1954), 188

Crane, Stephen, 73

Crawford, Joan, 206

Creature from the Black Lagoon (film, 1954), 207

Cresap's Landing (fictional town), 4–6, 55, 73; Grubb's sketch of, 65, 65; Preacher's arrival in, 135, 167; religion in, 169; small towns of 1950s films and, 209

Crescendo (TV production), 212

criminal psychology, 120

Crisp, Donald, 132

critics, xix, xxvii, 30, 193–94, 199–201; on Grubb's novel, 49–52; on Laughton's prospects as film director, 213; reassessment of *Night of the Hunter* by, 215–16; variety of responses from, 206

Cronjager, Henry, 127

Crosby, Bing, 176

Crowell, Josephine, 130

Crowther, Bosley, 200, 213

cult movies, 217

Cult Movies (Peary), 217

Cunningham, Miz (character), 47, 48, 57, 146, 184; in Agee's screenplay, 77, 81; secondhand shop in Grubb's sketches, 68–69

Currie, Finlay, 203

Damico, James, 120

Darwell, Jane, 54–55, 69, 179

David Copperfield (Dickens), 49

Davies, Marion, 178

Day Lincoln Was Shot, The (film, 1956), 174, 243n2

Dead Man's Gulch (film, 1943), 180

Death in the Family, A (Agee), xx, 73, 91

"Death or Glory" (Clash song), 217–18

DeFore, Don, 195

Dell Publishing, 199

DeMille, Cecil B., 202, 208

Depression (1930s), xix, 4, 73, 79; description in Grubb's novel of, 116; Grubb's childhood during, 8; represented in Agee's screenplay, 74–75

Devil and the Deep (film, 1932), 10

Dickens, Charles, 21, 30, 48–49, 103, 210

Dieterle, William, 11–12, 115, 212

Dollmaker, The (Arnow), 50

Don Juan in Hell (Shaw), xxiii, 3, 19, 21, 24; musical aspects of, 22–23; press attention to, 26

Dorsey, Tommy, 15

Dos Passos, John, 213

Do the Right Thing (film, 1989), 218–19

Double Indemnity (film, 1944), 80, 121

Double Life, A (film, 1947), 187–88

Douglass, Thomas E., xxiii, 42

doulos, Le (film, 1962), 216

Dracula (film, 1931), 118, 119

Dracula (Stoker), 35

Dream of Kings, A (Grubb), 9, 56

Driscoll, Bobby, 206

television adaptation, 219. *See also* Graves, Peter

Harper, John (character), 23, 122, 208; in Agee's screenplay, 75–76, 78, 81; basement-window iris shot and, 86; battle of wills with Preacher, 142–43, 177; bedtime story told by, 141, 144–45; carried in Pietà image by Rachel, 107; Chapin's performance as, 190–93; children's taunting song and, 93, 101–2; Christian teachings and, 37–38; in conflict with female characters, 78; double (stand-in) for, 108; dreamlike quality of film and, 135; escape from Preacher in boat, 130–31, 133; gothic tradition and, 31–32; in Grubb's sketches, 67, 68; Hamlet and, 47–48; interior monologues of, 38–39, 104, 141–42, 148; musical score and, 155–56, 160–61; narrative point of view and, 40, 61, 136; plot synopsis of Grubb's novel and, 4–6; at Preacher's trial, 135, 139; rejection of fathers/authority by, 139–40, 143–44; rite of passage into adulthood, 141–42, 146; river journey of, 39–40, 43, 68, 138; in television adaptation, 219, 220; watch as gift from Rachel, 145–46. *See also* Chapin, Billy

Harper, Pearl (character), 23, 31, 171; in Agee's screenplay, 75–76; basement-window iris shot and, 86; Bruce's performance as, 190–93; children's taunting song and, 93, 101–2; double (stand-in) for, 108; escape from Preacher in boat, 130, 133; musical score and, 155–57, 160–61, 169; plot synopsis of Grubb's novel and, 5–6; river journey of, 39–40, 43, 68, 138; secret of hidden money and, 94, 95, 124–25, 137, 177; story told to doll by, 141; in television adaptation, 219–20. *See also* Bruce, Sally Jane

Harper, Willa (character), 35, 43, 122–23, 124, 142, 186; in Agee's screenplay, 78, 79–80, 85; gothic

passion and, 34; in Grubb's sketches, 57; murder of, 61, 85, 86, 116–17, 162, 164, 165, 171; musical score and, 152–53, 161–66; naïveté of, 31, 47, 145, 165, 167; plot synopsis of Grubb's novel and, 4, 5; at revival meeting, 67–68, 70, 85, 92; sex channeled into evangelism, 203; in stage musical version, 221; in television adaptation, 220; underwater corpse of, 51, 67, 69, 81, 109–11, 123, 136, 159, 165–66; Winters's performance, 187–90. *See also* Winters, Shelley

Harper and Brothers, ix, 49

Harris, Jed, 13

Harrison, Rex, 212

Hartford, Huntington, 73

Hawthorne, Nathaniel, 35

Hayne, Barrie, 223

Hayworth, Rita, 202

Heaven and Hell to Play With (Jones), xx, xxv, 87

Heimrich, George A., 169

Here Comes Mr. Jordan (film, 1941), 181

Higham, Charles, xxiii, 74, 78, 106

highbrow art, 4, 26

Highbrow/Lowbrow (Levine), 208

histrionic code, 193

Hitchcock, Alfred, xxii, 102, 106, 174

Hoberman, J., 217

Hobson's Choice (film, 1954), 101

Hodiak, John, 22

Hoffberg, Sy, xxv, 190

Holden, William, 175

Hollywood film industry, xix, 13, 53, 149, 237n61; biblical epics and, 202–3; horror stories and, 35; hypocrisy of, 167; sentimental endings and, 172; standard practices of, 101; styles and genres of the past, 216; television and, 215. *See also* Breen Office

Hollywood Reporter, 196

Holt, Tim, 105, 180

Holzhauer, Jean, 49

horror, literature of, 30, 31, 34

horror films, xix, 118–19, 134, 200, 206; art cinema blended with, 208; "seven branches" of, 207

film and, 195–96, 199; readings by, 19, 25, 26–27, 28, 210; realism in mode of Griffith, 122–29; recordings, 19; Schumann's collaboration with, 148–50, 170; stage productions, xxiii, 11–13, 23, 212–13; as storyteller, 26–29, 223; stylized effects and, 59–60, 64; supporting cast and, 180–83; on television, 17, 25, 228n3; unified synthesis of film and, 135; Winters and, 188–90. *See also* Agee–Laughton partnership; Grubb–Laughton collaboration

Laughton–Gregory partnership, xxii–xxiii, xxvii, 3–4, 12, 13, 14, 223; balance in, 24; end of, 211–14; first meeting, 17–19; *Naked and the Dead* and, 209–11, 213–14; stage productions and, 13, 19–24

Lean, David, 101

"Leaning on the Everlasting Arms" (hymn), xx, xxv–xxvi, 46, 101, 138, 172; "pagan motif" of, 150; Rachel's duet with Preacher, 167–68, 169, 170; as secondary theme associated with evil, 153; as sound of terror, 159–60. *See also* musical score, for *Night of the Hunter*

Lee, Russell, 127

Lee, Spike, 218–19

Legion of Decency, 204

Lemmon, Jack, 174, 243n2

Lenhart, Jason Burton. *See* Gregory, Paul

Leontovich, Eugénie, 13

LeRoy, Mervyn, 203

Let Us Now Praise Famous Men (Agee), 73, 76, 79, 116

Levine, Lawrence W., 208

Levy, Emanuel, 209

Lewis, Matthew, 32, 35, 36

Lewis, Sinclair, 9

Library Journal, 200

Library of America, xxiv, 24

Library of Congress, xix, xxvi, 43, 54–55, 197, 216

Life of Galileo, The (Brecht), 12

Life of Moses, The (film, 1909–10), 202

Life on the Mississippi (Twain), 39

Lloyd, Harold, 126

Lloyd, Norman, 73

Lodger, The (Lowndes), 30

Look Homeward, Angel (Wolfe), 39

"Lord Arthur Savile's Crime" (Wilde), 105

Lorre, Peter, 118

Losey, Joseph, 13

lowbrow art, 4

Lowndes, Marie Belloc, 30

Lugosi, Bela, 119

lynch mob scene, 37, 46; actual incident as basis for, 45; in Agee's draft, 86, 183; expressionism and, 61, 119; horror film genre and, 119; musical score and, 150, 155, 158, 168, 170, 183; as narrative anticlimax, 182–83; Spoons in, 6, 34, 168, 182–85, *186*

Lynn, Emmett, 180–81

M (film, 1931), 46, 117, 118, 126

MacAndrew, Elizabeth, 31

Macdonald, Dwight, 91

MacMurray, Fred, 121

Magnificent Ambersons, The (film, 1942), xx, 105, 107, 109, 110

Mailer, Norman, xxvii, 209–11, 212, 213

Major Barbara (Shaw play), 212

Making of "Citizen Kane," The (Carringer), xxiv

Making of "The Wizard of Oz," The (Harmetz), xxv

Maltese Falcon, The (Hammett), 51

Man and Superman (Shaw), 19

Manheim, Ralph, 13

Mann, Delbert, 205, 243n2

Manners, Dorothy, 193–94

Man on the Eiffel Tower, The (film, 1949), xix, 105, 106

Manson, Charles, 217

Marcus, Greil, 217

Margaret Herrick Library, Academy of Motion Picture Arts and Sciences, xxiv, 56

Marriage-Go-Round, The (Broadway play), 212

Marsh, Mae, 130

Martin Chuzzlewit (Dickens), 48

Naked and the Dead, The (Mailer),
  xxvii, 209–11, 212, 213, 214
Napoléon (film, 1927), 85
Narration in the Fiction Film
  (Bordwell), 207
Nation, The, Agee's film reviews in, 73
National Film Registry, xix, 216
nature, 43, 111, 122–23
Negri, Pola, 178
Nevada (film, 1944), 180
Newmar, Julie, 212
New York Film Festival, xx, 216
New York, New York (film, 1977), 216
Night of the Hunter, The (film, 1955):
  actors in, xxv, xxvi, 13, 17–18;
  Agee's screenplay for, 74–81, 183;
  as anomaly of its time, 201–9; as
  children's fable, xx; Christmas
  coda scene in, 94, 170–71, 203;
  church organizations offended by,
  19; classic status of, xix–xx, xxvii;
  comparison with other films,
  175–76; critics and audiences,
  initial reception of, xix, xxvii, 56,
  58–59, 195–201, 213, 214; critics
  and audiences, reassessment
  by, 215–16; as cultural artifact,
  217–19, 222; enduring appeal of,
  222–23; German expressionist
  influences on, 113–22; novel re-
  created faithfully by, xx–xxi, 51,
  80–81, 96, 141; pastoral realism
  in, 122, 134; preproduction of,
  42, 98, 156; production crew for,
  xxv, 21, 98–104; "road-show"
  release plan for, 25, 26; scholarship
  on, xxi; shooting script for, 75,
  81–82, 92–93, 131, 145–46, 147; as
  silent talkie, 129–34; soundtrack
  recording of, 26–27; television
  broadcasts of, 222; as unified
  synthesis of sources, 135–48;
  videotape release of (1988), 137.
  See also cinematography; lynch
  mob scene; musical score, for
  Night of the Hunter; outtakes, from
  Night of the Hunter; river journey
  scene; screenplay, for *Night of the
  Hunter*

Night of the Hunter, The (novel), 4,
  131, 187; Agee's screenplay and,
  75–76, 78–79; as best-seller, xix,
  10, 50; comparison with Grubb's
  other novels, 8–10, 34; in context
  of American cinema, 11; critical
  reception of, 40, 41, 49–52, 200;
  filmic quality, 51; in galleys, 29;
  "Gentleman Friend" as origin of,
  45–49; gothic fiction and, 31–38;
  hymns in, 168; John's interior
  monologues in, 141–42; later
  adaptations of, xxvii; literary genre
  classification of, 30–31; lyricism
  in, 38–44, 62; as myth and fairy
  tale, 42–44; narrative economy of,
  3; promotion of film and, 197–99;
  reader expectations and, 206; river
  journey scene in, 116; Ruby in,
  166; screenplays compared with,
  94–96; spiritual conflict in, 48–49;
  stage musical version of (1996),
  221–22; synopsis of, 4–6; television
  and stage adaptations of, 219–22;
  writing of, 10
Noa Noa (Agee), 76–77, 87
Nolan, Lloyd, 21–22
North by Northwest (film, 1959), 198
Nosferatu (film, 1922), 118
Not as a Stranger (film, 1955), 196
"Notes for a Moving Picture: the
  House" (Agee), 87
"Notes on the *Auteur* Theory" (Sarris),
  xxii
Novels into Film (Bluestone), xxi
Nunn, Bill, 218

O'Connell, Arthur, 13
O'Connor, Flannery, 36, 37, 38
Oedipal theme, 46–47
"Oedipus Again" (Bauer), 136
Ohio River, 5, 6, 75, 104, 146;
  expressionism in starry night scene
  on, 115; importance to Grubb, 7,
  39; as virtual character in the film,
  124–25
Ohio Valley, 56
Oklahoma! (musical film, 1955), 201

screenplay, for *Night of the Hunter:*
Agee's first draft of, xx, 19, 74–81,
144, 169, 183, 185; comic touches
in, 84; Laughton's, 87; newspaper
serialization of, 198; nighttime sky
in, 96; silent-film techniques and,
82, 84–85
Sea Hawk, The (film, 1940), 154
Secret Beyond the Door (film, 1948),
118, 119
Seiderman, Maurice, 110–11
Server, Lee, 83
Seurat, Georges, 107
sex, 36, 38, 201; biblical epics of 1950s
and, 202; burlesque scene and,
57–58, *62,* 64; denial of, 34, 47; in
Harpers' marriage, 79–80, 203;
musical code for lust, 167; *Night of
the Hunter* as study in repression,
203; Preacher's revulsion toward,
32–33, 153, 203; religion and, 140–
41; Ruby's assignations in town,
166–67; in Spoons' marriage,
182, 185–86, 203; switchblade as
symbolic phallus, 64, 92, 96, 120;
Willa's longing, 187–88
Shadow of a Doubt (film, 1943), 174
Shadow of My Brother (Grubb), 9
Shahn, Ben, 127
Shakespeare, William, 11, 25, 116, 210
Shaw, George Bernard, xxiii, 19, 22
Shelley: Also Known as Shirley
(Winters), 197
Shelley, Mary, 35
Shock Corridor (film, 1963), 105, 109
Shore, Dinah, 25
Shurlock, Geoffrey, 144, 170
Sibelius, Jan, 162
"Siege of 318, The" (Grubb), 34
Sight and Sound magazine, xxii, xxiii, 87
Sign of the Cross, The (film, 1932), 176
silent films, 82, 84–85, 122, 124, 126;
biblical epics of 1950s and,
202, 203; closed style of films,
208; Gish's acting in, 173, 178;
"histrionic code" of acting, 193
Silver Chalice, The (film, 1954), 202
Simenon, Georges, 106
Simpsons, The (TV show), 219
Since You Went Away (film, 1944), 105

Singer, Kurt, 23
Singin' in the Rain (musical film, 1952),
134
Sirk, Douglas, 209
Sjöström, Victor, 122, 124
Small-Town America in Film (Levy), 209
Smollett, Tobias, 31
"Snow White" (Grimm fairy tale),
43–44
Sorrows of Satan, The (film, 1926), 104
sound, expressionistic use of, 85–87
Southern gothic, 36–37
Spartacus (film, 1960), 212
Speicher, Charlotte B., 200
"Split Cherry Tree" (Stuart), 41
Spoon, Icey (character), 4, 47, 119,
128, 142; casting for, 55; as foolish
woman, 167; gothic passion and,
34; John's conflict with, 78; lynch
mob scene and, 183, 184–85,
186; musical score and, 152–53;
plot synopsis of novel and, 5, 6;
postcard from Preacher to, 138,
184; in stage musical version,
221; in television adaptation, 220;
Varden's performance as, 183,
184–86
Spoon, Walt (character), 4, 47, 128, 173;
in Agee's screenplay, 77; Beddoe's
performance as, 181, 182; gothic
passion and, 34; plot synopsis of
novel and, 5, 6; postcard from
Preacher to, 138, 184; in stage
musical version, 221; submission
to Icey, 185, *186;* suspicions about
Preacher, 142, 185
Sprecher, Paul, xxiv, 75
Springsteen, Bruce, 218
Stalag 17 (film, 1953), 182
Stam, Robert, xxi
Stanwyck, Barbara, 121
Steamboat Bill, Jr. (film, 1928), 126
Steichen, Edward, 104
Sternberg, Josef von, 12, 212
Stevens, Edmond, 220
Stewart, James, 10
Stoker, Bram, 35
Story-Teller, The (Laughton recording),
25
Stroheim, Erich von, 63, 200